GETTING
CARTER

GETTING
CARTER

TED LEWIS AND THE BIRTH OF BRIT NOIR

NICK TRIPLOW

NO EXIT PRESS

First published in 2017 by No Exit Press,
an imprint of Oldcastle Books Ltd, PO Box 394,
Harpenden, AL5 1XJ, UK
noexit.co.uk

Editor: Steven Mair

A CIP catalogue record for this book is available from the British Library.

Front cover illustration: Michael Caine and Ted Lewis on the set of
Get Carter. Photographer unknown.

ISBN
978-1-84344-882-2 (hardcover)
978-1-84344-883-9 (epub)
978-1-84344-884-6 (kindle)
978-1-84344-943-0 (pdf)

2 4 6 8 10 9 7 5 3 1

Typeset in 12.75pt Minion Pro
by Avocet Typeset, Somerton, Somerset, TA11 6RT
Printed in Great Britain by TJ International Ltd.

For more information about Crime Fiction go to @crimetimeuk

It began with the laughter of children, and there it will end.
'Drunken Morning' – Arthur Rimbaud

Contents

Prologue

I'd exchanged emails with Mike Hodges about *Jack's Return Home* – Ted Lewis's punchy, defiant, distinctly non-metropolitan noir novel written in the twilight of the 1960s, which he'd adapted, then directed, as *Get Carter* in eight white-hot weeks in 1970. After the acclaimed dramas, *Suspect* and *Rumour*, made for television, it had been Hodges' first feature film, his first adaptation, and the film that established his reputation as a great British filmmaker. For the cinema-obsessed Lewis, quite simply it had been a dream come true.

I met Mike in Hull in November 2013. I'd been invited to host the Q&A following a screening of *Get Carter* as part of that year's Humber Mouth Literature Festival. Mike didn't want to watch the film so we went to a nearby restaurant along with festival director, Shane Rhodes, the writer, Kevin Sampson, and music consultant, Charlie Galloway – Kevin and Charlie were friends of Mike's from Liverpool, in town for the event, and Charlie had played a key role in the reissue of the *Get Carter* soundtrack in 1998. Over dinner, we talked about Lewis, his relationship to Hull and the Lincolnshire towns across the river where he'd lived and where *Jack's Return Home* was set. We were back in time for the film's final scenes: Jack Carter kidnapping and murdering Margaret in the grounds of Kinnear's country house, exacting revenge on those responsible for his brother's death, then the Fletcher brothers' call to an anonymous hitman famously in place from the opening title scene. Mike wrote in the screenplay: *The deserted beach is like the end of the world... Eric is halfway along the beach, struggling in the mud. Carter closes in on him.*

From the rear of the gallery we watched Michael Caine and Ian Hendry's chase along the slag-blackened beach of Blackhall against a grey North Sea backdrop. It looked incredible, as it always does. Mike said, 'It's like watching someone else's film.'

Afterwards, a group of us walked to the pub. The wind whipped off the Humber near Victoria Quay where the ferry once moored and a 16-year-old Ted Lewis commuted between art school and his mum and dad's home in Barton-upon-Humber. The pub, the Minerva, was his regular pre-crossing haunt. It features in his first book, *All the Way Home and All the Night Through,* and the 1971 novel, *Plender.* As the barman poured the pints, I thought about the times Lewis would have stood at the bar as we did and I wondered what he'd have made of Mike being there. I had a sense of this being the final stretch of some great circumnavigation, as if somehow I was bringing the story home. A few days later Mike emailed and asked, what was the name of that pub?

The Minerva.

Ted Lewis's story is as much about these unfashionable, unheralded places and how they fed into his work as it is about the zeitgeist-riding moments: 50s trad jazz, the Beatles' *Yellow Submarine*, the dark corners of 1960s Soho, the creation of Brit noir, *Z Cars* and *Doctor Who*. It's also about what happens when a good-looking, jazz-loving, cinema-obsessed kid from a small town on the banks of the Humber writes his way into history then drinks his way out again.

That Lewis remains in the public consciousness at all is mainly down to a small band of dedicated admirers in Britain and America, and, of course, that *Jack's Return Home* was the basis for the greatest British crime film of the 1970s, arguably of all time. Truth is, ask a room full of people to raise a hand if they've heard of *Get Carter* and you'll witness a sea of hands. Ask, do they know the name Ted Lewis and you'll be lucky if there are one or two. But without Lewis there is no Jack Carter, Sir Michael Caine is short of one career-defining iconic role, and the course of British crime fiction is changed forever.

When I moved to Barton-upon-Humber from London in 2001, my knowledge of Lewis extended no further than a dog-eared *Get Carter* paperback and a DVD of the film. For me, it was a one-way ticket to a place I'd never known. I had no idea it had been Lewis's home town. I learned more when his name came up in interviews for a social history book I was researching in 2007. Broadly speaking there were two responses: the first, usually delivered with bluff Northern Lincolnshire dismissiveness, was that he'd left, moved to London, made and lost a fortune and returned home with his tail between his legs and died of drink. The marginally more sympathetic view was that he was a local lad who'd done well – *'he wrote that film with Michael Caine'* – but whose boozing and philandering in later years had made him difficult to like. As one notable local told me, 'Barton is a small town and small towns have long knives'. More than once I was reminded of the lack of any formal recognition of him in the town. The Civic Society, guardians of Barton's heritage, pin plaques on the homes of notable local citizens. At that time Lewis had not been so honoured. I asked around. The suggestion was that he'd been too controversial a figure to warrant the tribute.

What really stirred my interest was an interview I recorded with the novelist Karen Maitland for a regional arts magazine in January, 2008. Karen's first mediaeval crime novel, *A Company of Liars,* had just been published and we spoke at length about the story, its inspirations and its journey to publication. Our conversation turned to crime writers we admired, specifically Ted

Lewis. Some years previously, Karen had worked as a librarian in Barton. At the time, the library kept a virtually complete collection of Lewis's books locked away in a metal cabinet. When the county of Humberside broke up in 1996 and local libraries were placed under the authority of North Lincolnshire Council, a team from the Central Library arrived in Barton to review the stock. They told the staff to throw Lewis's books on the tip. 'They were old and battered,' said Karen, 'and they couldn't think why we were wasting valuable cupboard space keeping out of date novels by a local author no one had ever heard of.'

To begin with, it seemed Ted Lewis had left little other than his published work and the memories of those who knew him. People entered and left his life with regularity and only a very few can claim to have been close for any length of time. Others suffer from the vagueness of memory that advances with age and the after-effects of 1960s and 70s lifestyles. Some are fiercely protective of his reputation and reject any enquiry. Others were hurt by him with the same outcome – he could, it was said, 'turn on a sixpence': charming, entertaining, boyishly attractive one minute; obnoxious, paranoid, self-destructive and abusive the next. For those closest to him, raking over the past is frequently a painful experience. I've sat down with friends, lovers, schoolmates, drinking pals, neighbours and colleagues; I've met with his ex-wife, his daughters, and his literary agent, Toby Eady. I've collected scraps of reviews and interviews from long defunct magazines. Primary sources are scarce. Verification is rarely straightforward. No formal archive or collection of correspondence exists, only a few pieces written about him for magazines and websites. Lewis didn't keep a diary for most of his life and the majority of his papers and personal documents were destroyed after his mother's death in 1990.

Yet the popularity of contemporary British crime fiction can be traced directly to the aesthetic he pioneered in *Jack's Return Home*, found again in *Plender* and *Jack Carter's Law*, and took to new levels of dark intensity in his final novel, *GBH*. That unflinching mix of tawdry underworld violence combined with an unerring eye for detail, an evocative connection with landscape and the reek of the authentically domestic, the brutal and banal, dark and psychological, and a gift for crafting language like no one who came before him, helped define the concept of present-day British noir. So why had he fallen into relative obscurity? Why, since his death in 1982, had there been no significant posthumous rediscovery? Why are his books, with the obvious exception of *Get Carter*, out of print in his home country?

For much of his life, Lewis exhibited the virtues and flaws of a classic noir antihero: nobility, infidelity, weakness, sickness, sex, cigarettes, love, booze and bad choices play a part. He was the star of his own film, damaged and dangerous. As a writer, he achieved an astonishing amount in a short period of time, though never enough to satisfy his expectations. His fall, when it came, was rapid. I've tried to fill the gaps and provide a narrative certainty, but there remain ambiguities, complexities, mysteries and half-remembered fragments which I've agonised over and learned to reconcile, avoiding the temptation to neaten loose ends on his behalf.

Interviewed shortly after the publication of *Jack's Return Home* in 1970, he said he'd tried to 'make it real'. The least I can do is to follow his lead and tell it straight as I've found it.

1

Heartache
1940–1951

Ted Lewis had a sense that something had been missing. Born on 15 January 1940 in Stretford, Manchester, among his imperfect and chaotic wartime recollections it was his father's absence that resonated. A space which, for the first five years of his life, was dominated by his mother, Bertha, and his maternal grandmother's matriarchal presence. In this his experiences were no different to those of countless other wartime babies and young children, their consciousness formed in an uncertain and austere time of absent fathers, air-raid warnings, rationing, bomb-damaged streets and the filtered realities of war reported each evening on the BBC news. A rare family snapshot from the period, taken while his father, Harry, was home on leave from the Royal Air Force, shows father and son together. Harry Lewis is on his haunches, tanned and healthy in the uniform of an RAF Corporal. His broad hands encircle his young son's waist. Perhaps a little more than a year old, Edward is pale, blond and chubby-cheeked, smiling and alert in the sunshine.

By the time Harry returned home from active service for the final time in 1945, his son, christened Alfred Edward, but always known as Edward to his parents, was a fit and energetic five-year-old. Readjusting to home and family life after the war proved difficult. For a short time, Harry went back to work at the Manchester Ship Canal Company where he'd been employed as a shipbroker's clerk before the war, but his experience had equipped him for greater responsibility. When the opportunity of a management position arose at one of the company's subsidiary concerns across the country in Lincolnshire, he accepted.

In early September 1946, the Lewis family migrated 100 miles west to east from Manchester to North Lincolnshire. Harry Lewis took out a mortgage on 118 West Acridge, Barton-upon-Humber, a modest three-bedroom semi-detached in one of the town's most established streets. The family moved in and Harry took up the post of manager at Elsham Quarry some ten miles away, one of several similar works peppering the landscape south of Barton which provided raw materials for building, engineering and railway industries.

The Barton that welcomed the Lewises was a small, insular market town on the south bank of the River Humber, some 25 miles from the fishing port of Grimsby to the east and 20 miles from the steel town of Scunthorpe to the west. They knew no one and the town's few thousand inhabitants were, in the main, families which could trace their local heritage back generations. The town had built up around two distinct geographical locales: the Waterside area close to Barton Haven, a busy inlet from the River Humber, where once a ferry had connected to Hessle on the opposite bank of the river a mile and a quarter away; and Top Town, which centred on two mediaeval churches – Saint Peter's with its Saxon tower and nearby Saint Mary's. A few local shops and half a dozen pubs led up to the town square, home to the weekly market. Beyond its own boundaries, the town had made its name through Hopper's bicycle factory whose machines were exported around the world; Hall's Barton Ropery which made ropes for the Royal Navy and the Empire for 150 years; and for the manufacture of bricks and tiles – there were a number of traditional works dotted along the river's south bank making use of Humber clay.

Across the river, accessible only by ferry from New Holland, a short train journey from Barton, or a lengthy detour inland by road, the lights of the city of Kingston upon Hull represented a distant world. The house in West Acridge gave Lewis a clear view of the river and the city beyond. After Trafford Park's industrial grime, Barton was an idyllic setting for the Lewises. Nestling in the hillside as the landscape scoops from the outer edge of the Lincolnshire Wolds to the wooded fringes and pebbled beaches of the Humber foreshore, it would have felt clean, its broad outlook offering an uncluttered panorama of the wide river, its air unpolluted. It was a free and safe playground for the young Lewis. In his first novel, the autobiographical *All the Way Home and All the Night Through*, Lewis wrote his observations of Barton, describing the easy pace of living and the ordinariness of the town, concluding that although the youth complains about the claustrophobia of life, 'hardly anyone leaves the place'.

In 1947, Lewis was enrolled at Barton County Primary School on Castledyke. Although he felt some affection for his headmaster, a quiet man called Jack Taylor, the bulk of the teaching staff were, according to childhood friend and classmate, Nick Turner, 'formidable old spinsters'. The most draconian was Miss Crawford, a strict disciplinarian who inflicted liberal doses of corporal punishment on her young charges. Children were terrified of her. Turner remembers the consequences if Miss Crawford suspected someone had broken wind. 'She would walk round smelling our backsides until she found the culprit and then slipper them in front of the class.' Miss Crawford's comeuppance came while attempting to teach the children to bunny-jump during a PE lesson when she fell on her back and had to be carried out. After the comfort of home, the sensitive Lewis was unsettled by the severity of Miss Crawford and the other teachers. They upset the sense of fairness he had come to depend on with his mother and grandmother and he withdrew, quietly shielding himself from the school's worst excesses.

Lewis's days at Barton County were curtailed abruptly when, in 1948, he contracted rheumatic fever. In pre-antibiotic, late-1940s Britain, cases were still fairly common, particularly among children. The disease was a major cause of death until around 1960. It would attack the heart's mitral valve, causing it to leak, often leaving the sufferer with chronic heart problems. In addition to its effect on the heart, it was a highly debilitating illness – we know from friends that Lewis suffered severe pain in his joints. In extreme cases, rheumatic fever could lead to brain damage. Recovery was primarily dependent on the ability of the patient's immune system to fight back and it was generally accepted that, if the sufferer kept to a minimum any potential strain on the heart, the disease would be less likely to cause lasting harm. Whilst the exact severity of Lewis's bout of rheumatic fever isn't known, it was certainly a grave cause for concern, serious enough for Bertha to ensure her son received complete bed rest for many months. Throughout the latter part of 1948 and into the spring of 1949, he remained at home, convalescing.

When it was suggested to John Dickinson, whose parents had become good friends of the Lewises, that he visit this young chap who was ill in bed, he found a pale boy a couple of years younger than himself, quite shy, and with a mop of blond hair, his bed littered with comic books and a pencil and paper constantly to hand. Dickinson recalls 'he would draw all the time, always these figures of people'.

With recurrences of rheumatic fever as common as the disease itself, particularly in the years immediately after the first incidence, Harry and Bertha would have been told that another episode could cause lasting and serious, possibly fatal, damage to their son's heart. But, as Lewis's ninth birthday approached, Bertha dared to hope the worst was over. Thinking a birthday party would raise his spirits, she made a cake, iced with the family's saved sugar rations. The boys who sat on the edge of the bed at his party have a clear recollection of Edward Lewis, sitting up in bed and 'holding court'. It was as if the illness had conferred a degree of celebrity.

The friends drawn to Lewis around this time called themselves the Riverbank Boys. Barton was no different to many towns where discrete areas became territories for loosely associated groups of friends. The Riverbank Boys were hardly a gang in any contemporary sense, more a bunch of lads who played together, shared interests and made a point of looking after each other. Lewis was welcomed on board. Along with Nick Turner and Alan Dickinson, he was one of the youngest of the group that included Martin Turner, John Dickinson, Mike Shucksmith and Neil Ashley. They were Barton born and bred and came from similarly respectable families. Here, for the first time, Edward Lewis of 118 West Acridge became Ted Lewis of the Riverbank Boys after Nick and Martin Turner's father, Arthur, decided Edward was too effeminate a name. Ted was 'more manly'. Lewis's friends called him Ed or Eddy. Bertha would make sandwiches for the boys and they'd sit around in her son's room, talking, drawing, reading comics, usually with Lewis as the centre of attention. Sometimes Harry set up a hand-cranked film projector, plugged into the light socket with a bulb behind it for the boys to watch cartoon films screened against the blank wall at the foot of the bed.

In hindsight, Lewis's rheumatic fever and the enforced period of recuperation and reading which followed, gave him a degree of knowledge and insight beyond his years. Temporarily released from the constraints of formal education, in its place, encouraged and supported by Bertha, his natural artistic ability was given licence to flourish. In the dull rhythms of convalescent days, he discovered an inner world of imagination, invention and story. Escape from the everyday came first through the wireless, particularly radio thriller serials like *Dick Barton – Special Agent*. Lewis was an avid listener.

He was also a keen reader of comics. While British comics of the time were, for the most part, limited to the traditional – *Beano*, *Dandy* – and boy's own titles like *Hotspur* or *Eagle*, increasingly Lewis's older friends were attracted to glossier American titles from the Entertaining Comics (EC) stable of crime, horror and science fiction. *Crime Patrol*, *War Against Crime!*, *Vault of Horror*, *Tales From the Crypt*, *Weird Fantasy* and *The Haunt of Fear* were captivating reads, particularly for lads raised on a diet of Desperate Dan, Biffo the Bear and old-fashioned heroes and villains of Empire. EC comics were no ordinary adventures. These were stories of violent revenge, punishment, guilt and retribution. *Death's Double Cross*, *Under Cover* and *Snapshot of Death* and countless stories like them delivered a jolt to Lewis's pre-teenage imagination. He was enthusiastic about the vivid colours and graphic narratives, the more horrific the better. The byline of his and Nick Turner's favourite comic featured a gleefully sadistic character hunting roadkill in dark city streets spouting the mantra: 'Blood and guts all over the street, and me without a spoon to eat.'

Retrospectively viewed as a highpoint in pop culture in

the period before concerns about juvenile delinquency in the United States prompted senate hearings to neuter their alleged impact on American youth, early EC comics have a parallel in the pre-censorship film industry of the early 1930s. Eventually, they would be codified and sanitised. They were bold, entertaining and featured tough heroes, deviant victims, good stories, sharp dialogue and eye-catching artwork. Some stories, like those of artist Johnny Craig, were naturalistic and had moral undertones. Others were gratuitously violent or overtly sexual. Lewis was enthralled by torture scenes, double-crosses in shadowy alleyways, gangsters in fedoras and hard-bitten detectives. They also began to influence the way he wrote, finding expression in the pages of his drawings. His comic strips and fictional characters were more colourful and they now had speech balloons.

An American comic in Barton in the early 1950s would have seemed a wildly exotic item and a prized possession. Although Bertha enthusiastically provided her son with whatever he needed to keep him happy and occupied, it is unlikely she would have been able to find, or would necessarily have approved of, the comics had she been aware of their content. Buying comics was a challenge for Lewis and the other boys. Often they were handed on by the older members of the Riverbank Boys, those with pocket money, part-time jobs or paper rounds. It was said they could be bought from sailors who came through the docks at Hull and Immingham. Martin Turner remembers buying them from a novelty shop in Cleethorpes – a thriving holiday resort and popular destination for daytrippers an hour or so from Barton on the train.

Lewis was absent from school for several months. Illness had left him physically fragile. It had also deepened the already close bond between mother and son. In later years, he told one friend of a game they played in which Bertha would ask, 'Who are you going to marry?' To which he would answer, 'You, mummy'. Bertha was determined he should be back to full health before returning to school. On warm afternoons, she set a chair in front of the house and allowed him to sit outside. Friends remember passing on their way home from school, stopping to talk to the boy swathed in blankets. He became something of a curiosity, the illness marking him out as different. When they asked why he wasn't at school he told them he had 'heartache'.

A school class photo, taken in the summer of 1949, shows a group of children, smart, but perhaps a little dowdy in hand-me-downs or the best that clothing coupons could buy. Lewis sits at the front, distinct, with his longish blond fringe swept across his forehead. He looks healthy, smiling. By the time he left Barton County in the summer of 1951, a promisingly bright boy, perhaps a little more fragile than most and extremely shy, the strict regimen of schooldays had sown the seeds of a quiet rebellion. As he regained strength, Lewis spent more time with friends, exploring the landscape and absorbing his surroundings: the River Humber, its windswept shores, rolling grey-brown tides, hidden nooks, disused tile and brickworks, jetties, broad bays and river-borne traffic were fertile grounds for the imagination. Here in the riverside wilderness, he found freedom from illness and a place to play.

2

Voice of America
1951–1956

THE BARTON GRAMMAR SCHOOL WHICH OPENED its gates to Lewis in September 1951 had been founded, like so many others, on principles borrowed from the public school system. Conservative by instinct and ethos, it sought to produce young men and women of sound learning, high academic achievement and traditional values. Established in 1931, the school had done much to elevate the town's standing. Its teachers were among the most respected members of the community, their status as educators and moral guardians unquestioned. Entrance was by no means a formality. Earning a place at 'the grammar' was an achievement, an indicator of aspiration for the children of Barton's working class and lower middle class families. For Lewis's friends, Nick and Martin Turner, John and Alan Dickinson, Mike Shucksmith and Barbara Hewson – all former pupils – schooldays are recalled with mixed feelings. For some, Barton Grammar was the passport to opportunity their parents had worked for, fought for, and on which they'd staked their children's futures; but it could also be intolerant of any pupil who did not, or could not, fit the mould socially and academically.

The school population, mainly from Barton and nearby villages, had been increasing year on year. By the time Lewis arrived, student numbers had risen to around 300. The proximity of the war and its after effects continued to shape the way people lived. Clothes were only available on coupons and food was still subject to rationing. Boys bragged of their shrapnel collections and told stories of the bomber crews from RAF Kirmington and the godlike American fighter pilots who had frequented local pubs – the RAF station at Goxhill had been transferred to the US 8th and 9th Air Force in 1942. Sixth former John Grimbleby would describe how he had found the impression of a German airman in the earth in a field outside Barton, the victim of a failed parachute. Luftwaffe raiders had routinely used moonlight reflecting off the Humber to navigate into Hull, turning home over the south bank. Barton people remembered the drone of bombers night after night when it had seemed as though the entire waterfront and city of Hull was ablaze. John and Alan Dickinson's father, a wartime fireman, told stories of how his fire crew had been strafed by a German fighter at New Holland quayside – most credit went to the 'heroic' Salvation Army officer who continued to serve tea throughout the raid. At school, teachers returning from the services had resumed their careers, readjusting to civilian life in the classroom. Physical education and geography teacher Jack Baker still wore his khaki battledress jacket to classes, just as he had for his job interview.

The school's headmaster, Norman Goddard, was a modern languages scholar. Hard-featured, with cold grey eyes, a Mozart specialist and strict disciplinarian, Goddard had established a fearsome reputation on his arrival in the spring of 1951. Martin Turner remembers that 'within a week, he had tamed the school'. Boys were expected to lift their caps to senior teachers; minor uniform, timekeeping and homework indiscretions were routinely punished, with one hundred lines the standard penalty. At the conclusion of each morning's assembly, Goddard took his place in front of the stage and read the list of names of those he wished to see. 'If he wanted to see you at lunchtime,' says Nick Turner, 'it was a ticking off. If it was break time, you might be able to talk your way out of it. But if he wanted to see you straight after assembly, you were in big trouble.' Goddard caned boys across the hand, a punishment from which girls were exempt, but which seemed only to make his verbal and psychological admonishment of them more severe. Teachers used the threat of being made to stand under the clock opposite the headmaster's office to deter bad behaviour. It came with an ever present fear of interrogation should the door open and Goddard demand to know why you were there. Nick Turner remembers, 'Say you'd been talking in class, he'd ask, "Why were you talking?" That was his thing, he'd say, "Why? Why? Why? Why?" again and again until you were an abject mess and you'd say, "Because I'm stupid, because I'm a fool." He'd wear you down with the same question over and over.' When the rumour circulated that Goddard had spent the war working for British Intelligence, interrogating captured German prisoners, no one had difficulty believing it.

In September 1951, Edward Lewis arrived in his new navy and light blue quartered cap, stiff navy blue wool blazer, polished shoes, striped tie and grey flannel trousers. Still finding his feet a few days into the new term, he was leaning against a wall near the boys' entrance to the playing field, hands in pockets, hair uncombed, tie loose around his shirt collar. Taking exception to this apparently insolent attitude from one of his boys, particularly a first former, Goddard walked purposely towards him. *Lewis, 1M wasn't it?* After a sharp ticking off, Goddard slapped him hard across the face. The shock of the assault caused

Lewis to wet himself. Goddard continued with his lunchtime inspection, leaving the new boy to clean himself up.

For the pupils, many of whom had recently arrived from village primary schools, none of whom had witnessed anything quite like it, this was a salutary lesson. They might have been used to corporal punishment – in common with most lads, Lewis had been 'walloped' by his father for misdemeanours in the past and there was the memory of Miss Crawford – but this was different. Goddard had decided to make an example of him. News spread through the school that 'Ed Lewis had pissed himself'. Inevitably, for the next few days he ran the gauntlet of snide comments. For the most part, his friends recall that these did not last and he was treated with sympathy; others, you suspect, were less kind-hearted. A new boy in a new school, he was humiliated and now vulnerable, knowing the incident was in reserve for the opponent in any argument. While Harry and Bertha may have disapproved, they weren't about to challenge their son's new headmaster and the episode was to remain with Lewis for the rest of his life. In his 1975 novel, *The Rabbit*, he included a graphic retelling of the story of the headmaster's slap, the sickening sensation of wetting himself in public and locking himself in the toilets until everyone had gone home.

Lewis's introduction to the school could hardly have been worse. The quiet distaste for authority he'd begun to nurture at Barton County grew deeper and he withdrew further. As others fell into line, conforming to the everyday rigours of school life, the injustices – real and perceived – hurt him deeply. Unfortunately, his place in the modern language form 1M brought him into regular contact with Goddard who would take the class for German lessons. Here Goddard reserved special treatment for boys not paying attention, pulling up the dcsk lid at the same time as sharply pushing the boy's head down. Inevitably, there were bloody noses. For entertainment one Friday afternoon, he sat them to attention on PE benches in the school hall and played an LP of Mozart's *Eine Kleine Nachtmusik*. In the verbal examination that followed, Nick Turner remembers, he asked, 'Had we heard this part or that? And if not, why weren't we listening?' For Lewis, always nervous in Goddard's presence, lessons like these were unbearable.

Reading Enid Brice's book, *A Country Grammar School Remembered*, which tells the story of the school, there are former pupils who consider Goddard embodied a necessarily 'strict but fair' brand of school discipline. It was hardly unheard of for 1950s schoolteachers to be authoritarian and corporal punishment was commonplace, but this seems different. Years later, on being told he had terrified one former pupil, Goddard said, 'Ah, but it worked, didn't it?' Mike Shucksmith thinks otherwise. 'There were tough teachers, and you respected them. I got it a couple of times for being a silly bugger, but Goddard was a shit. I hated him.' Interviewed by the *Manchester Evening News* in 1970, Lewis would recall an occasion he'd been seen eating fish and chips in the street and was publicly rebuked by Goddard for 'eating comestibles out of a paper bag'. It was not the kind of thing a Barton Grammar School boy ought to do. Lewis warmed to his theme, 'If you weren't a machine storing up maths, French, and anything moving away from the arts, they'd frown on you. I've written three novels and the first, about school, was rejected. The publisher I took it to at the time considered it libellous.'

Life outside the school gates offered plenty of distractions. In July 1952, the Lewises moved from West Acridge to a larger property at nearby 46 Westfield Road, a few doors down from the Shucksmiths. The new house, bought for £1,500, had previously belonged to a local doctor, Charles Hawthorn. It had a sizeable basement and attic and, in the front room, stood a newly bought upright piano on which Lewis began having lessons with a local teacher, Harold Johnson. Outside there was a small piece of adjoining land with an orchard and a few chickens. In the garden, which had a small, deep dip-pond filled with foul-smelling water, Lewis and his friends were soon making the most of the space, experimenting with homemade artillery, firing rockets along a length of drainpipe through an old dustbin lid. Health and safety was of the 'duck when you see one coming' variety. Past the pond and through the orchard, there was a collection of outbuildings in various states of repair, accessible via an old carriage drive from West Acridge.

With the extra space in the new house, Bertha's mother, Mrs Shaw, came to live with the family on a permanent basis. It was not a comfortable arrangement for Harry. In truth, as Lewis eased into adolescence, Harry was rarely around. A nine-hour day, six-day week at the quarry kept him from home. Travelling to work in the lorry that picked up and dropped off workers in Barton station yard, the boys would see him walking home of an evening, covered in a film of white limestone dust, visibly exhausted, trilby tilted on the back of his head. John Dickinson remembers him as a tall, dour, deep-voiced Lancastrian with a dry sense of humour, calling wearily, 'It's alright for you lads, you ought to be doing a bit of this digging in the garden.' Lewis would invariably give him some chat back.

For Harry, the new house marked a change in status, an aspirational step towards something more than respectable working class. He accepted an invitation to join the local masonic lodge and, in doing so, became one of a group of influential local businessmen with a keen – some have said controlling – interest in the town's affairs. Able to favourably interpret or circumvent the rules as suited their interests, there were rumours of good turns given and received, and planning consents for business premises in the town granted without question. By all accounts, Lewis found the masons and their arcane customs faintly ridiculous. He would refer to 'that lot up there', goading Harry about his visits to the lodge on Brigg Road, and threatening to read and expose the secrets in his mysterious masonic handbook.

Westfield Road became a home from home for the Riverbank Boys. Bertha provided an endless supply of tea and would also turn a blind eye if they smoked. She and Harry were heavy smokers and the kitchen was routinely a fug of cigarette smoke. Lewis and Nick Turner had been 12 years old when they bought their first pack of 10 Robin cigarettes from Mr Rowley's shop at the corner of Newport and Fleetgate and made their way to the riverbank, hiding in one of the disused brickworks kilns to smoke all 10. At school, a smokers' circle congregated behind the groundsman's hut at break times, which led to a running battle with the school groundsman, Mr Stamp, who frequently threatened to report the 'little bastards', but never did.

The easy availability of cigarettes was due, in part, to local shopkeeper, Bill Doughty, who sold them in singles from his shop in Market Lane. He kept a room at the back of his shop for his boys to smoke in and there were usually one or two dragging away. He also sold lemonade in a penny or twopenny glass and after each boy had finished drinking would take out a dirty rag and wipe the glass for the next.

Around this time, Lewis became 'Lew' to his friends. No one can quite remember how it came about, other than it sounded more American, like the names he'd heard in films. Cigarettes became a prop, adding to the image he was cultivating, the careworn private eye with a cigarette clamped between his lips. He adopted the smoking styles of screen stars he admired.

Often he would smoke in the two-storey stable block beyond the orchard with its horseboxes and hayloft. It became the boys' de facto headquarters and Lewis christened it 'Kexby Hall'. It allowed him a superficial independence whilst remaining under Bertha's watchful eye, although the carriage path from West Acridge meant a surreptitious entrance and exit could be virtually assured. Kexby Hall also housed Lewis's collection of pornographic magazines. Not, as it turned out, the safest place to store them. On a slow day at the quarry, Harry sent workmen to the house to clean the stable block. By the time Lewis found out, it was too late to retrieve the magazines. He was horrified, later telling Martin Turner, 'Have you ever stood and shivered at the awful realisation that there's something you *really* didn't want anybody else to see?' Petrified the workmen would find the magazines and tell his father, he said, 'I just froze.' If they were found and if Harry was told, Lewis never ascertained.

A mile or so outside Barton town centre, close to the river, is the site of what was once the Adamant Cement Works. Monuments of the river's industrial past reveal themselves; remains of buildings and kilns, a brick border underfoot, remind you that this riverside waste ground was once a working factory. If you break off the main path and work your way through the bracken and brambles until it opens to the foreshore, you'll come across an expanse of stony beach and the wide grey river. There you'll find cement set in the shape of the sacks, the sacking long since rotted away, which marks the place where barges would dock to load cement and tiles to be transported upriver to Goole, or across to Hull docks and beyond.

The 'old cements' and 'pebbly beach' were important places for Lewis and his friends. They spent countless days, weekends and school holidays setting up camp with the Turner brothers' ex-army pup tents pitched end to end, a groundsheet and a couple of blankets. They cooked beans, sausages, eggs and bacon on an open fire. In season there were wild strawberries and blackberries. Water for a brew came from a nearby spring. Away from prying eyes, says John Dickinson, they would 'go wild'. Just how wild is open to conjecture. When the old wooden jetty, known as Ferriby Goss, burned down, a rumour circulated that the fire had been started by the Riverbank Boys. The surviving boys, now in their 70s, are saying nothing. Evidence remains in remnants of weatherworn wooden piles on the riverbank a few hundred yards west of the Humber Bridge. On desolate winter mornings when the fog is at its thickest, the wooden spars and pilings of the wrecked jetty stick out from the sucking mud like Normandy tank traps. On those mornings it feels like a haunted place.

In *All the Way Home and All the Night Through*, Victor Graves describes the roofless and decaying works with their peeling paint and plaster, loose bricks tumbling. He speaks of their darkness and mystery, concluding that they were 'holy places', sanctuary from long days at grammar school, where he and his friends could truly be themselves. A collection of black and white snapshots captures what now seems like a last blast of childhood lived out in roughhouse re-enactments at Ferriby Cliff or the old cements: Lewis and Neil Ashley's re-creation of Sir Edmund Hillary and Tenzing's final ascent of Everest in 1953; a horseplay battle in progress – the life and death manhunt for the meanest hombre in town; and a group photo of Lewis, the boys, and Jane Guymer and Pat Parkin, two Barton girls invited for the evening.

For a group of energetic adolescent boys used to making their own amusement, the Humber bank, the old brickworks and its surrounding wilderness held limitless ways to have a good time. Here they played endless games of hunter and hunted and made hand grenades from damp clay moulded around bangers, with the fuse left exposed. Lines scored in the clay as it dried made them look like Mills Bombs. 'You'd light the fuse, wait, then throw the grenade,' says Nick Turner. High quantities of gunpowder made for impressive explosions.

The only rules were those they agreed amongst themselves. There were occasional fallings-out. Once, when Lewis came across *E LEWIS* in chalk graffiti on the wall of one of the deserted tileworks buildings, he was incensed, shouting, 'Fucking hell, everyone knows me, I'm gonna get the blame for this.' Mike Shucksmith picked up the chalk, adding a 'T' and 'H' in front of the 'E'. Eventually the graffiti read *THE LEWISHAM ART CLUB* and Lewis was placated. Neil Ashley, suffering with a headache, was tormented by Shucksmith chasing him up and down the foreshore, banging on a dustbin lid with a rock. Nick Turner remembers he and Lewis would stand at the river's edge, close to the navigation channel on the south bank, and taunt barge skippers in cod pirate accents, 'What be yer cargo? Be it shit?'

Time was immaterial. One summer morning Neil Ashley was due to cycle down as soon as he'd finished his early morning paper round. At camp, the others got up, had breakfast and 'buggered about' for a few hours and were finishing lunch when Ashley arrived on his bike. They asked where he'd been. 'Doing me job,' he said. They asked why he hadn't joined them for the morning. He said, 'What d'you mean? It's only nine o'clock.' When darkness fell, the boys told ghost stories by the light of a hurricane lamp, taking turns to 'scare the pants' off the youngest, usually Alan Dickinson. Sometimes Gandi Smith from nearby South Ferriby visited and the Barton boys made up horrific tales, then watched Gandi cycle home in terror, his bike's rear light deviating erratically across the riverbank path until it disappeared into the darkness.

Pinning an exact time and place to Lewis's first taste of beer takes you to those days on the riverbank. Older than Lewis by a couple of years, Martin Turner, Michael Tink and John Dickinson were served in local pubs from the age of sixteen or seventeen. For camping weekends, the closest pub was the Nelthorpe Arms in South Ferriby. From there they would buy bottles of beer, smuggling them out to the more obviously underage Lewis, Nick Turner and Alan Dickinson waiting in the car park. Or they'd take the beer back to camp. At The George in Barton, landlady Lila Harrison would serve the older boys and Lewis drank pints of bitter bought for him. He had no great capacity for alcohol and after three or four pints would make his excuses, go outside, throw it all up and then carry on drinking. Other times, the boys went to village pubs in nearby Winteringham or Elsham where they weren't so well known. Later, there were holidays at Butlins, one illustrated in a photograph of an obviously sloshed Lewis, suited, booted and grinning from ear to ear as he leans on Martin Turner's shoulder. He looks no older than fourteen or fifteen. Friends recall he began to use beer as an antidote to his usual shyness. He was more sociable and less self-conscious, but after a couple of pints, could become uncharacteristically argumentative.

On the corner of the High Street and Fleetgate, stood the Star cinema; the Oxford cinema was nearby in Newport Street. Both were a few minutes' walk from Westfield Road, or a smart gallop if you'd seen a western. From the age of nine or ten, Lewis had adored the thrill of an afternoon at the pictures. His first heroes were the cowboys: Roy Rogers, Gene Autry and John Wayne. Walking home, the boys would keep the stories going, excitedly imagining scene after scene. Sometimes a tethered horse grazing in a field on the way home found itself playing a role in re-enactments as they took turns riding bareback, shooting imaginary renegades.

Of the two Barton cinemas, the Star had earned a reputation as something of a fleapit; its down at heel quality wasn't helped by frequent projector malfunctions. The manager, 'a pompous little man', would take to the stage to offer apologies to a tirade of catcalls from the boys in the stalls. But with two performances on Monday, Tuesday and Wednesday, beginning with a cartoon or a short – the Three Stooges were firm favourites – followed by a ten minute Pathé News Reel and a main feature; then a change of programme for Thursday, Friday and Saturday, the pictures were a cheap diversion from school and homework. A sixpenny stalls seat in the Star wasn't much of a dent in Lewis's pocket money. At every programme change, he would take his seat in the darkened auditorium, revelling in outsider stories of the American frontier, imagining himself as John Wayne in *The Searchers* or James Stewart in *Bend of the River*. He loved gangster films, the more hard-hitting the better, favouring flawed tough guys like Lee Marvin in *The Big Heat* or *The Wild One* over the clean-cut, smooth mannered heroes who dominated the posters. Lewis preferred the kind of men for whom violence was second nature, capable of sadistically crushing weaker characters without a second thought.

Lee Marvin had walked out of Lee Strasberg's Actors' Studio in 1950, reputedly with a 'fuck you' to the venerable acting coach. He'd already established himself as Lewis's favourite film actor when Edward Dein's *Shack Out on 101* showed at the Star. *Shack* was one of a series of low budget red-peril paranoia B-movies. For Lewis, the politics was a marginal consideration. Marvin played 'Slob', a wisecracking short-order cook in a rundown roadhouse on the eponymous Route 101. Violent, mouthy, vindictive, revealed to be acting as a courier in the sale of state secrets from a nearby government establishment to an unnamed foreign power, Marvin steals the film entirely and bags the best lines – 'It's a good job I'm not wired, you could push me around like a vacuum cleaner'. In the week it played, Lewis saw *Shack Out on 101* enough times to memorise much of Slob's dialogue. In the film's climactic scene, to avoid discovery, Slob roughs up all-American girl and Shack waitress, Kotty, played by Terry Moore. He shoves her head through a window, then makes to stab her with a cook's knife, before meeting his match on the business end of a harpoon gun. Only then do his treacherous secrets come tumbling out.

Taking his lead from dialogue like Marvin's, Lewis was acquiring his own way with a one-liner. In a tender moment from one long-forgotten film, as the hero cradled a dying woman in his arms, Nick Turner remembers a voice calling out, 'Fuck her while she's warm!' Smart throwaways and sharp-tongued putdowns became part of his repertoire and a useful teenage defence mechanism.

Lewis's interest in cinema bordered on obsession. He bought *Picturegoer* magazine and shared a subscription to *Films and Filming* with John Dickinson. He immersed himself in the minutiae of filmspeak, memorising names and functions of those involved in the production as the credits rolled, staying in his seat until the final frame, delaying the moment he would have to rejoin the real world. Afterwards, it was as if he needed to carry the stories with him from the cinema. Talking about them kept them real and alive.

Once the early Saturday house had finished around eight o'clock, the boys would walk up the hill to Westfield Road where Bertha waited with tea and sandwiches. She'd sit with them in the kitchen, giggling at in-jokes and stories about how they'd got on with girls. Some nights they played three card brag for pennies and ha'pennies at the kitchen table. Lewis might be persuaded to play the piano, improvising or playing tunes from memory. Mostly they went upstairs to the attic sitting room to smoke and go over that evening's film with Lewis leading long conversations and pulling the plot to pieces, dismantling the action scenes, glorying in the violence. 'This was the best bit' or 'this was the cruellest'.

In his room at Westfield Road, film books, magazines and annuals competed for shelf space alongside the crime and horror comics and detective novels. Gathering detailed knowledge of the directors, writers, actors and designers – the people who made films – was just as important as knowing the stars. To most people they were remote figures, names and functions scrolling past as you tipped your seat and collected your coat, but for Lewis, by the time *Shack* showed at the Star, they represented his burning desire to work in film.

The second of Barton's cinemas, the Oxford, was marginally more sophisticated than the Star. It had an upstairs balcony with double seats for couples and a small foyer of its own, attended by an usherette, usually the formidable Mrs Haddock. A couple of ancient sofas with zigzag patterned upholstery and a standard lamp gave the foyer the feel of a slightly dowdy 1930s lounge. Afforded a little more discretion, the Oxford was the place Lewis began to take girls.

The shy, good-looking blond boy who had a way with words and could make you laugh then cut you dead had no shortage of offers to hold hands. Lewis had a succession of on-off girlfriends, most of them adolescent affairs over almost as soon as they began. He rarely broke off one relationship before assuring himself the next girl was waiting in line. Sometimes the chase was all that mattered. The affections and attentions of girls seemed to fulfil his need for reassurance. With friends he might not have lacked confidence, but alone or with girls, he could be deeply insecure. He was certainly self-conscious about his teeth, which he considered imperfect. He developed the habit of keeping his mouth closed when he laughed. It didn't seem to bother anyone else, other than the time he had a cold and a closed-mouth sneeze landed projectile snot on the sweater of the girl he was chatting up.

This phlegmatic attitude to girls changed when he met Jean Walker. She was a year or two older than Lewis. Her brother, Michael, had been on the fringes of the Riverbank Boys' friendship group for a while. On visits to the Walkers' house when their parents were absent, Jean and Lewis would disappear upstairs where, according to one friend, 'She taught Ted all he got to know about sex'. A group photograph taken at what looks to be a Christmas party shows Lewis sitting front and centre, every inch the young adult in suit, shirt and tie, flanked by his friend, Barbara Hewson, on his right and Jean on his left. He and Jean angle their bodies towards each other, somehow separating themselves from the others, as if in their own photograph.

Being with Jean had had a profound and lasting effect on Lewis and played a part in shaping his expectations of other girls. For the year or so they were together, he was as close to smitten as anyone had seen him. In the not-quite-liberated Barton of the mid 1950s, when sex for most fourteen-year-olds meant a kiss and fumble in the double seats at the Oxford, going all the way carried something of a risk, of pregnancy, of discovery, of ruined reputations. Later, writing in *The Rabbit*, Lewis's literary avatar Victor Graves would be terrified of casual sex. Along with the beer and the girlfriends, friends remember Lewis going through intense periods in which he'd lose himself in impenetrable moods for days at a time. He was sullen, unreachable, even to his close friends. The moods lifted, Barbara Hewson remembers, often with 'a wink or a dirty note passed across the desk'.

He may have been troubled by the emotional consequences of his childhood brush with mortality, although he seemed to have recovered physically and had proved himself a useful cross-country runner. A photograph, taken as a race ends, shows a wiry figure in white plimsolls, shorts and t-shirt, sprinting for the finish line, applauded by a blurry gathering of female spectators.

Certainly the residual effects of his early encounter with Norman Goddard were never far from his thoughts. With each subsequent meeting came the threat of a put-down or punishment that might lead to more humiliation. In a script for the unproduced *Thirteen Women – Mary: 1972*, in all likelihood written for television sometime between 1975 and 1977, he would draw on the events of a school trip to Stratford-upon-Avon to see a production of *Othello* – the cast included Paul Robeson, Sam Wanamaker as Iago and Mary Ure as Desdemona. Stratford was memorable for a number of reasons, not least of which was witnessing Goddard, who had taught one of the minor cast members, disappearing backstage to meet the actor, displaying a cultural sensitivity that astounded the Barton group. The play itself had a lasting impact. 'Taking us to see *Othello* was one of the few good things Goddard did,' says Nick Turner. 'It made a great impression on me and my future life, and on Ted. We talked about it for ages afterwards. I can still remember whole passages.'

But when Lewis recalled the trip in *Thirteen Women*, Victor Graves remembers his headmaster's disapproval of his mode of dress, a sky blue windcheater jacket with white piping and blue jeans. 'Gosforth', a thinly disguised Goddard, looks Vic up and down, examining his clothes:

GOSFORTH: Yes I imagined your parents to be the kind of people to approve of such attire.
VIC: But of course Henry clocked this and when he got on the bus he walked the whole length of the bus to where we were all sitting on the back seat and he said: Hello, Blue Boy.

'Henry' was Henry Treece, head of the school's English Department, and one of a handful of more enlightened members of staff who recognised Lewis's creative potential and to whom he increasingly turned for guidance. A celebrated poet, novelist and essayist, Treece saw promise in the remote, restless boy and was doubtless aware of the consequence of Goddard's criticism.

Treece's own education had been an uneasy combination of the traditional and experiential. As a pupil at Wednesbury High School, he'd won a scholarship to Birmingham University, where he began to write poetry, acted in university productions and boxed. A student of English, History and Spanish, he had been at university in Barcelona in 1936 at the outbreak of the Spanish Civil War, witnessing at first hand the beginnings of the bloody struggle between Franco's fascists and the fractured leftist loyalists. These events greatly influenced his thinking on politics and modernity. On his return to England, Treece began a career in teaching, first in Leicestershire, then at Cleobury Mortimer in Shropshire. When he took the post at Barton Grammar School in 1939, he had already produced *38 Poems*, the first of five volumes of poetry, subsequently published by Faber and Faber. Breaking off from teaching during the war, Treece served as a Flight Lieutenant Intelligence Officer with RAF Bomber Command.

Treece had been a leading light in the short-lived Apocalyptic

Movement of the late 1930s and early 1940s. This was a loose association of poets and essayists, a number of whom featured in the anthologies *The New Apocalypse* (1939) and *The White Horseman* (1941). The third collection, *The Crown and the Sickle*, which appeared in 1943, had effectively marked the end of the movement. The contributors who, in addition to Treece, included JF Hendry, Dorian Cooke, Norman MacCaig, Nicholas Moore, Philip O'Connor, Robert Melville, the critic Sir Herbert Read and, on the margins, a distinctly unwilling-to-be-associated Dylan Thomas – Treece had tried to recruit Thomas, but the poet was unwilling to sign the Apocalyptic Manifesto, some of which he had liked and some of which he had found 'manifestly absurd'. Adhering to no single form or style of writing, the Apocalyptics represented a generalised counterpoint to the political commitment and machine-age writing of poets such as Auden, Spender and MacNeice. George Orwell had described them as 'surrealists with the brake on'. Much of the writing displays surrealist and romantic qualities and makes use of mythological motifs to convey a belief that European civilisation was destined to collapse – a justifiable position, given the polarisation of politics and Europe in full retreat from the Nazis in the late 1930s. The movement is not well remembered; neither, in truth, is much of the writing it produced and it suffered by comparison with the later, earthier approach of the Movement poets who came to prominence in the decade after the war. Treece's own contributions were widely published, but did not generally fare well, with one critic characterising his poems as 'banal and sentimental'.

In 1942, an association with George Orwell had helped Treece to enter the world of BBC radio broadcasting, mainly through productions of his own verse plays, short stories, and poetry readings for *Voice*, Orwell's literary magazine for radio.

Treece's final collection of poetry, *The Exiles*, was published in 1952; followed later that year by his first novel, *The Dark Island*. From now on, he would commit himself to teaching and writing historical and mythical fiction.

For Lewis, along with others of his and future cohorts of Barton Grammar School pupils, Treece had virtual hero status. A well-built man, he carried himself with the confident poise of the boxer he had been in his youth. Ever-present dark glasses added to his charismatic appearance. Likewise, his individual dress code of bright yellow ties and socks and thick crepe sole shoes, coupled with a love of jazz – he was rumoured to have known Django Reinhardt – marked him out as something of a bohemian. In a school where many staff saw no further than the perpetuation of uniformly conservative, class-ridden thought personified by Norman Goddard, Mike Shucksmith remembers Treece's approachable style carried redemptive power:

> Put it this way, a small country grammar school is a bit like an amoeba in that it reproduces its own kind. All the staff were fairly narrow in their horizons, but Henry had been elsewhere and done other things. He had a broader view of life and was much more interesting to talk to than most of the other masters. I sat with him on a bench at the edge of the field at the staff versus school cricket match and he told me he'd been with Guy Gibson and the Dambusters squadron as Intelligence Officer. [No.5 Group, Bomber Command, included 617 Squadron, based at RAF Scampton in Lincolnshire.] He didn't make much of it, but as lads we were goggle-eyed.

Treece had the distinction of being the only teacher to whom Norman Goddard deferred. He'd also written the words of the school song *Keep Faith*. Set to music composed by Goddard and first sung at a speech day in 1953, the song was etched into the memory of every Barton Grammar School pupil thereafter.

Alongside the traditional grammar school fare of Shakespeare and classical poetry, Treece introduced a passion for storytelling into the classroom. *Bran the Bronze Smith* by Joyce Reason, a hero tale of pre-Roman, Bronze Age Britain was Lewis's first taste of historical fiction and was followed by more of the same. Treece brought his own books in for discussion. Remarkably prolific, his Celtic and Viking stories were plot-driven page-turners whose characters made more than enough use of swords christened 'Brain Biter' and 'Widow Maker' to create the kind of action Lewis and his classmates adored.

Treece set great store in the unconventional, the encouragement of original thought. Entering the classroom reading a copy of *Woman's Own* he'd picked up one morning, he devoted the lesson to a discussion about an article he thought interesting. He consented to digressive flights of argument or political debate prompted by pupils (one sure-fire distraction technique was to turn the conversation to boxing). Occasionally, he could be persuaded to tell stories of nights on the booze with Dylan Thomas. Lewis would later write that he'd once met Dylan Thomas at Treece's house, though he'd only been twelve at the time.

One hot afternoon, with sun streaming through the tall windows in his classroom at Baysgarth House, then serving as an annex to the main school, Treece told the class he was 'knackered' and asked them to 'carry on with something'. He pulled his striped knitted pullover over his head and went to sleep. For the double lesson of an hour and twenty minutes, no one made a sound. At the end, one of the girls gently tapped him on the arm and said they had to go. He was, by all accounts, an exceptional and inspirational teacher and proved as much, winning pupils' affection and consistently achieving the county's best 'O' level English results.

When Treece brought a Raymond Chandler novel into the classroom, revealing himself as a fan of hardboiled American fiction, reading Philip Marlowe in a wise-guy accent, Lewis was awestruck. Here was someone who shared his passion for all things tough and American, granting the stories equal billing with CS Forrester and Charles Dickens. Reading *The Big Sleep* defied school convention. Lewis recognised someone willing and able to raise a metaphorical two fingers to the loathsome rules and restrictions. He became a regular visitor to the Treeces at their home on East Acridge. Treece encouraged him to write, instilling the belief that it was a worthwhile pursuit, perhaps even a way to make a living.

One story from each of Lewis's third, fourth and fifth and final years survive by virtue of having been published in the school magazine, *The Bartonian*. Edited by Treece, they reveal Lewis's evolving influences and preoccupations. The first story, *Inside Information*, with its dark halls, themes of bloody revenge from beyond the grave and a ghostly twist, might have been lifted directly from the pages of an EC horror comic. Liberal use of gore and terror reveal the 14-year-old Lewis's affinity with Victorian gothic; and his concluding address to the reader: '*You ask how I escaped death? But you see, my dear friend, I didn't! No, I didn't…*' suggests late evenings spent with Edgar Allan Poe.

The second story, *The Legend*, published a year later in 1955, shows signs of a more distinct writing style. Alongside 1950s Cold War preoccupations with the atom bomb and its potential aftermath – doubtless a subject encountered in classroom debate – Lewis's post-apocalypse parable has something to say about urban and rural tensions. Here the city represents mystery and potential danger for its young protagonist; to visit is to risk death. A conflicted father and son relationship tells of an adolescent boy seeking to spread his wings in a world of restricted opportunity, surely a codified expression of Lewis's own feelings.

The final story, *Double Shuffle*, from 1956 takes us directly to B-Movie noir territory. Complete with subways, bellhops and wise-guy characters named 'Siegel' and 'Maguire', here is the first sign of Lewis in thrall to 1950s film, to Chandler, Spillane and American crime writing. Further evidenced by an uneasy collision of voice, smart-ass dialogue, and a bid to hardboil the narrative. Of the three stories, this is the most self-conscious attempt to write with a coherent stylistic idea. *Double Shuffle* lays down a marker, a statement of intent from its 16-year-old author. The preoccupation with the dangerous city persists, albeit in a more recognisable form. Here the danger is in the guise of friends who aren't friends, who steal your money and beat you to a pulp in alleyways. Lewis's first person monologue reveals the central character's inner psychological life. There is also a sympathetically written mother character, supportive of her son and his ambitions in the big city. In a telling contrast with the previous story's portrayal of a less than understanding father, here the father is already dead.

At the end of March 1955, Lewis played the part of Duncan in the school production of *Macbeth* – he'd previously played a boy scout in Percival Wilde's *The Dyspeptic Ogre*. According to John Dickinson, he 'did okay', but was never likely to pursue a stage career. Although, with the play coming at the end of the spring term, Lewis had more on his mind than remembering *So well thy words become thee as thy wounds*. He was looking forward to a school trip to Luxembourg during the Easter break, led by science teacher, Mr Smithson and French teacher, Mr Brice. The party set out on 12 April. A photograph taken at Barton Station and later printed in the local paper shows the fourteen-strong group with identical haversacks and sensible outdoor clothes. Lewis, on his haunches at the left of shot is bequiffed, nonchalant, in stout shoes. Next to him are John Dickinson and, in the rear rank, Nick Turner and Alan Smith.

Staying in a hostel near the town of Echternacht, close to the Sauer River, the location of heavy fighting between the US 4th Infantry and Armoured Divisions and German forces in December 1944, the boys spent their time walking in the surrounding countryside. (The US 4th Infantry Division had been commanded by General Raymond Barton, and had been assigned Ernest Hemingway as war correspondent.) Nick Turner remembers the fascination which met their frequent discoveries of discarded World War II debris. In woods outside the town, they came across the wreck of an aircraft and a blown up Sherman Tank adorned with the legend 'Blood and Guts'. In a photograph dated 18 April, the boys have grabbed themselves posing space on the tank, some on the turret, others above the tracks. Lewis, described by the caption, is 'reclining' to the left of a front machine gun port. The pictures recording the trip were published in *The Bartonian*.

Teddy Boys had been catching headlines since the early 1950s. The emergence of that most English personification of working class delinquency with his drape jacket, bootlace tie, brothel creepers, seat-slashing, street-fighting and petty violent associations had seen caricatures of menace-dripping Teds added to Lewis's drawing portfolio. Lewis, whose fascination with 'anything a bit rough and tough' was well established amongst his friends, might have fixated on Teds, but in Barton they were distant figures, newsreel bogeymen for his parents' generation.

Lewis's antidote to the monochrome world of austerity, the institutional straitjacketing of grammar school and Barton's small town conformity, had come through comics, books, pulp literature and film. Always film. He had seen and appropriated the *Blackboard Jungle* look – sky blue jacket and blue jeans. He certainly identified with the attitude. For a teenage film addict, 1955 was a big year. Lewis fixated on James Dean's character in *Rebel Without a Cause*, connecting strongly with the unsettled Jim Stark, yearning for the love and understanding he doesn't receive from his middle class family. That year also saw landmarks in noir cinema: *The Night of the Hunter* with Robert Mitchum; *Bad Day at Black Rock* with Spencer Tracy; *The Big Knife* with Jack Palance; and *Kiss Me Deadly*, Robert Aldrich's film of the Mickey Spillane novel. They would all have shown at the Star or the Oxford. If not, Lewis would have taken the ferry to Hull to see them there. On the eve of his sixteenth birthday in 1956, the *Lincolnshire Times* reports that *Night and the City* made a return showing at the Star – Lewis would have been too young to see it on its release in 1950. It was that rarest of things, a film about a London hustler played by an American actor, down at heel, delusional and irascible, another of Lewis's favourites, Richard Widmark.

America pervaded Lewis's art and influenced his thinking. It also provided the musical soundtrack to his own quietly subversive revolution. First to capture his imagination had been Count Basie, Duke Ellington, and a roster of big bands, most of whom could be heard regularly on the *Voice of America Jazz Hour*, often in association with US State Department-sponsored tours. These were the real deal. A far cry from the BBC's ersatz versions of dance band music or pop standards. Here again, the jazz-loving Henry Treece was undoubtedly an influence, as were countless American movies using jazz as a signifier of gritty urban cool. Westfield Road was the meeting place as Lewis and his friends broadened their horizons beyond the big band swing their parents would have recognised, listening to Dave Brubeck, Oscar Peterson, George Shearing, Stan Kenton and Gerry Mulligan. The records were difficult to find. Pinchbeck's in Barton sold a few popular and classical LPs, but never any real jazz. Grimsby and Scunthorpe were little better. Buying good jazz records required an expedition further afield to Gough and Davy in Hull. With the increasingly broad appeal of the music, as he had with cinema, Lewis needed to know everything.

It was a good time to be a fan of live music. In the days when bands would travel across Britain to play hundred-date tours in provincial venues, the Baths Hall in Scunthorpe was a regular gig. A trip to 'the baths' or across to the City Hall in Hull to see a great jazz player was an occasion; there were girls, booze and great music. Lewis, by then a capable, if not virtuoso pianist, could talk knowledgeably about the musicality of jazz. Inspired by musicians like George Shearing, he began to try out improvised jazz pieces. Later he would develop a greater ability, taking on, but never quite mastering, the technical complexities of modern jazz.

Through art, writing, music and especially film, Lewis was casting himself adrift from the rigid patterns of thought and expectation that had dominated his life. He'd ended one argument by calling his father 'a sanctimonious old sod'. Facing up to the repressive influence of his upbringing was one thing, but to actively and openly pursue rebellion wasn't his style. Ultimately, he cared about his parents and what they thought of him; he wanted to please them, to do the right thing.

As he carved out a niche for himself, reconciling the demands of the final months of his time at school with his own free-spirited creativity, he was not alone in finding the claustrophobia of Barton prompting him to look, or at least, think, further afield. In the days when most of his contemporaries' ambitions were limited to the end of the street, Lewis and the boys who had grown up together were outgrowing their town. 'Everybody knew what you were doing,' says Mike Shucksmith. 'There's nothing worse as a teenager, going to see grandma on a Sunday and being asked, "Who's the girl you were out with last night?".' It wasn't just the girls Lewis went out with, but the pubs he was drinking in, often ending the evening conspicuously drunk.

As the end of the fifth form approached, there was a final encounter with the headmaster whose bullying of 'the wrong sort' continued unabated. Lewis's treatment at his hands had instilled a deep empathy with others who suffered similar humiliation. When Albert Coleman's mother died and Albert came to school dishevelled and wearing a dirty shirt, Goddard hauled him up in front of the school, berating him for 'looking like something fallen off a dustcart'. Presumably the headmaster had been unaware of Coleman's loss, but Lewis seethed. Goddard's treatment of David Storey's mother and father at a parents' evening epitomised the snobbery he found intolerable. Storey's father had suffered as a Japanese prisoner of war, withdrawing into virtual silence as a result. Each day he came home from his job at the chemical works to sit in a kitchen chair by the fire, his baccy and cigarette papers close by on the mantelpiece. Mike Shucksmith remembers, 'If you went in, he'd say hello, but that was it. He'd pulled a curtain down between him and the world'. Everyone knew it had taken a great effort for Mr and Mrs Storey to attend school parents' evening. Mrs Storey was herself a quiet and reserved woman. When they encountered Goddard, he asked, who were they? When they answered, he said, 'Oh yes, David's parents. My best advice to you is get him to marry a career girl' and walked away. The story circulated and, once again, Lewis was outraged.

The difficulty he faced in expressing the indignation he felt was compounded by his, or at least Harry and Bertha's, desire that he continue at the school into the sixth form for two years. The decision was entirely in Goddard's hands. It was Harry's wish that his son enter a profession – accountancy has been mentioned as an unlikely career path – with a guaranteed job at the quarry to fall back on should he fail to achieve the requisite exam results. Lewis was horrified by the prospect and wanted to study for 'A' Levels, then university.

In the *Thirteen Women* script, Victor Graves recalls the exam results had been delayed that year. He returns to the sixth form in September in anticipation of their publication. As the returners arrived in the science lab, Gosforth (Goddard) is indignant that Graves is back at school, mocking the boy's ambition to be 'another Henry Treece'. In reality, when the results were finally published in mid September, Lewis had the necessary qualifications to stay in the sixth form, but Goddard refused him entry. The implication was that Harry's job as a quarry manager meant the family was not the 'right sort' for his sixth form. Even so, Lewis's open disregard for the school's ethos, and a lack of application had, in any case, given sufficient grounds for refusal. Nick Turner underwent a similar process of proving himself to gain sixth form entry (the Turners' father worked on the Humber ferries, which operated as part of the railway network). Harry insisted on accompanying his son to the interview with Goddard. Having attempted unsuccessfully to persuade the headmaster to change his decision, Harry had delivered a typically understated parting shot, 'Mr Goddard,

I've just one thing to say to you and that is that you have a most unfortunate manner.' But perhaps the most telling reflection of the end of Lewis's time at Barton Grammar is a speech the *Thirteen Women* script attributes to Treece:

HENRY: Look mate, if you're going to write, you're going to write. University won't make any difference to you. What do you want, to end up covered in chalk like me? Go to Art School. You can draw. Enjoy yourself for three years. At the end of it, who knows? You might be closer to the movies than you ever thought. Here, what's it going to be? Climbing the south face of Gosforth for two years? And then another three years after that? Christ, at that rate you won't have directed your first movie 'till you're at least 24.

At first, when Lewis broached the idea of art school at home, Harry dismissed it out of hand. Art was 'effeminate' and not, in his opinion, a suitable career. Besides, it would mean commuting to and from Hull every day, and that was out of the question. As a job at the quarry became a distinct possibility, Treece intervened and visited Lewis's parents at home. Speculating on the content of the discussion in the front room of 46 Westfield Road that September evening with the weighty formal presence of piano, armchairs, and Bertha's cat ornaments, I wonder would Treece have realised the door was closing on the boy's future and intervened of his own volition, or had Lewis appealed directly for help? Had he made himself scarce for a couple of hours, or was he upstairs listening to the deep murmur of conversation, knowing what was at stake?

Of all the help and guidance Treece had given and would continue to give over the years, it's hard to believe there was a more important contribution as mentor and friend than to leave

Harry and Bertha with an agreement that Lewis could continue his education at art school in Hull. The story, told first by the Turners and John Dickinson and elaborated on at length by Barbara Hewson, was that Treece had fought Lewis's corner. No doubt he'd done so quietly and respectfully, persuading Harry to recognise his son's undoubted ability, giving reassurance that he would take his English 'A' level just as planned, and that the new skills he'd acquire were bound to lead to a career. Might they have agreed that at the quarry it would have been impossible for a boy like Edward to achieve his potential, just as it had been under Norman Goddard's bullying regime? All we know for certain is that Treece made the case convincingly and Harry Lewis relented.

Lewis enrolled at Hull School of Arts and Crafts in October 1956. He returned to school for speech day and prize-giving on 25 October – presumably to receive the commendation for his final story in the school magazine, although it equally seems an act of defiance. The group photograph taken that day shows regimented rows of prizeworthy pupils: the girls in white blouses, hands in their laps; the boys in uniform blazers and ties. Almost hidden in the back row, Lewis wears his suit, more than ready for the world beyond Barton.

3

Bo or Italian
1956–1960

IN 1956, THE CITY OF HULL was shaking off a sense of itself as the 'north east town' whose streets and suburbs had been scarred by a devastating wartime bombing campaign, anonymised in news reports and unacknowledged in the country at large. (The 'D' Notice prohibiting reporting of the bombing of Hull would remain in place until 1976.) Its docks, industry, proximity to mainland Europe, and location on Luftwaffe flight paths to northern and midlands industrial cities had combined with the rivers Humber and Hull as natural navigational aids to make it the most bombed British city per square mile of the war. There was national recognition of the suffering of people in Coventry and Exeter, London and Liverpool, but not Hull. The city's own newspaper, the *Hull Daily Mail*, had been subject to restrictions. Typically, a report on 20 May 1942 told of a 'Fierce Raid on a North East Town' in which a number of people were killed and injured when raiders dive-bombed residential areas. The last recorded Luftwaffe raid on the UK to cause casualties came on 17 March 1945 when a Heinkel 111 flew along Holderness Road, opening up with machine guns and dropping fragmentation bombs. Thirteen people were killed and 22 injured. By the end of the war more than 1,200 people had been killed and 3,000 injured. Nearly 95 per cent of the city's houses were damaged and 152,000 people left homeless. There was deeply held belief among local people that Hull's suffering had been ignored and now it was being left to dust itself down and carry on.

That it did was, in part, due to a collective spirit of defiance and, more discernibly, a thriving and profitable fishing industry. Hull's fleet of deep water trawlers landed a third of the fish which ended up on British plates. It took an army of skippers, mates, third hands, deckhands, decky-learners, engineers, cooks and radio operators to bring back the fish for bobbers, filleters, fish merchants and fish-house workers to unload and process. Fish came fresh from ship to dock to the railways and roads and away to customers in a matter of hours. Ships and men had to be maintained, supplied and fed. Fish came in and the city worked.

Fishermen, home briefly between trips, were characterised as 'three-day millionaires', earning a reputation as hardened drinkers and gamblers whose limited time ashore was spent in the pubs and clubs of Hessle Road, done up to the nines in tailor-made suits and silk shirts. High living was understandable: with the industry at its peak, the mortality rate for men at sea was several times that of any land-based industry, six times that of coal mining. Men lost fingers, hands, and worse. At sea, first aid was rudimentary at best.

Fishing was a family tradition with fathers, uncles, brothers making a living at sea. In a tragedy which left its mark on the fishing communities, in the winter of 1955, two vessels – the *Lorella* and the *Roderigo* – had iced up in severe weather conditions. Clearing the ice was impossible and the ships became top heavy. Both capsized and 40 men lost their lives. However tough the conditions, men still sailed to bring back cod and haddock from fishing grounds close to the Arctic Circle. Rewards could be considerable. Top skippers earned good money for themselves and their crews, gaining reputations on a par with the city's rugby league and football players.

As Lewis arrived at the Hull College of Arts and Crafts on Anlaby Road, a few miles away the poet, Philip Larkin, who'd arrived in 1955 to take up the post of University Librarian at the University of Hull, had begun work on *The Whitsun Weddings*, the poem inspired by a train journey from Hull to London the previous year. Interviewed some years later for the BBC's *Monitor* arts programme, Larkin said, 'I never thought about Hull until I was here. Having got here, it suits me in many ways. It is a little on the edge of things.'

The city's future was beginning to unfold. There were new shops, cinemas, pubs and clubs. Department store Hammonds had recently installed a 'Picadish' cafeteria on the third floor where you could take one of the high stools overlooking Ferensway and swing round with a bird's-eye view over Paragon railway station and the bus station. In his poem, *Here*, Larkin speaks of a 'fishy-smelling / Pastoral of ships up streets, the slave museum / Tattoo-shops, consulates, grim head-scarved wives'. For some new arrivals, it might have felt like the end of the line and was certainly a little 'on the edge of things', but for Lewis, after Barton it was quite the opposite.

Attendance on the National Diploma of Design course meant leaving Westfield Road at 7 o'clock each morning for the walk to Barton Station and the short train journey to New Holland Pier. From there, Hull was a 30 minute ferry crossing away. If, as sometimes happened, one of the three pre-war paddle steamers grounded on the shifting sandbanks, the journey might take an hour, maybe more. From Hull Corporation Pier, it was a brisk 15 minute walk to the main college building in Anlaby Road.

Before art school, a trip to Hull had been an occasional highlight. Lewis and friends crossed the river to buy records at Gough and Davy and for Saturday trips to the pictures. Downstairs in the ferry bar where licensing laws meant alcohol was served all day, in an atmosphere thick with smoke and the smell of warm Double Diamond and rum, trawler crews who'd docked in Grimsby would make their way home to Hull. One Saturday morning when a group of fishermen came on board, one of whom produced a battered pack of cards, Lewis stood close by as hands of brag were dealt and the men outbid and outbluffed each other. The kitty rose in pound notes – serious money when most local men earned an average three or four pounds a week. Lewis drew closer to the game. At the climax of the hand with a healthy pot on the table, one of the fishermen dropped his cards on the floor. Nick Turner remembers, 'The fisherman said, "That was an ace wasn't it?" Quick as a flash, Ted said it was. It wasn't, but the others folded. He'd taken his life in his hands; if they'd realised he'd lied to help this bloke's bluff, he'd have got hammered.'

Aside from fishermen and daily commuters, the ferry's main trade was carrying passengers and goods for Hull Market and daytrippers from the hinterland of Grimsby and Scunthorpe and the villages of northern Lincolnshire. Lewis absorbed the atmosphere, listening intently and picking up on idiosyncrasies of accent, turns of phrase and snatches of overheard conversation. When his classes stretched into the evening, he'd run from college to quayside to make the last ferry home. If there was time and he had a few shillings in his pocket, he'd sink a pint or two in one of the dockside pubs and then perhaps another on the ferry. Nick Turner recalls an evening with Lewis and two girls at the cinema in Hull. Before catching the ferry home, they stopped off for a couple of pints in the Minerva and came out to find a prostitute and her client 'at it' up against the pier. 'He was ramming away, she was still eating her fish and chips. She saw us watching and shouted across, "What's a matter, love, an't you ever seen one before?" Ted shouted back, "Yeah, but not big enough to crawl back into."'

Until now, Barton had defined Lewis, reining in his ambition. Across the water, Hull felt like another country. Art school was the focal point for aspiring musicians, writers and artists working across the city. For Lewis, it was an irreversible step from Harry and Bertha's best intentions of a white-collar profession. He found himself one of a post-war cohort of like-minded young people from relatively modest backgrounds who, with education, aspiration and self-belief, challenged convention in ways denied their parents' generation.

Lewis began studying the intermediate level of the NDD, known as the 'inter', as well as working for his English A-level, a prerequisite for students of illustration expected to pursue careers in the emerging commercial worlds of graphic design and advertising. He was taught drawing, lettering, typography, painting and illustration with an approach that placed emphasis on ideas and learning how to think independently and creatively. Lettering classes could be exacting, repetitive, but it was a long way from the rote learning of grammar school. Lewis was initially conscientious, thriving in the less regimented system.

The man who came closest to replicating Henry Treece's influence as artistic mentor, and whose eye for detail and character nuance is central to understanding the development of Lewis as an artist, was William Augustus (Bill) Sillince. Known primarily as a cartoonist, caricaturist and 'humourist-stylist', Battersea-born Sillince had come to prominence with his work for *Punch* magazine, for whom he was appointed art editor in 1937 – a position he retained until the early 1950s.

In 1950 he published *Comic Drawing*, a 'light-hearted but essentially practical study of the nature, function, and creation of pictorial humour'. In the book, Sillince, who'd studied at Regent Street Polytechnic and Central School of Art then worked in advertising before becoming a freelance artist and cartoonist, set out his philosophy, distinguishing himself and his work from that of satirists and other more politically barbed cartoonists. Self-portrait caricatures which appear in collections of his cartoons show an owlish man with horn-rimmed glasses, an image recognised by Lewis's art school friends. They recall Sillince teaching by encouragement and anecdote rather than overly formal instruction. His stock-in-trade had been making gentle observation in a series of cartoons, which mocked English stereotypes of stuffy civil servants, military buffers, society girls, pinny-wearing housewives and overweight bureaucrats. Immensely popular collections of his topical wartime cartoons for *Punch* were published in hardback in *We're All In It* (1941); *We're All Still In It* (1942); *United Notions* (1943); *Combined Observations* (1944); and *Minor Relaxations* (1945). By and large these are wryly observed morale raisers that bring out the best in his affectionate humour, making subtle points of propaganda. The *Yorkshire Post* said Sillince had 'a remarkable knack for snatching the topic of the moment and pinning it down in black and white mirth'; the *Observer* that he had 'a sense of humour which, even in these grim days, does not jar'. In a foreword to one of the books, Sillince writes with characteristic understatement that, if his pictures should leave the reader 'a little brighter than before then the object of my present effort will have been achieved'.

Drawing with 2B and 4B pencils on self-burnished, grained paper, Sillince's technique softened the image and, as a consequence, tempered any underlying sting of his cartoons.

He skilfully conveyed a completeness of story in a single frame, raising a smile from the set of a pompous general's jaw, implying stoical defiance in the roll of a sleeve on a rolling-pin wielding 'Mum' or humanising ''Itler' as a boxer, scrawny, defeated, and throwing in the towel. A window on the wartime world, the books had established Sillince as a firm favourite with readers and students.

Like Sillince, Lewis's painting tutor, James (Jimmy) Neal, was a Londoner new to Hull. The arrival of two distinguished London tutors may have had something to do with the increased incidence of respiratory illness in the capital at that time. Lewis's friend, Ron Burnett, recalls both tutors had come to Hull for their health. Many did, particularly in the aftermath of the London smog of December 1952, in which a thick, polluted fog killed thousands of Londoners. For those with asthma or other respiratory problems, the cleaner air from the east coast and Humber estuary was thought to be beneficial.

Neal had trained at Saint Martin's and the Royal College of Art and brought with him kudos, experience and a refreshing down-to-earth approach to his classes. On his death in October 2011, artist David Sweet wrote in the *Guardian* how he had 'told stories about characters he had known, and related facts from the biographies and scandals of artists of the past, particularly obscure, minor artists, to illustrate a point or amplify a comment about a student's efforts'. In a shakily handwritten note sent in response to enquiries about Lewis in 2009, Neal remembered he 'was always very tired'. In his mind, there was no doubt the daily travel and attendance at art classes amounted to 'a very heavy schedule for a young lad'.

For art school students from Hull or the towns and villages of the East Riding, finding their way around French painters' names was an adventure in itself. Life classes gave them their first experiences of the nude form. Lewis's classmate, Dick Armstrong, remembers a young female model 'covered in love bites and elastoplasts' collapsing as the session drew to a close. 'It was winter and the girl had been surrounded by electric fires. She'd been standing for some time and the air was thick with cigarette smoke.' Armstrong, still drawing the girl's feet, realised her legs were going. 'I looked up in time to see her collapse, caught her and guided her onto this plinth covered in sheets. The teacher rushed over – you weren't supposed to touch the naked model and I thought I was in trouble.' The next morning Lewis greeted Armstrong by asking, did he have his running shoes on?

From the outset, it was clear that Lewis had talent as an illustrator and artist. Tutors and colleagues thought well of his work. But after the initial burst of enthusiasm, he began to coast as he had at school, doing enough and no more, dashing off assignments at the last minute. Away from the classroom, he immersed himself in a thriving social scene. With the college building sandwiched between the Tower Cinema on one side and the Regent Cinema opposite, the temptation to skip classes was irresistible. Sometimes the art school crowd would go en masse when classes finished at six o'clock. But Lewis would already have seen one film in the morning then crossed the road for a matinee showing of another. He retained his love of American gangster flicks, B-features and westerns, and became interested in the new European directors, Godard, Rossellini, Bergman and Chabrol. In the art school, there were fresh audiences for his encyclopaedic knowledge of film and filmmakers and he was recognised as an aficionado among other cinema-loving students. When the college film society began regular Sunday afternoon screenings at the Dorchester on George Street, Lewis joined and developed an interest in the emerging new wave of

British writers and directors. Here, perhaps for the first time, he identified the characteristics of his own parents and their preoccupations in the films he watched and the books he read. Friends remember him being distinctly uncomfortable with depictions of this instantly recognisable world. When Richard Hoggart wrote about working class archetypes in kitchen sink dramas in *The Uses of Literacy* in 1957, he might have been describing Bertha and Harry Lewis: '"Our Mam" is a solid, asexual presence contained within and defined by the domestic sphere. "The mester" or father, by contrast, is a figure inscribed by the work he does, commanding respect from his family and the community rather than love.'

Although cross-country running, beery belligerence and a tendency to fantasise about himself make it seem as if Lewis was engaged in a private game of kitchen sink bingo, he was never quite John Osborne's prototypical 'angry young man'. His frustration was not political or overtly anti-social. He was too shy for that, at least when sober. But he did kick hard against the conventions of his upbringing. In later years, he would talk about how he'd detested having to attend social events in Barton. Usually these were connected with his father's masonic responsibilities where formal conventions were adhered to and the Lewises measured themselves against wealthier middle class Barton families.

Evidence that the new wave would influence the kinds of harder-edged genre films Lewis preferred came with *Hell Drivers* in 1957, directed by exiled American, Cy Endfield. In terms of tone and treatment, Stanley Baker's performance as ex-con, Tom Yately, confronted by Patrick McGoohan's road foreman, 'Red', and his gang of corrupt lorry drivers, did much to redefine the way in which leading men were portrayed on screen. Now they could be provincial, working class, and hard as nails. In *Hell Drivers*, everyone is on the take. Action rattles at pace on rough tracks and backroads from a greasy driver's caff to a quarry side wasteland, doubling as a battleground. The haulage industry was home territory for Lewis. He knew these lorry drivers, or men like them, from his father's and his own experiences of the goings-on at Elsham Lime Works. In Dave Rolinson's notes for the 50th anniversary edition of *Hell Drivers*, he quotes from an interview Endfield gave to *Films and Filming* – a magazine to which Lewis subscribed – in which the director refutes the suggestion that 'Hell Drivers could not happen in this country', pointing out that 'I researched the subject for a long while. And I say it could, and does, happen here.'

An unusually tough film for the time with echoes of James Curtis's socially-aware pre-war novel, *They Drive by Night*, *Hell Drivers*' earthy brutality broke new ground. Critics praised its 'rough, tough action' and its authenticity, particularly in the fight sequences. Realistic, as Baker explains in the documentary *Look In On Hell Drivers*, because he and McGoohan used their own experiences as amateur boxers. Aside from the 'bruises and loose teeth', the dialogue, particularly between the drivers, had the ring of truth. It was offhand, confrontational and bitterly humorous. When Lucy, the firm's secretary, asks Yately if he has been in prison, he makes no attempt to sugar-coat the fact: 'I wasn't framed, and nobody talked me into anything. And the judge didn't give me a raw deal. Happy?'

It didn't take long for Lewis to acclimatise to student life. As he made new friends, the art school's basement common room, where students went to smoke cigarettes and socialise, became part theatre and part playground. There was a raised, spotlit area where girls sat, drank coffee and chatted. Lewis would look in and select his 'target for tonight', echoing the wartime

RAF propaganda film. He might have his eye on a particular girl. Other times he would hold court in the common room, occupying one of a random assortment of battered, motheaten easy chairs, telling jokes and anecdotes to an attentive audience. Part James Dean, part Lost Boy, his stories were designed with the sole purpose of attracting girls. Judy Burnett remembers one Lewis line. 'He'd had some illness when he was a kid and he told them his heart was weak and that he didn't have long to live – only maybe a week or two. He said he was going to die and the girls fell for it.'

It worked. Frequently. There were variations on the theme of his own imminent death or his parents' impending divorce. Dick Armstrong remembers Lewis entering the common room ashen-faced, planting himself in an armchair, saying he'd been to the doctor and had been warned if he had one more cigarette he'd die. 'As he told this story, gradually there was a girl on one arm of the chair with an arm around him, then a girl on the other arm, and several in a kind of puddle around his feet. I saw him half an hour later and he was smoking as if nothing had happened.' On one occasion, Armstrong received a lesson from Lewis in the art of enigmatic attraction:

'I used to bring LPs, carrying them under my arm, we all did. He called me over once and said, "Dick, the way you carry those LPs everyone can see what you've got. That's really off, you shouldn't advertise what you've got." I said, "Well you carry yours under your arm." He said, "Yeah, but I've always got the cover to my body." The penny dropped, that by slightly disguising the artist or the LP, he'd be a bit more mysterious and they'd all think, "What's Lew got today; what's he listening to?"'

Once Lewis had set his sights on a girl, he was usually successful. If he lost interest, the girl would be dismissed, usually finding out by discovering he was seeing someone else. Armstrong ran into trouble when he began going out with a girl called Janet Camm:

'She appeared at college the same day I did and she was gorgeous. Anyway, Ted snapped her up. When their relationship ended, she transferred her affections to me. I was in the gents' toilets and found myself face to face with Ted angrily demanding to know what I was doing with Janet. He said he "hadn't finished with her yet". He was spoiling for a fight so I backed off. You see, the unwritten rule was that he'd do the ditching.'

Armstrong kept his distance for some time after that and when he and Janet did eventually get together, he asked her why she'd ended the relationship with Lewis. 'She said he'd been peculiar with his sexual demands, but I didn't take it any further.'

For the first two years at art school, when Lewis came home to Barton his friends who had been granted access to the school sixth form were still around. They were together, just as they'd always been, going to the pictures and listening to jazz records in Lewis's room at Westfield Road. In October 1957, when the Count Basie Orchestra played Scunthorpe's Pavilion Cinema, Lewis was there. In 1958, when the Dave Brubeck Quartet played at Scunthorpe Baths on one of the US State Department sponsored tours, Riverbank Boy, Pete Bacon – known as 'Streaky' and no great fan of jazz – was press-ganged into taxi duty. Seeing and hearing Brubeck and his band close up brought Lewis's admiration to a new level. Brubeck's 1959 LP, *Time Out*, would become a firm favourite.

In the long summer holidays between art school years, Harry Lewis arranged for his son, along with Nick Turner, to be taken on as casual labour in the quarry at Elsham. Their job as hammermen involved looking through newly blasted chalk rocks for pieces of flint that couldn't be ground down, then breaking the rocks to remove the flint. Lewis wasn't much good at manual work. He swung the hammer, but with little real effect. On these long summer days in a dusty white bowl of the quarry under the blazing sun, there was plenty of scope for skiving off to chat and play cards. 'If we came across something big enough to hit,' remembers Turner, 'we'd have a go.' The few pounds they earned came from Harry's back pocket.

Lewis was always observing, watching and listening to the working men from Lincolnshire villages. He liked to listen to one older labourer who told stories about his wife. 'When there's a thunderstorm, my missis goes to bed with a pair of wellies on, because she's frightened of electricity. Bugger me if last night she didn't go to sleep with my wellies on her arms as well.' It might have been a caption from a Sillince cartoon.

By the time Lewis returned to art school for the third year in September 1958, the daily commute across the river, always something of a hindrance to his social life, was becoming intolerable. He had argued for some time that he needed to move out and find digs in Hull. Not surprisingly, Harry and Bertha were against it, but Lewis persisted, arguing that he would be better able to work. Eventually they relented and he found a place in lodgings at 9 Ash Grove, Hull.

Ron Burnett had started the National Diploma in Design course a year later than Lewis. An accomplished trombonist, already an established player on the Hull jazz scene, Ron played in the Unity Jazz Band alongside a group of like-minded friends. The Unity, so named because their original line-up had rehearsed in the Unity Hall on Anlaby Road, rather than any notion of collective politics, were one of a clutch of new bands inspired to play New Orleans style traditional jazz. Dismissed by some as 'rumpy-pumpy dance music', characterised by improvisation on traditional themes, and revered by purists who saw it as jazz music's most authentic form, the music had a simplicity, freedom and rawness to it. The Unity had established itself as the art school band, although their followers included a sprinkling of undergraduates from the university and assorted friends and fans. Lewis became their piano player. Rock 'n' Roll may have alienated parents and inspired moral panic headlines as the coming of Elvis, Jerry Lee and Little Richard grabbed the attention of sections of British youth but, for Lewis, playing jazz fitted the bill perfectly and the Unity were among a number of local bands to ride the crest of the trad wave. Many were accomplished players. The Bay City Jazz Band from Bridlington included Mick and Chris Pyne, on piano and trombone respectively – Mick also played cornet and tenor sax. The brothers would later be invited to join Humphrey Lyttelton's band and Mick would tour as piano player with Stan Getz. The trad crowd followed British musicians like Chris Barber, Ken Colyer, George Melly and Kenny Ball, all of whom played in Hull at one time or another. For a few, chart success would follow as the 1950s gave way to the 60s. But for 'Lew' Lewis, Ron Burnett, Tony Dugdale – clarinet, Eric Dobson – banjo, Alan Peacock – trumpet, Norman Wilson – double bass, Brian Thompson – drums, and Nick Marling – van driver, roadie, sometime manager and general factotum, playing trad to rooms full of sweaty dance-crazy students for beer and a few shillings was like being in a pop group.

Lewis's art school years saw the rise and fall of a generation of rock, pop and skiffle sensations, a few would-be stars and plenty who never quite lived up to the hype. Hull was a regular stop on the package tour circuit. Promoters made the most of the latest singing sensation by setting them up with a 15 or 20 minute closing spot on a bill largely dominated by middle of the road variety acts, comics, ventriloquists, crooners, TV personalities and the occasional local band. In the late 50s, rock 'n' roll and skiffle groups were guaranteed to fill theatres. Among the largely forgotten Terry Denes, Gary Millers and Charlie Gracies, you could have seen the Platters, Lonnie Donegan or Buddy Holly and the Crickets at the Hull Regal, later the Everly Brothers, and Gene Vincent; at the Cecil you could have screamed for Marty Wilde, Adam Faith, and Cliff Richard and the Shadows. Ron Burnett remembers the Unity played support to Marty Wilde at a university student union fundraiser. Touring dates suggest this was at the end of March 1959 as Wilde was riding high in the charts with *Donna*. Lewis was deeply envious of the cowboy gunbelt the rock 'n' roller wore on stage that night.

Lewis and Ron Burnett became firm friends, sharing Hemingway, Steinbeck and Chandler and the short stories they read in *The New Yorker*. They were a double act whose instant rapport and sparky, instinctive patter was at the heart of the band and the social group that formed around it. Their verbal interplay, inspired by the Marx Brothers, the Goons, Spike Jones and *Mad Magazine*, became a kind of band in-speak among the art school jazz crowd. Lewis was also a fan of the radio show, *Hancock's Half Hour*. Ray Galton and Alan Simpson's scripts were clever, funny and melancholic, predicated on the doomed-to-fail self-awareness of Hancock's character. For the episode first broadcast on 8 April 1958, and later included on the LP, *Pieces of Hancock*, the show celebrated the centenary of the fictional East Cheam Festival of Arts. *The East Cheam Drama Festival* – 'direct from the stage of the scouts' hall, Cheam' –

consisted of three short playlets performed by Hancock and his repertory company. The first playlet parodies the once popular Victorian melodrama of identity and duplicity, *East Lynne*, and is titled *Jack's Return Home*; the second takes a knowing swipe at the kitchen sink preoccupations of contemporary theatre in *Look Back in Hunger* by the playwright John Eastbourne; finally the evening falls into complete chaos as Hancock celebrates *The Life of Ludwig van Beethoven and the Song that Made him Famous*, hurried to a conclusion because Hancock is keen to get home for the 'boxing on the telly'.

Lines from radio shows found their way into Lewis's and Burnett's knockabout lingo. Or they'd make up their own. Former art student, Harry Duffin, remembers their response to a chance comment overheard in the art school gents' toilets:

'I was in the men's toilets downstairs at college. There used to be a bit of a scrum to get at the mirror. I was pretty vain and had a good crop of hair and I was standing combing my locks when Ted and Ron were there and I made some off the cuff comment to a mate about my "sheer physical beauty". I thought nothing of it until the next session of the Unity Jazz Band I was at. It was in a large school hall and a guy called Graham [Ron Burnett recalls it was Graham Palmer], who was a mate of Ted's, went to the microphone and announced that Ted had written a new song which the band were about to perform. The band struck up a riff and Graham began to sing – "*The sheer physical beauty of Harry Duffin, makes the girls go ooh-la-la.*" That was the song, the riff and just those words repeated over and over. It got a good laugh and, for a while, the band played it every time I turned up at a gig.'

Ron's mum, Gwen, and his dad, also called Ron, ran the Station Inn on Hull's Beverley Road, a short distance from Lewis's digs, and the Unity crowd often congregated there before going out. If it wasn't the Station, it would be the Argyle or the Midland, a favourite hangout before college gigs. After hours, Gwen, fondly remembered as a 'proper landlady' by Lewis's friends, hosted parties long into the night.

With a network of pubs, clubs, gigs and parties, it was easy to tap into Hull's jazz scene and find like-minded music fans. Jackie Scoble, who first saw the Unity at an outdoor gig at Little Switzerland – an open space on the Humber foreshore at Hessle – remembers 'these really dishy looking guys, playing brilliant music, out for a good time with the girls. Lew was like a film star, so was Tony (Dugdale) and the others, and jazz was *the* thing. The music was enough to get us on a real high. You got up and danced, and you were worn out at the end of the evening.' Lewis's film star credentials are on display in a photograph taken by Graham Palmer at around this time. Palmer had taken a few shots of the band, but the portrait is of Lewis alone, posed in candy-striped open neck shirt, tweed jacket, and with a carefully combed quiff. A good looking boy. Every inch the 1950s matinee idol.

Whatever its musical merits, trad jazz was an expression of youthful abandon; an energetic alternative to the mainstream influence of dance band music, watered down rock 'n' roll and pale pop ballads. For the Unity and their audience, it meant good times, drinking, dressing up and playing simple, accessible dance music. Ron Burnett is the first to admit the Unity were learning their trade as musicians. Lewis, he remembers, was fairly accomplished. Mike Gordon played piano in the university jazz band and recalls Lewis teaching him to play the Jelly Roll Morton classic, *Dr Jazz Stomp*, taking him through the chords, trademark cigarette dangling from his lips. The Unity regularly filled the floor at their Friday night residency at the Blue Bell, the stomping ground of many local jazz bands. In a narrow room over the pub, packed with fans and drinkers, the band played two sets a night. Charge for admission varied between sixpence and a shilling, depending on the bands playing. Lewis was cool, one of *the* cool, according to followers of the band. He revelled in the possibilities of jazz, beer and girls who would sleep with him. As Jackie Scoble says, 'every girl in the crowd was in love with somebody or thought that somebody was wonderful'. She remembers a night Lewis missed the last ferry. A friend was waiting for her father to give her a lift home. She offered Lewis a lift back to her parents' house in Cottingham and he stayed over in the spare room. In the middle of the night, the girl crept into his bed. Not surprisingly, he didn't say no.

The 2.19 Band was a rival outfit from the art school architecture department, playing a regular gig in a pub off Hessle Road. They would arrange to go out together, to the cinema, to dances or to jazz gigs, or to see and be seen at the Picadish. Fellow student Neville Smith, who would later write the classic thriller *Gumshoe*, had come to the University of Hull from Liverpool. He remembers the most important question for an evening out would be, 'Are we going Bo or Italian?' 'Bo' meant bohemian, an Anglicised beatnik look of baggy sweaters and drainpipe trousers associated with trad jazz fans. Italian was inspired by the continental and Ivy League stylings of modern jazz players. The art students tended to have a foot in both camps. For the most part, they were bohemians by necessity, affecting a careless scruffy appearance. They didn't have the income to pull off the Italian look with any confidence, although Ron Burnett was known to tour what he referred to as the 'dead men's shops' for good suits and have them altered. He remembers his first encounter with Neville Smith and Brian Case on the steps of the art school. 'Nev asked me were there any bohemians in Hull?'

Growing up in south east London, the son of a policeman, Brian Case would acquire legendary status as a writer on jazz, film and crime fiction for *Time Out* and the *NME*, as well as being the author of several landmark books and a highly regarded novel, *The Users*. He and Neville Smith met at the University of Hull. They would remain good friends for many years.

In July 2015, back in Hull's Central Library for a reading and conversation session on the launch of his interview memoir *On The Snap*, Case shared his memories of the city. 'It could be a dangerous place – drunk decky-learners, dreadful Tetleys beer, you couldn't buy decent jazz records. It wasn't so much rock 'n' roll, it was more Teddy Boys, awful long jackets in maroon, zigzag pockets.' Case had seen his first Teddy Boy in Deptford and been awestruck by the style, the confidence, the sharpness. But he was very much an Italian suit man. 'It was all very exact. London had places where you could get your stuff – Old Compton Street, I'd get stuff in there. You tried to go for American import suits. Ivy League suits. Like the jazz men. Which was natural shoulder line, not tapered, three buttons. It was all very technical. I used to go to Maison Alpha in Old Compton Street, seven shillings and sixpence for a Gerry Mulligan haircut, swept to the side like a longish bob.' He remembers hitching to Leeds to see Art Blakey and to Manchester to see John Coltrane. In Hull, he and Neville Smith frequently found themselves at Unity gigs. Smith has perhaps the most vivid memory of Lewis the trad piano player:

'Every Saturday night in the late 1950s, the Unity Jazz Band, under the leadership of trombonist Ronnie Burnett, played in the Common Room of Hull University Students' Union. Their band uniform was a Victorian version of Italian suits, with pointed shoes, drainpipe trousers, high-button jackets, stiff Victorian collars with rounded ends and slim ties. At the piano, with dark rings under drooping eyelids, blond hair falling over his face, sporting a pearl tie-pin, and with a permanent fag between his lips, sat a man I came to know as Lou. (In my mind, Lou is always how I have spelt the name.) Lou, to my envious eyes, never looked anything other than utterly shagged out.'

There were bohemians in Hull, of a sort, but Lewis was not one of them. Quietly conventional and 'quite dapper' in his own way, according to art school friend, Keith Riseam, Lewis was 'slight, not a big lad, lovely blond hair, cheeky, a good sense of humour. He played trad and enjoyed playing it, but he would go into rooms and sit and listen to modern jazz'.

For Colin MacInnes, whose 1959 novel, *Absolute Beginners*, threw the spotlight on the styles and customs of the two diametrically opposed jazz tribes, the culture was a teenage declaration of independence. The Dean is a 'sharp modern jazz creation' with 'college-boy smooth crop hair', a 'neat white round-collared Italian shirt' and 'short Roman jacket *very* tailored'. By contrast, writes MacInnes, the Misery Kid with his 'horrible leanings towards the trad thing' is full-on bohemian. His hair is long and 'brushless'; his shirt has a 'white stiff-starched collar (rather grubby)' and his short jacket is old, 'somebody's riding tweed, most likely'. In contrast with Hull's more integrated jazz scene, MacInnes' tribes are rarely, if ever, seen together in public.

In August 1959, Lewis and his resolutely trad bandmates piled their gear into Alan Peacock's dad's Humber Snipe and travelled to Leeds for a recording session. The resulting five tracks are the only surviving recordings of the Unity: *My Daddy Rocks Me*; *Travelling Blues*; *Marching through Georgia*; *Shine*; and *Black and Blues* showcase a mix of live favourites and New Orleans standards made famous by, among others, Louis Armstrong and Trixie Smith. All are given the Unity treatment. The band seems loose and relaxed, particularly letting go on the uptempo numbers. For the session there was no bass, which wasn't unusual. Stand-up basses were expensive and hard to come by, hence skiffle groups making do with the tea-chest variety. Eric Dobson's banjo and Brian Thompson's drums were the rhythm section. The quality of the recording is basic at best, but the performance swings enthusiastically. This is music made for the joy of it. Lewis's piano drops in and out of the mix, but where it shines through on solos he shows himself an instinctively rhythmic player, picking out licks and more than holding his own.

The art school calendar was punctuated by regular social events: freshers' dances, riverboat shuffles, Christmas parties, and summer fancy dress balls. The riverboat shuffles began as a novelty with four or five bands playing for an evening. The organisers would hire one of the Humber ferries, sailing from Corporation Pier as far as Spurn Point at the mouth of the estuary, before turning – a manoeuvre which made for some particularly choppy, piano-sliding-across-floor moments – and making the return trip, arriving back in Hull around midnight. One night, they didn't have a piano. Ron remembers, 'Ted was distraught so we went to a nearby pub, just off the pier, borrowed a piano and pushed it onto the boat and pushed it back afterwards'. On a good night, there might be 600 passengers on board. Brian Case remembers, 'You had to be pissed to enjoy them. They were *very* Dixieland. Like with all those things, after an hour you wanted to get off but you were trapped.' Another night, the Unity backed jazz legend, George Melly. 'Someone suggested we get someone to guest with the band and we asked George Melly,' says Ron Burnett. Melly had sat in with bands before, memorably on one drunken evening in a pub on Anlaby Road, most likely the Argyle. 'It just appealed to him, so he came up to Hull and sang with the band at this golf club in Melton.' Martin Turner has a memory of the infamously hedonistic Melly in a radio interview some years later saying the best pianist he'd ever heard was a student called Ted Lewis from Hull.

When the Unity played, they would invariably meet in the pub for a pre-gig pint or two. For many of the gigs, including those at the college and the Windsor Hall, there was no bar; but the students always found places to stash drink and ways to get drunk. Early in 1959 there was a short-lived craze for preludin, a prescription diet pill that worked as an appetite suppressant and upper. Keith Riseam recalls, 'You'd take a couple of those and go for twenty-four hours'. But the phase didn't last; three-day hangovers were barely worth the high. Lewis's friend, Mike Shucksmith, also refused entry to Barton Grammar School sixth form, had been called into the RAF for two years' National Service. He'd visit whenever he could and remembers the preludin fad taking its toll on Lewis:

'Not being a very robust guy physically, Ed was like a skeleton on these things. Apart from juicing him up so he could go and live the life of Riley with the band and everything else he got up to, he didn't eat much. I remember, if he was going home for the weekend, he would call in at my house to see what I was up to, if I was home or not. And my mother used to say he looked like a man of forty. This was when he was about seventeen or eighteen.'

For the most part, Lewis and the trad scene's drug of choice was alcohol. Ron Burnett remembers a night out to see Gerry Mulligan and his band at Hull City Hall. 'We met at a pub before the gig for a few drinks, then stopped on the way at another pub, then another. We were late by then so we ran to the next pub, the Punch Hotel, opposite the City Hall. Lew threw up and said straight away, "Right, let's go and have another drink."'

The new wave films, piano playing and jazz clubs, combined with a louche style and good looks, added to Lewis's carefully cultivated mystique. Judy Burnett remembers him as 'physically small, slight. The girls would think he was so sweet. He wasn't a strong man, sweet face, cigarette hanging on his lip, bottle of beer on the piano.' It's an image captured in a handful of grainy black and white photos from the time.

The combination of drink and an almost compulsive need to chat up women brought Lewis into conflict with even his closest friends. One night he made a play for Ron Burnett's mother at the Station Inn. Lewis had also known his friend was keen on a girl named Catherine, but it didn't prevent him chatting her up and taking her back to his digs. A few days later, Lewis apologised. 'He said he was drunk and didn't know what he was doing.'

Jan Chesterman was a regular on the Hull jazz scene. She recalls being at a party where Lewis had a fling with the girlfriend of a member of the 2.19 Band:

'Lew took her off this guy, so he filled a vodka bottle with *2001* carpet cleaner, put it on the table and said, "That's mine, no-one touch it" knowing Lew would pinch it. I remember being told Lew had drunk the vodka. I was really concerned, so I took him back to my house and made him drink loads of milk. I don't know how much of it he'd had, but it was a close call.'

When friends from Barton came across for weekends, Lewis set them up with blind dates. John Dickinson remembers 'He was having a great time, we were quite envious; art school made our lives seem a bit humdrum.' At one art school Christmas party, Lewis set Dickinson up with a girl who smoked a pipe. 'It was Chinese themed night and I remember going into the gents and there were all these Chinamen strewn around the floor.' Lewis's girl-chasing exploits – Alan Dickinson describes them as 'an extension of his athletics career' – almost came to a dramatic end when he was discovered in bed with one young girl. Nick Turner remembers. 'Her father threw Ed out the house, chased him down the street and said he'd nail his balls to the college door if he ever saw him again.'

In September 1959, Lewis began his final year at art school with the preparatory work for the portfolio he would present to Bill Sillince. As usual, he had applied himself at the last minute, finishing as term started. Sillince was impressed with the drawings, most of which had been inspired by Lewis's home and garden at Westfield Road, the orchard and the north Lincolnshire landscape around Barton and the Humber foreshore. With the college year barely into gear and his work accepted, the pressure was relieved and his social life could once more take priority. He cast his customary eye over the new student intake. There was Heather Morton, his current girlfriend; she was pretty, affectionate and loyal. Judy Burnett remembers, 'She dearly loved him, but he was rather cruel to her.' A wonderfully disorganised group photo of the art school crowd taken on the beach at Fraisthorpe earlier that summer evokes those days of beer, sunshine, picnics, pretty girls in summer dresses and skinny lads with windblown hair and good sunglasses. Lewis is in swimming trunks, a bottle of beer and a cigarette on the go, Heather at his side. Shortly after the new term began, Lewis ended their relationship. He would later rename her 'Hilary' in his novel *All the Way Home and All the Night Through*, writing that, after the break-up, she'd confronted him at the freshers' dance where the band was playing, that he'd ignored her, and she'd become drunk and hysterical, wailing and sobbing uncontrollably. Heather doesn't remember the scene being quite as dramatic, only that she'd been upset at being let down.

At seventeen, Juliet Raahauge had gone to great lengths to persuade her parents to allow her to attend art school. Her mother and father, with a house in the affluent village of Kirk Ella and a family connection to the 'county set', had thought it a bad idea. Juliet had never had a steady boyfriend, at least not one who'd taken her beyond adolescent hand holding. The art school, with its reputation for parties, jazz, booze and bohemian behaviour was not considered appropriate. If Juliet was to attend, her mother would decide the terms.

To begin with she kept her distance from Lewis. He was, she says, 'a big name' in college, someone whose reputation as an art school lothario preceded him. With her mother's strict rules, she had less freedom than most of her contemporaries. For Lewis, this made finding ways to chat up Juliet far more of a challenge than he was used to, but he'd made his mind up she was the one. His pursuit signalled a departure from his usual technique of feigning uninterest and expecting the girl to do the chasing. But Juliet didn't fall at his feet. She was, remembers Judy Burnett, 'an English rose who arrived at college in twinset and pearls', from a world that Lewis had rarely encountered. He had fallen in love with someone very different from himself. The layers of mystique fell away as he let slip the film star nonchalance he'd created over the preceding three years.

In a memorable scene in *All the Way Home and All the Night Through*, Lewis's literary stand-in, Victor Graves, discusses his feelings of class insecurity with 'Philip', home from medical school. Lewis identified himself as being working class, aspirational perhaps, but not quite middle class. It shouldn't have mattered, but it did. Lewis was anxious, inhibited, and knew he needed to overcome his anxieties or risk losing Juliet altogether. And, if that wasn't complicated enough, there was Juliet's mother's approval to gain. Mrs Raahauge needed to be convinced, particularly since a family friend had passed on gossip about the jazz-playing blond boy with a succession of girls in tow. But when Juliet invited Lewis home, he arrived, immaculately dressed in his Prince of Wales check suit, and turned on the charm. 'She adored him,' Juliet remembers. On a shopping trip to Hull, she and her mother met Lewis in the street. 'Ted had these long eyelashes and my mum asked, could she take a cutting from them? I was so embarrassed.'

On several occasions, Juliet made the trip across the river to stay at Westfield Road. Bertha and Harry welcomed her warmly, as did his grandmother. 'You could tell he had a great affection for her. She and William the cat were such an important part of his life.' Juliet remembers Mrs Shaw as a large lady who spent her time sitting in the corner of the room 'radiating calm and love'. Bertha doted on him. 'His mother got all dressed up and had her hair done when he came round. She always made him his favourite sausage sandwich and would hover about like a tiny bird making sure that he was happy.' Harry she remembers as 'laconic, gangly, but quite a wit'.

From the beginning, Lewis and Juliet's relationship was intense. They began to wear beatnik black, visiting the cinema to be alone with each other rather than attending classes. Juliet's mother's rules were tested to the limit, then broken. The courtship was not without flashpoints, more often than not driven by Lewis's drink-fuelled insecurity. Drinking excessively made him difficult and, as Juliet remembers, he began to have blackouts. 'He'd end up paralytic and in a corner being sick or not knowing who he was. It was exhausting. He was a demon, like a Jekyll and Hyde character, accusative, rude, violent, and aggressive for no reason.'

Intoxication made Lewis jealous of any relationship Juliet had with other male friends, even if they were his friends too. At a Wild West themed art school dance, Lewis had dressed as Doc Holliday, complete with model six-shooters, bootlace tie and cowboy hat. The band met at the pub as usual and began drinking. Lewis had convinced himself Juliet wouldn't be coming, that she would leave him. By the time she arrived – Hiawatha in a short fringed buckskin dress – he was drunk and thoroughly obnoxious. When the band were due to play, Lewis was incapable and they went on without him. He wandered through the college looking for Juliet. She and Keith Riseam had escaped for a coffee at the Wimpy Bar. Keith remembers, 'It was about ten o'clock by the time we got back. Ted was beside himself and I thought I was dead. He thought I'd pinched Juliet.'

At some point in the evening, Lewis had punched through a window and his hand was bleeding quite badly. He'd also fallen down the art school stairs, dragging some Gaudi drawings on loan from a London gallery off the wall as he lost his footing. With the help of friends, Juliet managed to get him to Hull Infirmary to have the wound dressed. She had arranged to stay with Judy, but ended up spending the night with Lewis on a friend's sofa. Early the following morning the phone rang at Judy's. It was Mrs Raahauge. She wanted to speak to Juliet. Judy said she was still in bed, but Mrs Raahauge insisted she be allowed to speak to her daughter. A terrified Judy had to come clean. She passed on the phone number of the house where Lewis and Juliet had stayed. Mrs Raahauge arrived by car and took Juliet home. After a considerable period of contrition and some careful persuasion, Juliet convinced her mother to allow her to continue to see Lewis. The relationship carried on into 1960 and what would be Lewis's final year in Hull.

Increasingly, the prospect of leaving college, his friends, the band and the city weighed heavily. Lewis, Ron Burnett and others began to make their way to London for weekends, hitching a lift south, going to the theatre, seeing films, and visiting jazz clubs. They regularly took in sessions at Ronnie Scott's and the Cy Laurie jazz club in Soho's Ham Yard – Laurie and his band had played in Hull and the club he ran would go on to become the legendary mod club, The Scene, in the early 60s. Ronnie Scott's was renowned as a real jazz club; there it was all about the music. 'There were no hassles to buy beers or drink up,' says Ron. The jazz on offer included the best touring bands from the US. Consequently, the Hull crowd were on the spot for some of the greatest performances of the era, catching, among others, Zoot Sims, Stan Getz, and Art Blakey and the Jazz Messengers.

As well as giving the art students the opportunity to take in shows and exhibitions, trips to London gave Lewis a taste of the adventure he craved. Soho, with its sex shops, Maltese gangsters and prostitutes was, as George Melly said, 'perhaps the only area in London where the rules didn't apply'. Less of the bohemian no-go area and artistic enclave it had once been, it was still a place you could be bad and pretty much get away with it. Lewis and his friends drank in pubs like the Blue Posts and ate cheaply at The Star, an Italian Restaurant where they'd buy a plate of spaghetti Bolognese for three shillings and sixpence. A stone's throw away in Meard Street, The Gargoyle,

Soho's infamous pre- and post-war hangout for artists, poets, bohemians and pornographers had been bought by a couple of Soho businessmen with an eye for the main chance. Jimmy Jacobs and Michael Klinger soon reopened the place as a strip club, the Nell Gwynne Revue. Lewis was enthralled by the opportunities on offer in London. He and Ron saw *Beyond the Fringe* at the Fortune Theatre and *One Over the Eight* with Kenneth Williams at the Duke of York's. Ron remembers a night out at the newly opened Establishment Club: 'You felt you could do all these things, go anywhere, and do anything.'

As the end of term approached, Lewis submitted his final portfolio. In the summer student rag parade, the art school crowd were on floats along with students from the university. Lewis was wearing nothing more than a pair of swimming trunks. When the float reached Queen's Gardens, Juliet needed the toilet. She went into Hammonds department store and then got back on the float, not realising Lewis had followed her into the store. By the time he emerged, the floats had gone and Lewis had to walk the mile and a half back to the university in his swimming trunks. When he arrived, he was fuming.

Art school ended. Lewis played a final few gigs with the band. Juliet left on a family holiday for a fortnight. When she returned, after two weeks in which Lewis's insecure imagination had taken hold, he felt something had changed and no amount of reassurance could convince him she hadn't been unfaithful (he had slept with another woman at his farewell party). A few weeks later, at a friend's party, he drank even more than usual and accused Juliet of imagined infidelities. In a drunken rage that night, Lewis hit Juliet, ending the relationship once and for all. Later, he would reflect on the events of that night in Victor's guilt-ridden internal monologue at the key moment in *All the Way Home and All the Night Through*, writing, 'This is going to be dreadful and you are too drunk to realise how vicious and painful it's going to be... you want to hurt her because she is true and in hurting her you will hurt yourself in payment for your cheating.'

Juliet still struggles to understand what fuelled Lewis's insecurity. 'He'd had a good childhood, his mum and dad loved him and he was well treated. But he told me all sorts of things, that his parents were getting divorced, that his heart was bad and he had months to live. He just said things to get sympathy and he didn't need to do that.' With the relationship over, it seemed her friends were only too willing to admit that Lewis had been going with other women. 'I realised he'd been much more of a bad boy than I ever thought. Other people would be only too pleased to tell you, but I was mortified.'

Juliet had been Lewis's first real love. He was miserable, telling Alan Dickinson the relationship ending was 'the end of the world'.

Lewis left art school with his National Diploma in Design. Friends had assumed he would go to London to work in illustration. He applied for jobs without success and moved back home for the summer, supported by his parents. His dream of living and working in London in the film industry seemed more distant than ever. He was drinking a great deal and attempting to reconcile himself to the self-inflicted failure of the relationship with Juliet. He began to write, initially drawing on his earliest memories and the experiences of his father's wartime absences. He would later tell William Foster of *The Scotsman,* 'First off, I was all set to write my whole life story. All about my childhood during the war when my father was away and Manchester where I'd been born.' In the event he was drawn to the raw, confessional passages which dealt with Juliet and the final year at art school. With hindsight, it seems a literary penance. Lewis was in Barton, his friends mostly working or studying elsewhere, and the relationship which mattered beyond all others had been sacrificed to drink and insecurity. What was he to do but unsparingly write it all?

His design and illustration portfolio had been sent to several employment agencies. Finally, in what feels like something of a last-ditch solution, when a job offer did come through with Westland Aircraft in Somerset, he took it. It wasn't what he wanted or where he wanted, but if he wasn't to remain adrift indefinitely, he had no choice other than to pack his bags and head west.

4

Lone Ranger
1960–1966

O F THE CULTURAL TOUCHSTONES THAT WOULD inspire
and influence Lewis's writing – EC crime comics, pulp
novels, American noir, Westerns, B-movies, the British new
wave, Spillane, Chandler, Greene, Sillitoe – it's important not to
overlook two landmark British crime movies made as the decade
turned. Released in April 1960, *Hell is a City* was directed by Val
Guest, adapted from a streetwise 1954 novel of the same name
by former Manchester policeman, Maurice Procter. The first
in a series of police procedurals featuring Detective Inspector
Harry Martineau, Procter's writing delivers a healthy dose of
reality and makes liberal use of features common to the hard-
boiled school:

'Robbery with violence at the busiest time of a fine Saturday
morning. A sudden shout, a scream maybe, a rush of feet, a
slamming of doors followed by the snarl and squeal of harshly
used brakes and tyres: momentary overtones in the city's
roar. A slick, quick crime, obviously. A city crime committed
by city denizens. Denizens of the underworld. Rats. Like rats

they crept out of their holes to attack and steal, and scurry away.'

Guest retained the novel's earthy tone and, importantly, its locations in and around Manchester (Procter names it 'Granchester' in his novel) to create a credible and largely successful northern British crime movie with distinct noir sensibilities. In a departure from British cinematic conventions of the gentleman detective, Stanley Baker brings a violent unpredictability to the character of Martineau on the trail of hardened criminal, Don Starling. When Starling escapes prison, Martineau knows he'll go to any lengths to make good his escape. We follow the pursuit with a growing unease. Martineau is fallible, edgy, quick-tempered, and morally compromised, knowing he needs to be as tough as the man he's chasing. Guest's direction and grimy *mise en scène* bring a documentary realism to the drama. Shooting in black and white, he moves at pace from Martineau's failing marriage and troubled home life to Manchester's sleazy pubs, shabby backstreets and bleak rural settlements skirting the moors at Oldham Edge and Saddleworth.

Joseph Losey's *The Criminal* premiered in September 1960. A visually stark social commentary on the prison system, ridden with institutional collusion and sanctioned mob violence, it tells the story of professional villain, Johnny Bannion; Stanley Baker based the character on his friend, Soho gangster Albert Dimes, who also acted as advisor on the film. On his release from prison, Bannion comes into conflict with Mike Carter, played by Sam Wanamaker. Carter is a sophisticated operator, a shrewd corporate crook, embodying a new way of running criminal enterprise. In Carter's world, Bannion's old school villainy has no place.

In common with Cy Endfield, who'd directed Stanley Baker in *Hell Drivers*, Joseph Losey had been making films in Europe since being blacklisted by Hollywood in the early 1950s. In many ways typical of the outsider looking in on the established order, he would later explain how he'd set out to explore failings in the British penal system and 'to show life in prison as it really was'. In doing so, he produced a distinctive, stylised Brit noir and a milestone in the depiction of the criminal underworld.

Taken collectively, *Hell Drivers*, *Hell is a City* and *The Criminal* illustrate a fundamental shift in the representation of crime in British cinema, effectively wrapping up the immediate post-war period and signalling a move away from officer-class casting, spiv-stereotypes and pre-war concepts of law and order and its portrayal. Lewis must surely have recognised that, for the first time since *Brighton Rock*, here was a credible British crime/noir aesthetic rooted in working class and underclass experience, grounded in real language, set in the backstreets of northern English cities, tawdry suburbs and inhospitable rural backwaters. American exiles, Endfield and Losey had a different view of things. There were few, if any, sympathetic characters and plenty of weak, guilt-stricken ones. Baker's emergence as a kind of British Lee Marvin wouldn't have been lost on him either – a belligerent, brooding presence in whom the viewer senses a constant threat of violence. Baker's characters didn't care if you liked them or not. Lewis would have revelled in ultra-real fist fights in formica-tabled caffs, the suspense of racetrack heists, brutal beatings, inevitable double crosses, and Johnny Bannion's lonely death in a frozen field.

Shortly before Christmas 1960, Harry sold the house at Westfield Road and the Lewises moved to 84 High Street, Barton, a shop with accommodation attached, opposite the

Star Cinema. Soon afterwards, they opened as a tobacconists and confectioners. Bertha was a familiar and friendly presence behind the counter for a generation of children. With Lewis having left home, almost certainly for good, the shop provided a useful diversion as well as a much needed source of income. Whether, as some have suggested, the move signalled a downturn in Harry's fortunes, the new home met the family's needs and relieved the burden of upkeep of house and garden at Westfield Road.

In January 1961, Lewis returned home for his twenty-first birthday party. Having expected to take his talents to London, he was effectively marooned in the drawing office of Westland, whose base at Yeovil in Somerset must have seemed a world away. The work was not well paid – he later claimed he'd been earning £3.00 a week, a modest pay packet even by 1960 standards – but it had a kind of steady respectability. Interviewed some years later, he would recall 'a terrible job' that placed him far from fulfilling his promise as a graphic artist and further still from his film directing ambitions. The small consolation of time on his hands meant he continued to work on the autobiographical novel he'd begun after college. Writing longhand on the firm's headed paper was a minor act of defiance.

On return visits to Barton, his first port of call was invariably Henry and Mary Treece. Their relationship had lasted throughout art school; Lewis later recalled spending an afternoon drinking in the Volunteer Arms with Treece, his father, and the American poet, Henry Roskolenko, with whom Treece had a longstanding professional and personal friendship. A series of heart attacks had forced Treece to retire from teaching in 1959, but he remained a guiding influence in Lewis's life, encouraging his literary ambitions as mentor and friend. In his *Thirteen Women* script, Lewis wrote a vivid description of a scene from around this time. He sits side by side with Treece at the piano in the drawing room at East Acridge House – Barbara Hewson remembers the room 'appeared to be endlessly shelved with books' – the French windows open to the lawn surrounded by elm trees. Henry's son, Richard, sits on a footstool by the piano, accompanying the piano duet on acoustic guitar as they play a four-handed version of *Honky-Tonk Train Blues*.

Treece maintained a prolific output of historical fiction, attaining a degree of popularity without ever achieving bestseller status. In 1961, Brockhampton Press published his children's adventure novel *The Jet Beads*, which featured illustrations by Bill Sillince. There's no knowing whether Lewis had made the introduction, or if Sillince and Treece had known each other before Lewis enrolled at art school. Or, indeed, if Treece had sought Sillince's help to secure Lewis's place.

When he'd finished work in Yeovil, Lewis spent most evenings in the pub, sometimes writing alone – barstool writing was to become a lifelong habit. Other times he would drink with a crowd of local lads, some of whom accompanied him on weekend trips to London, taking the train on a Friday afternoon, pulling into Paddington in time for a few pints with old mates before last orders. John Dickinson was studying medicine at Guy's Hospital and met the Yeovil crowd. 'We were out near Kew somewhere and in the middle of the rush hour, one of them – they called him Spoons – wrapped a towel around his head like a turban, put a mat under his arm, walked out into the middle of the road, laid the mat down and started praying. He stopped the traffic for miles.' As a hungover Lewis sat on the slow, Sunday evening train as it rolled west, he must have thought about what he'd left behind at art school: the band, good times among friends, and Juliet.

Little else is known about Lewis's time at Westland other

than how it ended. After a night's drinking in a local pub, he was one of a group which left, a little raucously, along a quiet lane. When they stopped to relieve themselves in a hedge, the police arrived and they were arrested. Lewis was charged with a public order offence. He pleaded guilty and was fined. Later, he told Ron Burnett that someone he'd upset in the pub had blown the whistle on him. Whilst he could handle a brush with the law, Lewis was terrified his parents would find out, especially if the case were somehow to find its way to the local paper. In Bertha's eyes he could still do no wrong and he was keen to keep it that way. There is no record of the news ever reaching Barton and he left Westland not long afterwards, quite possibly encouraged to find alternative employment. He would later play down the affair, saying, 'I threw the job up when I got a cheque in the post for £70 for illustrating a book, a job that took two weeks'. The incident was never mentioned.

As Lewis concerned himself with avoiding the potential embarrassment of his public order offence, Harry was dealing with legal issues of his own. On 28 October 1961, under the headline, 'BARTON MAN IS ACCUSED OF CORRUPTION', the *Lincolnshire Times* reported that 'Harry Lewis (52), of 84 High Street, Barton, an executive of the Elsham Lime Products Co., Ltd.,' had been committed for trial at Nottinghamshire Assizes on a charge of bribery. He was one of seven men sent for trial at Newark on corruption indictments. Three of the men, former senior employees of Bellrock Gypsum Industries, Ltd., based in Jackson Road, London N7, were accused of receiving bribes. Four other executives of firms in Lincolnshire, Staffordshire and Sussex, of whom Harry was one, were alleged to have paid bribes ranging from £16 to £125 to obtain orders for their companies. There was to have been an eighth (unnamed) defendant, the director of a Nottinghamshire firm which supplied tools to Bellrock, but he had been found dead on the day of the Newark hearing.

Harry's 'inducement' dated back to 1959 and amounted to an alleged bribe of £37 10s – effectively a sweetener paid to a man named Kirkland, manager of Bellrock Industries, in a deal to buy 15 metal skips from Elsham Products. Kirkland told the police he'd arranged to receive an additional £2 10s cash for each skip purchased.

Harry maintained the commission paid on the sale of the skips had not been out of his pocket, but had been paid through the firm, coming off the selling price not Bellrock's purchasing price. 'Kirkland asked me if there was anything in it for him – would I give him a personal commission.' He was released pending the hearing at Nottinghamshire Assizes the following month on bail 'in his own recognisance of £50'. He said he would plead not guilty, and reserved his defence.

At the November Assizes, the case collapsed. Harry and his co-defendants were acquitted (the *Lincolnshire Times* report neglects to explain on what grounds). He told the court that, in his 37 years with the company, 'nothing like this has ever happened before'.

It's hardly the murder, mayhem and corruption of *Hell Drivers*, but the Bellrock case does provide an insight into Harry's world. Described in court by one detective as a 'very respected citizen', he may have remained above any or all dubious practices, but it would be naïve to think they didn't occur in his line of work, or that he would have been unaware when they did. In an era before tight regulation, the haulage industry had its own ways of operating off-the-books transactions and backhand payments. There's no record of Lewis having found out about the case and none of Lewis's friends recalls it coming up in conversation.

His visits home were becoming more infrequent since his

first illustration commission enabled the move to London. *The Hot-Water Bottle Mystery* by Alan Delgado was published as a set text for Scholastic Book Services in 1962, with drawings credited to Edward Lewis – this was surely Treece's influence once again, facilitating the initial contact with a publisher. The book showcased Lewis's loose-lined, characterful drawing style and remained a much-used text well into the 1970s. As well as funding Lewis's move to London, it helped to justify the decision to leave Westland. In London, he found employment with relative ease, taking a job in the Central Display department of Wembley-based shelving company, Dexion ('Storage solutions to suit your needs!'), designing and illustrating the inhouse magazine.

Over the next few months, Lewis re-established contact with friends drawn to the capital to work or study; these included Tony Dugdale, Mike Shucksmith and John Dickinson. Ron Burnett and Keith Riseam made regular trips south and stayed with Lewis on a number of occasions. Nights out tended to start with a few pints at the Lamb and Flag in Covent Garden before moving on to the nearby Yates' Wine Lodge, and from there to Frith Street, Soho, and Ronnie Scott's jazz club. Riseam remembers coming out of Ronnie Scott's in the early hours one morning and encountering a man beating up his girlfriend. Lewis crossed the road to intervene, playing the 'knight in shining armour'. The woman he was trying to help turned on him, beating him over the head with her shoe. 'He wasn't a big lad,' says Riseam, 'not a scrapper, but you could see London changing him'.

Living in London revitalised the sense of freedom Lewis had experienced at art school. He earned decent money and there were plenty of opportunities to spend it. The Barton and Hull contingents formed the nucleus of a social group that was added to by regular weekenders and new arrivals from Humberside as others finished their courses. There were many lost weekends of drinking and jazz clubs and the flow of visitors ensured stories from London returned to Hull.

A couple of years Lewis's senior, Mike Shucksmith had completed his national service in the RAF before studying to become a pharmacist. Graduating in 1961, he made his way to London and reconnected with Lewis. They shared a flat in Seymour Place, Marylebone – the first in a series of rented lodgings. Shuckmith recalls 'an interesting relationship'. Lewis had changed little from their schooldays in that 'if things got difficult he avoided them'. Over the next few years, Shucksmith would often find himself coming to Lewis's rescue. Sometimes the issue would be money as Lewis was notoriously profligate. Usually it was a case of being ready with an alibi for whichever girl had been kept waiting or jilted. There were inevitable scrapes which made life with Lewis interesting and he had charm and charisma that meant people accepted his shortcomings. He would often ring Shucksmith at work and ask, pointedly, was he planning to go straight home:

'Knowing what he meant, I'd say I was going to the pub first. He'd arrange to meet me there at half-past seven. That meant he had someone lined up. We'd meet up at the pub at half-seven and this girl would appear. One I may have seen before or one I hadn't; or he might turn up alone and say, "She's gone home." By which time another one would appear. I've known it happen three times in an evening, he had three women on the go. Once or twice he tripped up, but he was a very accomplished liar and he appeared quite innocent, which is how he got away with it.'

His old friends, the people with whom the naturally shy Lewis could feel comfortable, knew him well enough to accommodate his silences, his unpredictable moods, his unreliability and, for the most part, the extremes of behaviour when he drank to excess. Often, they'd see him creating a character for himself, particularly with women. 'He shot them a line all the time,' says Shucksmith, 'but he was so plausible.' He had an undoubted sexual magnetism. Shucksmith had been working in a pharmacy and, after he left, began a relationship with a woman who worked there. After Lewis had come in the shop, Shucksmith asked her, what had she made of him? 'He was only 22 and she must have been 30 and had been married – and her words were, "I shouldn't like to be left alone in a room with him." She wouldn't have trusted herself. There was something about him that snapped their knicker elastic. I couldn't see it, but whatever it was, he had it.'

Meeting women was never far from his mind. Dick Armstrong remembers an evening at Lewis's Baker Street flat. He was reluctant to put the lights on as dusk fell, telling Armstrong cryptically that he should 'wait and see'. Lewis took him to the window and they watched as the two women living in the flat opposite made themselves ready for the evening, stripping down to their underwear for a shower, emerging naked and walking between rooms before getting dressed to go out. Armstrong recalls, 'We were glued. I told him I could see why he lived there. He just grinned and said, "Yeah, I'm never going to live anywhere else".'

The consequences of Lewis's serial relationships and the emotional debris left in his wake came when one of Lewis's girlfriends fell pregnant. There was never any question of marriage; neither Lewis nor the girl were remotely ready to become parents. But in the early 1960s, terminating an unwanted pregnancy was illegal. Backstreet abortions carried immense risk and Lewis didn't have the cash to pay for one of the more discreet clinics – there was one a few hundred yards along the road from the flat in Seymour Place. Mike Shucksmith lent his friend the money and the termination went ahead.

Whichever crowd Lewis was drawn into, most people liked a drink, but around this time on his visits to London Ron Burnett noticed a change in Lewis. 'He was going to the bar to buy a round of drinks and ordering himself a whisky first, downing it while the rest of the pints were being pulled.' Lewis frequently drank until he was out of control. On one occasion, Shucksmith's former pharmacy course colleagues were invited to their digs – by then they had moved to a rented flat in West Hampstead. Lewis passed out, head hanging over the back of an armchair, with his mouth open. After a while they realised something was wrong. 'All you could see was the whites of his eyes, they'd rolled back.' They tried to rouse him, but couldn't. 'We thought he'd gone.' Eventually, after a few minutes, Shucksmith and his friends managed to bring him round. When he was drunk, Lewis looked for trouble. At one party in an old Victorian house, there was a heated argument, something to do with Lewis stepping out of line with another man's girlfriend. He was thrown down the stairs, top to bottom, smashing his nose. As Shucksmith says, 'He wasn't big enough or fit enough to get stroppy with people, but he was full of himself'.

Under considerable pressure from nights on the drink and maintaining multiple girlfriends, on visits home to his parents Lewis kept up the pretence of still being a clean-living boy. He took girls home, including his one steady girlfriend for most of this period, Joan Higgins. Three or four years younger than Lewis, the beneficiary of a convent school education, she too was revelling in a new found freedom working for a literary agency in Covent Garden. There's no record of how she reacted to Barton or Lewis's parents. During what Shucksmith refers to as the 'Joan period', he and Lewis were drawn into a round of tedious bring-a-bottle house parties. Lewis was in his element, surrounded by outwardly innocent, sexually adventurous former convent girls who, in his words, had been 'let off the leash'. In a later list of prospective book titles, Lewis alluded to these 'Young Ladies of Good Standing'.

He was invited for weekends at the Higgins family home in Henley-on-Thames where, as always, he was charming when the situation demanded, and presented himself well, gaining a degree of acceptance. Still, it came as a surprise when Lewis announced that he and Joan had become engaged. There's little doubt in Shucksmith's mind that the engagement came at Joan's instigation, perhaps under a degree of parental pressure, although there is some question as to how serious Lewis was about the relationship. As usual, there was no point at which he wasn't seeing other women.

Lewis began to find further success with some hard-won commissions for freelance work as an illustrator. John Dickinson remembers him arriving at his basement flat in Eccleston Square with a set of illustrations to complete for a new version of *Alice in Wonderland* – Lewis often slept over if one of Dickinson's medical student housemates went home for the weekend. The drawings were due the following morning and he hadn't started. Dickinson made him coffee all night as he worked to complete drawing after drawing. It was simply his way of working, riding the deadline. He was commissioned to illustrate a second Alan Delgado book, *Hide the Slipper*, early in 1963.

Through the winter of 1962/63, Lewis shared a flat in Fellowes Road, NW3 with John Dickinson, Tony Dugdale and Mike Shucksmith. That year saw one of the coldest winters on record. The water pipes and the water in the toilet froze and their landlord disappeared to Majorca. Dickinson was working for final medical examinations and found Lewis a far from ideal study partner. 'He'd say, let's not go in, let's go to the pictures.' Sometimes he would announce he had 'the doom', which manifested itself in going to the pictures and not going to work. Increasingly, when the doom came, Lewis turned to drink to lift himself. 'That's just what we did,' says John Dickinson. 'It was only lack of money that saved our livers.'

Unearthed at a charity book sale in Barton in April 2015, a burgundy leather-bound desk diary, identified as having belonged to Lewis, gives some insight to his state of mind at the beginning of 1964. It begins prosaically enough with a list of parties in the run-up to Christmas 1963 and a reminder to take his corduroy jackets to the dry cleaners. He anticipates returning to Barton on the weekend before Christmas and plans a Thursday night visit to the Mandrake club.

January 1964 begins with a wistful reflection on Christmas at home and an indication that he's become disconnected from his roots since moving to London. Meeting old friends and neighbours made him feel he'd been away too long. He concludes: 'Although I'd lived in London, I'd been home frequently enough to make it seem from my point of view and theirs that I'd been in London only temporarily.' That was no longer the case. As the weeks pass, there are notes, presumably for stories and novels, alternating with well-intentioned reminders to do more work in the evenings. For his birthday on 15 January, he writes 'finish of novel', although subsequent entries say pretty much the same thing, suggesting the deadline came and went without the novel being completed. There are indications, too, that he was concerned about his health when he writes about frequent 'chest staring'. As winter gives way to spring, the diary ceases to function as a reminder of events or a journal of daily thoughts. Spread across two weeks at the end of March is a list of possible titles for stories: 'Girl in an office / Seymour Place, W.1 / My Grey Heaven'. The uptick is reserved for 'A Lunchtime Affair', though with whom is never mentioned and the story hasn't surfaced.

The deepest insights come across a dozen or so pages in April, May and June – although it's possible they were written some time later. There's a distinct echo of being written in the throes of 'the doom' described by John Dickinson; Lewis muses on the nature of death: 'Death happens. You don't know when it's around until you look down at your chest and then back into the mirror' and then, 'Death smiling back at you looks exactly like yourself. You cause it, maybe that's why. In my case, it's true, believe me'. He then takes an imaginative leap and, in a lengthy two-way conversation, 'Ed' and 'Death' perform a tragi-comic parody of Bergman's *The Seventh Seal* by means of sneering self-analysis:

DEATH: This is what worries me kid. You have, according to my Book, a good life, a lot going for you. You draw, write, play music. You know you could develop any of those into something really big. You know that. You should, too, have the incentive, the way them bitches shake it at you. God knows why, but it's down here, so that makes it true. People, the other kind, like you too. They'd like you more if you weren't so arrogant sometimes. So those are some of the things that make people like living. But not you. Why?
ED: I don't know. I've always been this way.

Trading one-liners, they debate Ed's ego, the lies he's lived and told and his 'screwing'. Lewis holds himself to account with extreme prejudice, ripping his character to pieces as he instigates a discussion of love, sex and his own seemingly conflicted sexuality:

> ED: You and me could get along. We really could.
> DEATH: Watch it. The poets are always on about 'strange death' but I'm not that strange.
> ED: You know you've nothing to worry about with me in those quarters. And I use that last word hoping <u>somebody'll</u> get it.
> DEATH: So you're not queer?
> ED: I've <u>been</u> queer, but that's not the same. It was an experience. You know?
> DEATH: No, I'm afraid I don't.

It is the first suggestion that Lewis had relationships with men, something hinted at by friends, but never explicitly. The conversation concludes with a bizarre sequence of events in which Ed asks Death to kiss him 'Like a woman'. Unfolding like the grotesque frames of an old *Haunt of Horror* fantasy comic, Death agrees and becomes a woman, but not 'Berenice', the woman 'Ed' had expected or hoped for:

> Her hands move to his throat. He begins to burn. As the fingers tighten the flames leap over his body… the girl opens her mouth but instead of words a tongue of flame darts across Ed's eyes.
> ED: (Screaming) Where is Berenice? You're not Berenice. She wants to be here, I know it. (But the flames are too far advanced. Ed's remains powder and fall to the floor.)

After a short silence, 'Ed' brings himself back to safety with the comforting smell of home: 'The smell of hedges and fields…

clean spring rain, the kind of rain you heard when you were a child, tap-tapping on a greenhouse roof.'

The writing in the diary plays to a sense of darkness and dislocation. There is no way of knowing the state of sobriety or intoxication he was in when it was written although, as the handwriting becomes progressively looser, it's easy to imagine a post-pub stream of consciousness. It isn't without humour and there's a degree of self-parody and boozy self-pity in the dialogue, particularly the conversation with Death. But it's striking that he pays attention only to those aspects of his personality he considers the worst. It's as if, at the age of twenty-four, he's already aware of the heavy price he's paying for his lifestyle.

Lewis was growing restless at Dexion. In what must have been one of his final pieces of work, he illustrated a company publication on the state of British industry. Continuing his dialogue with the macabre, its cover is a darkly comic graveyard scene complete with 'British Industry RIP' tombstone and deathly Victorian undertakers, one of whom looks to be a morbid self-caricature. Lewis has annotated the copy, making reference to those drawings he particularly likes, pencilling arrows to a photograph of 'a disgruntled reader', in reality his office manager, who 'makes more money from his M/C jobs than our manager'. The magazine would have been a significant part of his pitch to the advertising companies with which he was now seeking employment.

When Lewis arrived at the Vernon agency late in 1964, he joined a company that, in terms of the new ideas sweeping the world of advertising, remained resolutely middle aged, corporate and dull. Tom Barling, already on the creative team at Vernon's, remembers 'a shitty little agency' with a grim atmosphere, run by people with 'bad suits and bad expressions' who would have been better placed in the civil service. He says Lewis in those days was 'a pussycat, a kid from the north who loved film and came out of his shell when we went to the pub. All he wanted to do was go to the movies and meet girls in pubs.' It helped that the advertising industry did most of its deals in the West End on Friday nights. 'You'd go to the pub, meet someone, and they'd have a little job they wanted for Monday. Then you'd find out they'd want it shot as well so it'd be ready for Tuesday. You'd do the deal in readies there and then.' It meant conventional weekend drinking and social life was out of the question. 'That's when you'd earn your coin. If you were freelance that's what you did. Not all the time, of course; there were some lost weekends.' Dick Armstrong met Lewis for lunch on one occasion and recalls how Vernon's creative department was a law unto itself: 'Those buggers had lunch between eleven and three in the afternoon. I was in trouble when I got back'.

While Lewis was burning the candle at both ends and frequently in the middle, he was also conscious of the need to write; later he'd say that his mother had 'been on at me not to neglect my writing'. An initial relationship with an agent hadn't delivered and was quickly forgotten. One evening at the pub Lewis and Tony Dugdale joked about a children's book they'd written about a cat named 'Bramble'. In a fit of giggles they described the story to Dick Armstrong with Lewis chipping in expletives. How the cat went into the garden 'for a crap', at which point they collapsed into hysterics. Later in the evening, Lewis confided that he had been writing a novel, but when Armstrong asked him to elaborate he became evasive and wouldn't say any more about it.

It was typical of Lewis not to give much of himself away. His extraordinary capacity to retain detail and acute observational sense meant, for the most part, the specific events he was writing about in what would become *All the Way Home and All the Night Through* were recounted from memory, then filtered through his own imagination. By now, he'd abandoned the idea of a rambling autobiography and focused on the final year at college for the story of art student Victor Graves, bringing in a cast of characters, most of whom were friends and students. With Tony Dugdale's prompting, he adapted and included anecdotes based on experiences of other jazz bands. Ron Burnett suspects he must have kept notebooks, as much of the text gives a verbatim account of events and conversations. 'It was part of our training as artists – writing and recording things is a part of illustration.'

By all accounts Lewis was keeping up a three nights a week cinema habit throughout this period. Alan Dickinson remembers they had seats 'up in the gods' to see *The Longest Day* – Lewis later claimed to have tracked down John Wayne at his hotel in London and tried, unsuccessfully, to trick his way into Duke's suite. On another trip they went to see the new Lee Marvin film, *The Killers*. Directed by Don Siegel, *The Killers* was inspired by a prohibition era Hemingway short story in which two hitmen wait in a small town diner for the man they've bent sent to kill. Hemingway's killers are precursors of cliché wiseguys, passing time in conversation about what is and isn't on the menu. They wear 'tight overcoats and derby hats' and look like 'a vaudeville team'. They explain they are in town to kill an ex-boxer, 'the Swede' Ole Andreson, who always arrives at the diner at six o'clock. Hemingway feeds the underlying tension, as does Siegel, knowing that every menu option denied, sideways look, or misplaced comment could unlock the violence these men do for a living. In Siegel's film, it is this quality of the everyday, almost banal conversation that Lee Marvin (Charlie Strom) and Clu Gulager (Lee) trade in that makes the story tick.

Strom is troubled when the man they've come to kill, Johnny North, played by John Cassavetes, doesn't run. As Strom says, he's 'gotta find out what makes a man decide not to run… why, all of a sudden, he'd rather die'.

Memorable for a scene in which Marvin suspends Angie Dickinson from a fifth floor apartment window by her ankles, Alan Dickinson remembers he and Lewis thought the film was more like a 'second feature' – Siegel had originally made it for television, but it was considered too violent. There was, however, something interesting in the two hitmen, one fastidious, worried about his diet and appearance, the other a killer troubled by the passivity of the man he's sent to kill. Nothing here was quite as it seemed. Lewis watched the film, thought about how it worked. As a reader of Hemingway, he almost certainly knew the original story.

Lewis had kept in contact with his friends from Barton. They continued to holiday together, drinking and chatting up girls at Butlins, or boating, boozing and playing brag on the Norfolk Broads. On one occasion he joined Alan Dickinson on holiday in Majorca for a few days. 'He picked up this lady. To be fair, she wasn't the prettiest. I don't know what happened after that, I'd disappeared to another room.'

In a handful of instamatic snaps taken on a Norfolk Broads boating holiday in 1964, Lewis and his friends are larking about in each other's company as they've always done. In one shot, Lewis leans nonchalantly on the tiller, smoking. He has the look of a man who has slept in his clothes, his crumpled beige shorty-raincoat more suited for city streets than river cruising. It turned out not to be the best of holidays. Lewis was never the most domesticated person with whom to share a living space. He left his things lying around, avoided washing-up and was usually elsewhere when anything needed doing. Late one evening after a few drinks, Pete Bacon complained. The argument escalated into a blazing row with Lewis going toe to toe, daring Bacon to hit him, saying, 'You'd like to wipe the floor with me, wouldn't you?' When the others tried to calm him down, he jumped into a dinghy and disappeared into the darkened broad. That night the weather was appalling. Lewis was drunk, had no life jacket and almost no idea how to sail. Somehow, he made it back an hour or so later.

He'd taken the boat's forward single cabin, forgetting, as they approached a bridge, the mast would be lowered at an angle, which meant the counterpart below-deck lifting sharply. Lewis had left his suitcase in the way and it was broken in half. Later in the trip, the cabin flooded. Martin Turner remembers leaving him standing at Wroxham station 'wet through with the two halves of his suitcase'. His parting shot was 'Well that was a great holiday lads, we'll have to do it again sometime'. They never did.

When Hilary Bremner, an old friend (and briefly girlfriend) from Hull received a call from Lewis in anticipation of her coming to London, they arranged to meet. They rekindled their friendship, spending an evening at the Swiss Cottage pub near the Fellowes Road flat. Sometime later there was a lunchtime meeting at a pub in Shepherd Market. For Hilary, any romantic thoughts were short-lived. She found him 'too introverted, too quiet' for her liking. The meeting with Hilary worked its way into Lewis's creative thinking. As he was writing *All the Way Home and All the Night Through* and looking to name his characters, he renamed Heather Morton, his long-term art school girlfriend, as 'Hilary'.

It was a characteristic he would repeat throughout his writing career. While most writers create composites – screenwriter

Paul Abbott has spoken of his characters containing at least five real people – the thread of truth in Lewis's characters draws heavily from real life counterparts. Often he begins with a name of someone he knows well. In *All the Way Home and All the Night Through*, Juliet Raahauge became 'Janet', a mischievous reference to his previous love interest, Janet Camm; her family name 'Walker' referred to Jean Walker, his former girlfriend in Barton. Ron Burnett became 'Harry', Judy Burnett was 'Jenny' and Keith Riseam, 'Keith Rushton'.

Lewis's break as a published author came shortly after he was taken on by the highly regarded literary agent, John Johnson, who placed *All the Way Home and All the Night Through* with Hutchinson under its New Authors imprint, an established route for promising new writers. Publishing first novels on a profit-sharing basis, its economic viability was, to a great extent, reliant on considerable library sales and minimal outlay. Among those on the Hutchinson roster was the novelist Robin Cook – later Cook would be revered for his uncompromising take on British noir fiction, writing as Derek Raymond. His first novel, the semi-autobiographical *The Crust on Its Uppers*, published in 1962, told the story of a well-to-do young man adrift in London's underworld. Recalling meeting Lewis around this time in an interview reprinted in *Crime Time* magazine, Raymond said, 'I knew Ted Lewis – no I didn't, I only sat next to him. Nobody I knew ever knew Ted Lewis – it was impossible to get to know him, even superficially.' He paints a vivid portrait of the young writer in the Horse and Groom, the pub downstairs from Hutchinson's offices in Great Portland Street:

'Lewis invariably sat on his own at the far end of the bar, and I never saw him with a girl. He usually sat bent over in an attitude vaguely resembling prayer with his head on his arms; and none of us ever got to know him, because he was always totally drunk. He was blond, good looking, had a face I liked – and I wouldn't at all have minded a long talk with him or even a short one… I never managed it. You could say something to him, but he never talked back, and when you looked at him all you got in return was the mysterious look you might get from a stained glass window.'

Raymond writes that he believes this was around 1962 or 1963, but emphasises that this is his own observation, a memory 'and that a 28-year-old one'. It may well have been later.

For Lewis, the deal with Hutchinson for *All the Way Home and All the Night Through* was vindication. The writing impressed his editor, Giles Gordon, as 'a work of real lyrical romanticism', though he was less enamoured by the young author. When recalling their first meeting for an *Arena* magazine article nearly 30 years later, Gordon's strangely hostile memories were of a 'cynical little shit' and 'one of the most incredibly arrogant people I've met… with him it didn't seem to be an arrogance born out of insecurity. He really did think he was the best author who ever lived'.

Lewis might well have come across as difficult and his own diary suggests he was aware he could appear 'arrogant', but there is no doubt he was also deeply insecure about his writing. Since his schooldays, a superficial brashness had been one of two default positions when dealing with authority figures, especially after a few drinks – the other being a taciturn reserve more in keeping with Derek Raymond's Horse and Groom memories. Gordon's comments suggest there were tensions in the working relationship between editor and author, which may explain some of the more overwrought and under-edited passages in the published novel. Lewis acknowledged that, once he had decided the book would concentrate on his final year at art school, 'it wasn't too difficult filling it out'. However, once 'filled out', Gordon's advice might have been to pare down, cut one or two of the more superfluous scenes and overwritten descriptive passages. Consequently, the published novel has the feel of treading water in places and is perhaps a final edit short of finished.

There would be a final pre-publication drama for the *All the Way Home* manuscript: Dick Armstrong was working in an office in Fleet Street when Lewis turned up one afternoon in a panic and asked to use the phone: 'He'd left his manuscript in the back seat of a taxi and was ringing round trying to find the thing.'

All the Way Home and All the Night Through, with its Sillitoesque title and 'superficially hard boiled yet really sensitive' jacket quote, was published by Hutchinson in November 1965 as number 48 in the series of first novels. Lewis was paid a standard advance of £150 against royalties. The debut novelist with his racy tale of student love, jazz, beer and self-loathing in an unnamed provincial city attracted significant press attention in the run-up to Christmas 1965. Hutchinson was able to propel the novel into broadsheets for review. On 22 November 1965, Lewis gave his first major print interview to Stephanie Nettell, editor of *Books and Bookmen*, one of the Seven Arts stable of magazines. Nettell remembers the interview taking place in a pub. She found Lewis 'rather idealistic and romantic, and unaffected', confident of his talents, but 'no more so than any other published writer'. She wrote of a 'fair-haired young man... with a gentle face and a serious, almost earnest manner. The author of an unerringly sincere tale of young love, of that misguided but still agonisingly tender passion one suffers around the age of 19.' The interview appeared in the magazine's

December edition under the title *First Love Comes First for Ted Lewis*. Accompanying the piece was a photograph showing the 25-year-old Lewis sitting behind an open window. In part shadow, light trousers and dark jacket, bags under his eyes and hair keeping a trace of the quiff that is, perhaps, a year or two out of date. The look is classic early 60s pop-cultural iconic, like an image destined to find its way onto a Smiths record sleeve. It gives a visual sense of what made the girls fall at his feet. Imagine part boy author, part indie icon, with a trace of danger in the lips and brooding defiance in the eyes.

From the outset, Lewis acknowledged that *All the Way Home and All the Night Through* was 'frankly autobiographical'. Nettell writes:

Like Lewis, Vic is a student at the Hull College of Art, with a passion for the north Lincolnshire countryside where he lives. Like Lewis, he has to endure a spell of humiliating inactivity while he searches for a job when he graduates. Like Lewis, he drifts into a sullen life out of tune with everyone else – sleeping all day, dreaming at night.

Lewis seemed resigned to a negative critical response. '"The critics won't like it" he says with a brave, what do I care shrug; "it's bound to be dismissed as another one of those autobiographical first novels."'

When Nettell had phoned to arrange the interview, she found Lewis once more on the move. Having spent the previous few weeks 'designing a food chart for doggy gourmets', he'd been fired by Vernon's. In truth, it was no great loss and his new job as Art Director with the Alexander Butterfield agency was unquestionably a good career move. Butterfield's was one of the new agencies emerging in London in the mid-60s as British advertising started to find a new, young voice, described by social commentator Peter York as 'no longer Fifties deferential or mock-American, one that used our shared history, cultural references, music and sacred symbols to make advertising'.

Lewis had been appointed to a more creative role, one that gave him a connection to television and brought him a step closer to film. He was also keeping up a steady flow of freelance illustration work, including a book cover for fellow Hutchinson New Author Lee Dunne's *Goodbye to the Hill*, and drawings for a third Alan Delgado book, *Return Ticket*. He was commissioned to illustrate a comic book version of the film *Bridge Over the River Kwai*, for which he faithfully recreated still images from David Lean's film. The soft line drawings and detailed characterisations reveal Sillince's continued influence and Lewis's own well-practised observational techniques.

All the Way Home and All the Night Through was generously received, although one critic thought it would have 'benefited from some pruning'. *The Times* called it a 'fresh and original book'. However, Ian Hamilton in the *Daily Telegraph* felt the novel was 'too long' and that the 'excess of naturalistic banality' was 'sometimes stupefying'. In conclusion, Hamilton admitted that it said much for Lewis's writing talent that 'the wintry pathos of the story should come through strongly enough to register, in the end, a touching effect of innocence, tenderness and truth'.

The candour of *All the Way Home* came as a shock to many of Lewis's friends, particularly those whose stories were laid out in explicit detail. None more so than Juliet Raahauge, who found herself once more faced with the events of her year at art school. There had been no prior warning. When the book was reviewed in the local press, the *Yorkshire Post* described her character, unkindly, as a 'very innocent richie'.

Asked about his parents' reaction to reading about their son in his own book, Lewis said his mother had been 'a bit upset… not by what I said, but to think I'd gone through all that, being unhappy and everything'. Apparently, Harry hadn't said much at all. Lewis wasn't sure if his father had read the book.

All the Way Home is a more or less faithful retelling of the deepening insecurity and disillusion Lewis experienced at the dawn of the 1960s. Superficially, it's a tale of art school life, falling in and out of love at the pictures, Hammonds' Picadish on Saturday afternoons, Park Drive cigarettes, and sweaty jazz gigs at the Blue Bell. What distinguishes it from any number of would-be kitchen sink novels is the fearlessness of Lewis's writing. Victor's coming of age is honestly self-critical, particularly scenes in which he succumbs to alcoholic blackouts, episodes of possessive jealousy and violence. Lewis is unafraid of making Victor an unlikeable, self-absorbed character, his anxieties mediated through descriptions of the Humber's rural and post-industrial landscapes. No previous novelist had paid attention to this part of England, certainly not with Lewis's striking observational sense. The Humber is at the heart of the book. Lewis places the quietly repressive familiarity of home and family in Barton in sharp contrast to art school, music, mates, birds and booze over the river in Hull.

There is a key passage in the novel which, in terms of its style, places itself outside the main narrative. For eight pages, Lewis retells the story of the night of an art school fancy dress party. Writing in the present tense, he begins with the jazz band meeting pre-gig at the pub:

The Albert Hall. Dockers pub. Pro's pub. Licensed for singing in huge upstairs room. Rough pub. Annually invaded by fancy dress students. Miraculous lack of incidents between dockers and students. Only just though. Victorian pub. Drinking pub. Dedicated to drinking. Powder blue gaberdine suit pub, double-breasted twenty-inch bottoms white open necked shirt pub. Hard pub.

Lewis doesn't write with this stripped down narrative voice before these few pages and it doesn't occur again. The dockers and trawlermen suggest a barely suppressed violence. Dropped pronouns and clipped sentences emulate pulp novels. The ghosts of Chandler and Spillane offer a dramatic counterpoint to the naturalistic tone of the rest of the writing. Here, for the first time, Lewis alludes to what would become his singular voice, then abandons it, almost as if he feels, or has been persuaded, that it is insufficiently literary.

All the Way Home and All the Night Through was intended as the first in a series of novels drawn from episodes in Lewis's original autobiographical writing. During the *Books and Bookmen* interview, he speaks about a half-finished novel which tells the story of a group of close friends whose relationship disintegrates when one is suspected of rape. The second novel, whose half-completed manuscript Lewis says is 'tucked away in a drawer at the agency', is again the topic of discussion in William Foster's *Scotsman* interview. Provisionally titled *Thirteen Women*, Foster describes it as 'an even more intimate chronicle than his first, retailing the lust-ridden thoughts of a hero, suspiciously like Lewis, who enjoys lying in bed half the day planning the conquest of the female of the species'.

These were the drafts from which Lewis would write his autobiographical short story, *The Rabbit,* published in *Argosy* in June 1966. *Argosy* was a popular paperback format collection of short stories, articles, comment, crosswords and reviews – not to be confused with the US pulp fiction magazine of the same name. Lewis was billed as the 'new star writer' for June, placed alongside an interview with John Braine and reviews by Geoffrey Household. A sharply realised prequel to *All the Way Home* that would resurface a decade later as the basis for the novel *The Rabbit*, Lewis documents the growing disharmony between Victor, his old friends and his long-suffering girlfriend Veronica. His going-away to art school has altered their relationship. Back for the summer and working as a labourer at the quarry managed by his father, one evening Victor tries and fails to justify his lack of interest in Veronica. She isn't fooled, '"Don't wrap it up in Paul Newman language, Victor. It may help you, but it doesn't help me".' In the Wheatsheaf a few days later when his awkward attempts to curry favour with quarry workmate, 'Clacker' – 'the provoker in any punch up' – are ignored, Vic grumbles to Veronica and his old mates. Once again, Lewis reveals a harsh inclination towards self-criticism as Veronica exposes 'the definitive Victor Graves'. Vic is powerless as she wrecks the carefully constructed front he presents to the world:

That's a basic need of Victor's. To have what he considers inferiors surround him. So that he can prove what a great fellow he is with the proletariat. Prove that by being an art student, he's no better than they are. The sickening thing is he thinks he is better, but superficially pretends he isn't. He just wants everyone to think he's a good fellow, in spite of what he thinks of them... pretend to love thy neighbour, says Victor, because that cons them into loving you, into admiring you, so that you can think you're better than anyone else.

Victor picks a fight with Clacker, knowing he'll take a beating, but needing to prove himself tough enough to pick a fight and lose it. It's a wilfully foolish, self-destructive act. Defeated and humiliated, his only recourse is to withdraw, stop caring what his friends, or Veronica, or Clacker, or anyone thinks of him.

After initial press attention and an early flurry of sales, *All the Way Home* was barely promoted. Later in 1966 it would be published in paperback by Arrow, whose choice of an altogether steamier cover image and addition of the subtitle 'Ted Lewis – his bestselling story of an art school Casanova' seemed to recast Victor as a provincial art school 'Alfie'.

For Lewis, whose life in London sometimes seemed to be running in parallel to Michael Caine's cockney lothario, there was the day job, advertising campaigns to be planned with the Butterfield agency. One of the firm's commercial clients was bringing a new brand of wine into the British market. Lewis was overseeing the visual presentation and had arranged for a photo shoot with Brian Phipps, an established commercial photographer.

Josephine Roome was running Phipps' Shaftesbury Avenue office as a 'sort of Girl Friday'. The free-spirited daughter of a Metropolitan Police detective turned publican, Jo had not long returned from a year in the south of France where she'd lived and worked as an au pair for a wealthy French family. The days were long and the work hard, nevertheless she'd immersed herself in French music and culture. On her return to London and the family's Bayswater pub, the Moscow Arms, she was looking forward to travelling again. Working for Phipps was a way to save money for the trip. She remembers him mentioning the Butterfield's art director who would be coming in and who had written a book. When he asked if she'd like to read it, Jo took the book home.

Lewis and Phipps worked on the wine company shoot over a number of visits. Some weeks later, Mike, Butterfield's copywriter, rang Jo up and invited her to a party at their office. Jo remembers she and Mike were upstairs where there was space set aside for dancing, when she suggested they go downstairs to the bar. 'He made a point of drawing my attention to Ted who was with this very lovely girl.' After the party, Mike asked to see Jo again. They went to a local pub where he explained that, although he had wanted to go out on another date, he'd been put up to it by Lewis. Some weeks later, Phipps mentioned they'd been invited to Ted Lewis's leaving drinks. Jo wasn't interested, but Phipps insisted she accompany him.

At the leaving party, most people were outside. It was a sunny spring evening and the pub was crowded. Jo had one drink and told Phipps she was leaving. He said she should say goodbye to Ted first. 'I went inside and that was when he asked me out. I hadn't really paid him any attention before then, and he hadn't shown me any, but that's what happened. We were inseparable from then on.'

Lewis was modishly cool in black polo-neck sweater, corduroy jacket and desert boots. Jo was attractive, stylishly dressed, with her hair cut by Vidal Sassoon. They were well-matched, in love and happy. 'We'd get on the top of the bus, look at each other and just be laughing. We both knew it was absolutely right. And I'd been someone who was *never* going to get married.' On their first date, Lewis took Jo to see his new band in their Soho rehearsal rooms. He'd been playing piano in a quartet called Fresh Clean Taste. Ron Shapiro, brother of singing star Helen, played drums. 'They'd got a few friends in and I went along to listen. It was brilliant.'

Meeting Ted Lewis was not Jo's first encounter with aspiring writers. Before her year in France she had worked in the Bayswater office of Associated London Scripts (ALS), the company founded by Spike Milligan, Eric Sykes and others as an agency for comedy writers and performers. Her memories are of Ray Galton and Alan Simpson, then writers for Tony Hancock, whose brother Roger ran the office. When Hancock parted company with Galton and Simpson in a bout of career anxiety, Beryl Vertue took over management of ALS. Although there had been opportunities to progress, Jo was unwavering in her desire to travel.

Lewis's final farewell to the world of advertising in 1966 was largely down to Tom Barling. Having taken on the job of production designer with Soho-based animators Halas and Batchelor, Barling discovered he had 36 episodes of the cartoon series of *The Lone Ranger* to produce and needed people who could draw. He called on several artists he knew, including Lewis. 'I said, "Dear boy, all you have to do is walk along that corridor to the hissing Hungarian [John Halas] and ask for £75 a week." I think Ted bottled it and went for £60.' Whatever salary Lewis secured from Halas, he was working in television animation.

Halas and Batchelor was never less than chaotic, but Lewis was at last making a mark in the film industry, although not in the way he had expected. In Ted Pettengel, Paul Hayward, Tom Bailey, Chris Miles and David Elvin, he joined a team of young and talented animators. Elvin had been with Halas since 1965, a graduate of the School of Art and Design in Southend-on-Sea and St Martin's School of Art and Design. He and Lewis struck up an instant rapport through a shared taste in music, a love of Laurel and Hardy and an intimate knowledge of 1940s and 50s B-movies. They adopted the pseudonyms of two cowboy actors from the early 1950s. Elvin became 'Rocky Lane' and Lewis 'Monte Hale'. When Lewis gave Elvin a copy of *All the Way Home and All the Night Through* it was signed 'To Rocky from

Monte'. 'I just remember us laughing, enjoying each other's company. You couldn't wish for a better mate.'

The Lone Ranger series with its highly imaginative scenarios was scheduled for broadcast on CBS Television in the USA in September 1966. Tom Barling was employed as the European representative of Format Productions which then owned the rights to the character. Chris Miles had worked for Halas since 1964, primarily on their breakthrough productions, the *Hoffnung* series for the BBC and *DoDo, The Kid from Outer Space* for Lady Stearn Robinson. Lewis and Miles soon found themselves with increased responsibility following the departure of Tom Bailey and Ted Pettengel. 'We were background artists, although I think we'd prefer to be called designers, as our roles were more varied and complicated,' says Miles.

Format producer Herbie Klein and director Jules Engel – Engel was responsible for creating the *Mr Magoo* cartoon series – ran Artransa Park, a small studio in California. Needing to produce an initial 36 six-minute episodes of *The Lone Ranger*, work was farmed out to cheaper London studios. According to Barling, the only one Klein had any experience of was Halas and Batchelor. The Halas team produced an almost immediate uplift in standards. An extraordinary accomplishment, given that they were regularly drinking three or four pints during lunchtime sessions in the Dog and Duck. Barling remembers they were producing great work. 'All the backgrounds and colours were done. I was sending stuff off every week to California to keep them happy and then CBS changed the schedules. "Stop work on these, work on these." Half the time, I wouldn't see the storyboard until Monday morning and we were supposed to be rolling with animation to camera by Friday.'

David Elvin contends that Halas didn't really appreciate animation and that his interests lay in 'higher art'. Under intense pressure, Barling was promoting young artists and animators and they delivered. 'I brought them in and they did it. That series was put together mostly by people who had never been in the business before. Probably why the work was very, very good.'

Lewis had rarely worked to such unrelenting deadlines. With Barling, by his own admission, 'holding the hissing Hungarian down in one corner and the Americans in the other not making any sense', non-delivery and missed deadlines were not an option. 'Ted was doing lovely work,' says Barling, 'but I did have to kick his arse. One time I needed ten backgrounds for a Monday morning shoot and on the Friday night none was complete. I told him, "It's you who's got to do them so please don't let yourself down." When I came in on Monday morning, there were stale sandwiches, empty beer bottles, and fifteen beautiful backgrounds and I said, "Why couldn't you have done that before, you bastard?" I kissed him on the cheek and walked out. I don't think he ever forgave me.'

Lewis's time with Halas and Batchelor on *The Lone Ranger* was instrumental in his development as an animation artist, providing the high profile production experience he needed to establish himself in Soho's film community where word of mouth could win or lose you work. With the demands of *The Lone Ranger*, spending time with other artists, and making the most of the pubs and club scene in the West End, there was little time to work on new writing.

Within weeks of their first meeting, Lewis took Jo home to meet his parents. Lewis had told lovely stories about Bertha and Jo warmed to her immediately. She had the impression that Harry was very much 'the boss' and was horrified to see the diminutive Bertha struggle in with the coal bucket while there were two men sitting there. The formality of the occasion, combined with her own nervousness, caused Jo to lose her voice for the weekend. She remembers speaking to Lewis about it afterwards. In contrast to her own family life in a pub filled with noise and laughter, the Lewis household seemed stifling and traditional. 'Harry was the sort of man whose dinner had to be on the table when he got home, and you got the feeling nothing was ever good enough.'

On that initial visit to Barton, the first people Lewis took Jo to visit were Henry and Mary Treece. That afternoon, as they sat in the sunshine talking with Treece at the bottom of the garden, Lewis told them he and Jo were getting married.

Almost certainly they would have spoken about the lecture Treece was due to deliver at Hull College of Arts and Crafts at the beginning of June, the content of which would have been on his mind at the time of Lewis's visit. The carefully annotated manuscript notes of the lecture, *Notes on Perception and Vision*, represent the fullest account of Treece's philosophy of writing. Not all the notes written were incorporated in the script he eventually took to Hull, and from which he gave his lecture on 1 June 1966, but these give a particular insight into Treece and the influence he had over his protégé's writing and thinking:

May 17, 1966

I see the creative writer on two levels at least. In one he is the crippled god – the maker who in his non-literary life is, or feels himself to be, somehow incomplete, inadequate. Yet, being a creator, he has pride, and a stubborn despairing courage: so, he writes for himself a world in which the blind man sees all, and the cripple leaps over mountains.

On another more important of his levels, the creative writer is not the lame god, but the integrated observant man, using all his senses and his sense to understand and to set down archetypal patterns. Now this man will have only one essential tale to tell: and it will be the story of the seasons in their progression through the year – from the Sun's first awakening after winter to the burning of the stubble after the harvest. His vision will be directed to this ritual-dance of the months, the crops, the heroes; to their coming fruition and their death.

It is a primitive pattern, but it contains everything – the gentle colour of the primroses and the sound of roaring thunder. It is a pattern over which a roaring god (or goddess) other than the writer presides, and is acknowledged by him: and once this writer – who is the messenger of god – has perceived the pattern, surrendered himself to this vision – then he will know, without doubt, that all years are one year, all pleasures one pleasure, all disasters trivial, and all heroes expendable.

In a section dated 20 May 1966, Treece discusses what he refers to as 'a writer's basic and personal theme – that central thesis of his life which makes him different from other writers'. For Treece, the two principal themes in his own writing had been 'the Father seeking the Son (or the Son the Father) and the theme of the Distracted Woman, the woman drawn away from gentleness and mercy into other, perhaps more sinister paths; the Maenad, the Bacchante'. He concludes the section with a somewhat prescient (in terms of Lewis's future writing direction) discussion of theme and style:

Out of one's struggle to set down such themes grows one's personal manner of writing – one's *style* as it is called. Buffon said, 'Le style, c'est l'homme même.' Style is the man himself – that is, the man trying to record his struggle to make clear his essential and obsessive theme, the theory which makes him tick.

Yet there is a strong case for believing that the writer outgrows his own style as his vision develops. Looking back, the writer is dissatisfied with what he said, not because it was bad *in its day*, but because if he did it now, he would do it differently – because his perception has developed and the old words no longer represent his present development or change.

The writer is probably fighting a losing battle all his life, for his perception is perhaps always one jump ahead of his technique, his ability to set down the inner turmoil and its resolution.

The notes finish with a treatise on the importance of feeling in the writer's work, and its inevitable cost: 'It has long been an Article of Faith with me that the creative writer is born to awareness (if only partial) and to suffering (sometimes *in extremis*) just as the sparks fly upwards.'

Henry Treece suffered a final, fatal heart attack on 10 June 1966. For Lewis, the loss was profound. He attended the funeral in Barton. Treece had been an inspirational figure to many former pupils and was held in great affection, but for Lewis as an adolescent, and then a young man, he was confidant, friend and mentor. A constant. In many ways, a surrogate father. In a later magazine article, Lewis's friend Barbara Hewson remembered visits to the Treeces where they'd be 'regaled by tales of their friendship with Dylan Thomas and his wife Caitlin. Of the latter's famous and inexhaustible supply of Irish stew constantly simmering on the stove top. Of the day the four of them almost drowned off Laugharne, having imbibed a few too many in Brown's famous pub.' Barbara wrote of Treece:

All who met him were affected by his personality. He was a man larger than life, multitalented, who inspired loyalty and affection from pupils and friends alike. There is a word which describes him, often misused – charismatic. Henry Treece was bestowed with this rare quality in abundance, but then he was a rare spirit.

An indication of the depth of mutual friendship between Treece and Lewis came in a scene from the *Thirteen Women* script written a decade later. Mary Treece takes one of her husband's books from Victor's bookshelf. She opens the book at the flyleaf and reads the inscription, 'In you resides my single power of sweet continuance here.' It is signed 'H'.

Lewis married Josephine Roome in a traditional top hat and tails wedding at St Matthew's Parish Church, Bayswater on 17 September 1966, with the reception afterwards at the Moscow Arms. It was, as Lewis's friend and fellow animation artist Malcolm Draper says, 'really posh… when we arrived, we were announced; everything was done properly'. Lewis entertained the guests on the piano, although no one quite remembers what he played. Looking now at the wedding photographs, with family and friendship groups coming together amid some slightly questionable period fashions, Jo stands out as the epitome of mid 60s elegance. Lewis invariably has a cigarette in hand. Bertha and Harry seem detached from the main group, at odds with assorted art school alumni, jazz musicians, advertising executives, writers and artists. A more intimate reflection of the newlyweds comes from a set of photographs taken some time after the wedding, at their flat in Belsize Park. These have the air of a self-styled pop-art portrait. The couple pose together in their living room. Lewis sits in an armchair with Jo in front of him on the floor; behind them are books, an unframed group photograph, and a copy of the Beatles' *A Hard Day's Night* LP. In the second, they're both wearing cowboy hats, possibly someone's thoughtful wedding gift.

Jo recalls the importance of sharing each other's music in their early days together. 'There was lots of Oscar Peterson and Miles Davis in the collection, but mainly jazz piano.' They both loved the Beatles and Lewis was especially taken with classical music – Benjamin Britten was a favourite. They listened to the radio, spoken word as well as music, discovering they'd shared a childhood love of *Dick Barton – Special Agent*. Lewis would read voraciously.

Missing from the wedding photographs was Mrs Shaw, Lewis's maternal grandmother. She had become bedridden and in need of full-time care. For the wedding, it was decided she would be admitted temporarily to a nearby residential home. Mrs Shaw never left the home and died shortly afterwards. Bertha was grief-stricken and suffered an extreme reaction, losing feeling in her legs. For a while she was unable to walk. It was, she explained at the time, like an extreme and permanent feeling of pins and needles. Unable to leave the house, the family doctor, by then John Dickinson, who had returned to Barton as a general practitioner, remembers she used to complain that there was something tight around her legs. 'I could never find anything. It did bother her a lot, the pain.' At a loss as to the cause of the problem, Bertha underwent a lumbar puncture, later telling Jo, 'It was the most painful thing I've ever been through.' Over a period of time, she did regain the use of her legs, but remained bereft; her mother had gone and her only son was married and living in London. She was at home with Harry.

Jo was welcomed into her husband's family, but found the atmosphere in the Lewis household staid and repressive. Harry's most intimate exchanges seemed to be with the cat, which he would talk to 'as if they were having a real conversation'. It wasn't an ideal situation for a newly married couple to spend their first Christmas. Apart from the traditional drinks at Madge Dickinson's, Jo recalls the whole thing was a rather joyless affair. There was no love of food or celebration in the occasion. In comparison to Christmas in the pub where her family would 'sit around the table for hours and talk', at the Lewises they ate their meal and washed up. It was another job done. Jo swore she would never again submit to Christmas at her in-laws.

5

Making it Real
1967–1970

IN THE NEW YEAR, LEWIS WAS back at Halas and Batchelor working on *The Lone Ranger* – the show had been recommissioned and was scheduled to run until September 1969. By contemporary standards, *The Lone Ranger* appears crudely simplistic; the characterisations are one dimensional stereotypes, at odds with some surreal storylines. Lewis's backgrounds are reminiscent of John Ford's Monument Valley and Anthony Mann's western landscapes. With budgets and production values set in California, it was down to the Halas team including Lewis, Elvin and Chris Miles to innovate. Miles recalls:

'In those days all drawings were done on cells, but the backgrounds were usually painted using washes and water colours. In our case the background designs were drawn with a chinagraph sticky black pencil and the colours inserted under the cell level by using torn or cut coloured pantone papers. This was a faster way of producing a finished scene. Ted and I both designed *The Lone Ranger* films. Not as directors, but working out from our own illustrated storyboards the various camera angles and movement instructions that overlay the work of the animator.'

The methods employed on *The Lone Ranger* were certainly different. Dreamlike, almost gothic backgrounds complement what was by no means a conventional western series. It featured elements of science fiction, proto-steampunk machinery and some typically freakish bad guys. Lewis had begun to invent characters for the show and, having successfully created the 'Deadly Glass Man', was working on creative ideas for the new series.

In March, he arranged for Henry Treece's son, Richard, to travel to London for work experience at Halas. The 17-year-old had followed in Lewis's footsteps, studying graphic design in Hull at what was now the Regional College of Art and Design – renamed in 1962, but still on Anlaby Road. In an article in the *Lincolnshire Times*, Richard explains how he'd worked alongside Lewis for two weeks on 'cowboy backgrounds of cactus and hills' for a *Lone Ranger* episode featuring 'Dr Destruction'. The piece says that the TV series is the 'Number 2 top television show in America' where it was shown 'in colour'. In the UK, the first series had just begun screening in a Sunday teatime slot.

Towards the end of 1966 and into 1967, Lewis had achieved success with an assortment of short story commissions. *All the Way Home* and *The Rabbit* proved to be unlikely standard bearers for the kind of contemporary angst-ridden romance stories editors were looking for. Lewis found an off-beat fit with women's magazines. Commenting on Lewis's twin occupations of animator and writer, the *Lincolnshire Times* article explains that he had recently completed a story serialisation for the 'Petticoat girls' magazine'.

Petticoat was a new London-based teen weekly seeking to exploit the mid 60s explosion of fashion and pop culture. Janet Street-Porter and Eve Pollard were among the magazine's early editors. Lewis's story, *The Two-Sided Triangle*, was a slice of fictionalised autobiography serialised over three issues, published, with his own line-drawn illustrations, between horoscopes, ads for hairspray – 'If he knows it's there, we'll give you your money back' – and articles telling girls all they needed to know about working as a nanny – 'how Mary Poppins went mod'. The first instalment, published on 11 March 1967, told of the meeting between Alan, an advertising designer and self-doubting novelist, and Jill, the reassuring photographer's secretary with whom he falls in love. Their chance meeting, instant attraction, love, flat-sharing and marriage were ideal; a harmless tale from swinging London for a teen magazine aimed at the 'young and fancy free'. But Alan's self-destructive impulses threaten to undermine the relationship. Musing on his writing, he says, 'I'd never feel convinced anything I did was any good, never know whether it was right or wrong, never dare feel elated about what I'd written in case it was really terrible.' He struggles to come to terms with his girlfriend's success in a glamorous profession and is jealous of her male colleagues. Fretting that she earns more than he does, he insists they move into a rundown flat affordable on his salary alone. Just as the relationship looks to be going well, Alan learns of the rejection of his second novel, *The Shooting Party*, by the publisher 'Dickinsons'. The arrival of the news coincides with Jill's unexpected absence for the evening. Alan agonises over his book's failure and, as the evening wears on, based on nothing in particular, convinces himself Jill has been unfaithful.

The Two-Sided Triangle was a neutered version of the autobiographical self-reflection of *All the Way Home and*

All the Night Through. It told a largely faithful version of the story of his and Jo's meeting, their whirlwind romance and the rejection of his unfinished second novel. But the most notable aspect of the story is hinted at in the conclusion. After Alan has received the editor's rejection of *The Shooting Party*, his agent, presumably based on John Johnson, discusses their options in a letter, suggesting that, while he could try and sell the book on its completion to another publisher, Alan would, on the whole, be better advised to 'start completely afresh on that alternative idea we discussed some months ago'.

Assuming the not-quite-but-almost-real treatment of the subject matter, Lewis must, by now, have realised the undergraduate themes which earned him a deal with Hutchinson's New Authors would not work a second time. Pursuing an alternative idea was sound advice and it signalled the move towards writing more commercial fiction.

Aside from preoccupations with his uncertain literary career, the early months of 1967 were among the happiest Lewis had known. The flat he and Jo rented over the Odeon cinema in Belsize Park was spacious, relatively cheap and homely. Perfect, in fact, for a film-obsessive. Lewis's friend and colleague, David Elvin, remembers pet-sitting for their cats and a pair of chipmunks. When they weren't working, the couple would be out and about in pubs and with friends, going to the pictures and making the most of Sunday jazz sessions at the Tally Ho in Kentish Town. The pub had built a reputation as the venue for impromptu appearances by American jazz artists, many of whom would be in London for higher profile slots at West End clubs. Tom Barling often went along and remembers 'It used to end with Stan Tracey up there on piano playing Watermelon Man with two hundred people joining in.'

Bertha and Harry Lewis also paid a visit to London around

this time. Not ones for the bright lights, they insisted on their afternoon naps and remained diffidently self-contained. Tom Barling recalls how having his parents around changed Lewis. 'Ted wasn't speaking to them properly; there was a division, as if they came from two different worlds.'

It's a fair summation from Barling who would become a successful novelist in his own right, known primarily for a series of London gangland novels which included *The Smoke*, featuring fictional gang boss, 'Charlie Dance'. He recalls how he and Lewis would talk at length about their shared ambition to become successful authors. 'He wanted to know about East End villains and I knew a few so I used to tell him.'

In truth, in the spring of 1967, Lewis needed only to pick up a newspaper for an insight into the London underworld. In April, Charlie Richardson, his younger brother Eddie and their associates Frank Fraser, Tommy Clark and Roy Hall were on trial at the Old Bailey, following their arrest in a raid on the morning of England's World Cup win in July 1966. Referred to in the papers as the 'torture trials' in response to lurid stories of teeth pulled with pliers, savage beatings (after which Charlie Richardson would reputedly offer the victim a clean shirt to go home in), and electric shocks from Charlie's sinister 'black box', the courts examined every detail and newspapers reported each day's developments. The Richardsons might have lacked the Kray Twins' iconic profile, but the trial showed them to be equally ruthless and, arguably, just as successful as gangsters and criminal businessmen. Their legitimate interests included a string of scrap metal dealers, West End drinking clubs and stakes in South African mining companies. The latter involved dealings with the South African security services and an extreme right-wing organisation, the Afrikaans equivalent of the Ku Klux Klan, known as Der Broederbond. The Richardsons had a glamour of their own and their social circle included well-known entertainers, including the actors Stanley Baker and Diana Dors. Sentencing Charlie Richardson to 25 years in prison, the presiding judge, Mr Justice Lawton, branded him a 'vicious, sadistic, criminal'. Two years later, the Kray Twins would follow the Richardsons into the dock and receive equally severe custodial sentences.

What was clear to anyone reading reports from the Richardson trial, and later the Krays, was the extent to which London criminal interests had infiltrated provincial cities across England. A state of affairs made all the more workable with the 1960 Gaming Act which legitimised gambling in arcades, pubs and amusement parks. It offered a source of income to the criminal opportunist. The Scotland Yard hierarchy accepted that, if they were to tackle successfully London's professional criminal class, it would require the setting up of independent, uncorrupted units from outside the capital, as their own officers were all too frequently implicated.

Lewis was intent on working on his writing and bringing a second novel to fruition, but as spring gave way to summer, he received a phone call from Tom Barling with an offer to meet and discuss an opportunity on an upcoming animated feature film.

In London's animation community, Television Cartoons (TVC) were best known for producing the animated Beatles show that ran on Saturday morning television in the United States. The short cartoons, featuring mop-top characters with nondescript 'British' accents, were based on the Beatles' 1964 vintage, hopelessly out of step with the psychedelic pop princelings seen around London by 1967. Originally conceived as a cash-in on the band's success, the cartoons were tolerated by the Beatles' management as a means of extending the band's post-touring shelf life. The Beatles, understandably, hated them. Initially, when TVC announced there would be an animated Beatles film, it was assumed to be a feature-length version of the existing series, but *Yellow Submarine* was always going to be a different proposition. Tom Barling received an early approach from TVC. He found the production in chaos:

'I was painting the ceiling in my new house when they came and got me in a taxi – "quick, come with us, we need you" – I was in there a week and it was amateur night. There were three different units with three different directors who weren't speaking to each other. I was running round trying to get the layouts for this and layouts for that. There were some Americans on it who were bloody good, but the egomaniacs who were supposed to be directing…'

Barling lasted a week before quitting:

'I thought, what the hell am I doing here? I had Heinz Edelmann, this German designer, I mean his stuff was lovely on the flat, but you try animating the bloody things; everything was so flat. There wasn't a piece with three-dimensions in it – there was a fight between two dinosaurs. I started animating and key drawing them so they moved around a bit – like a boxing match. And it was like, "Where are the bubbles – it's under the sea!" John Coates didn't want to pay me – it was a joke.'

When Tom Barling told Lewis there was a major film project underway, he jumped at the chance. With his art school background, a track record in illustration, experience on *The Lone Ranger,* and a practised eye for detail, Lewis was

Harry Lewis and son – circa 1941-42
(photo courtesy Nancy Lewis)

Lewis and Martin Turner – circa 1955
(photo courtesy Nick and Martin Turner)

Riverbank Boys – Camping on the banks of the Humber circa 1953-54
(photo courtesy Nick and Martin Turner)

Ted Lewis and Jean Walker in centre
– Barbara Hewson on TL's right
(photo courtesy Barbara Hewson)

Barton Grammar School – Luxembourg Trip 1955

Barton Grammar School Luxembourg Trip 1955

**Ted Lewis in cross-country,
Barton Grammar School 1955-56**
(photo courtesy Barbara Hewson)

Hull College of Arts and Crafts – steps circa 1957 – Lewis 2nd right top row

Unity Jazz Band publicity shot at Beverley Racecourse – 1958-59 (photo courtesy Ron Burnett)

Unity Jazz Band at the Blue Bell 1959
Lewis at the piano 'utterly shagged out'
Ron Burnett in the foregound

Graham Palmer's portrait of Ted Lewis 1959

The art school gang at Fraisthorpe Summer 1959
Lewis front row, third from right, Heather Morton by his side

Lewis with Juliet Raahauge at Art School Wild West Dance 1960

Lewis at Art School Wild West dance 1960

Lewis drawing for Delgado book *Return Ticket* 1965

Lewis's first commission
The Hot-Water Bottle Mystery
by Alan Delgado 1962

Lewis illustration for *Bridge Over the River Kwai* circa 1965

Lewis photographed for Books and Bookmen 1965

Michael Caine and Ted Lewis on location
July 1970

Lewis on location Gateshead August 1970

Lewis in Barton circa 1975

Lewis at home January 1980

interviewed and appointed to supervise the *Yellow Submarine* animation clean-up process. There was a final piece of work for Halas, a film commissioned for the Government's Central Office of Information. Written by Joy Batchelor and directed by John Halas, *Dying for a Smoke* was a nine-and-a-half-minute animation aimed at warning children and teenagers of the perils of cigarettes. Voiced by actor Warren Mitchell, the devil, in the guise of 'Nick O'Tine', lures and enslaves unsuspecting children in his chain-smoking gang. Lewis, a thoroughly committed smoker, and Chris Miles are credited as background artists and the techniques pioneered for *The Lone Ranger* were once again to the fore.

Lewis joined the *Yellow Submarine* production in the summer of 1967. At his recommendation, John Coates and George Dunning interviewed Chris Miles. In September, Miles joined the team. As *Yellow Submarine* was to be created by an assortment of freelance animators and artists, all of whom had their own style of drawing, clean-up became an essential part of the design and production process. Lewis and Miles carried the responsibility of ensuring all drawings faithfully reproduced the work of art director, Heinz Edelmann. Miles estimates that, over the lifetime of the production, he and Lewis and their team, which at one time or another also included Ian Cowan, Richard Dakin and Ray Newman, handled somewhere in the region of 250,000 animation cells. Working side by side for long hours, the two became close. David Elvin was another arrival from Halas, joining the project later in 1967. 'All I knew about TVC and the Beatles was that terrible cartoon series. I'd been fraternising with John Coates in the Dog and Duck. He rang up and made me an offer. By the time I arrived, Ted was already on board.'

At the height of production, there were as many as 200 artists working on the film; many were students recruited from art schools across London and bussed in for overnight shifts. Others from outside London had come to the capital specifically to work on the project. Inevitably, there were anomalies in the quality of the work they produced. The film's animation director, Bob Balser, described the importance of Lewis's clean-up team in Bob Hieronimus's detailed chronicle of the production, *Inside the Yellow Submarine*:

> The difference in drawing ability was obvious when a scene was put together. So we set up a very efficient clean up control department and every single scene passed through the hands of a small group of excellent artists (not animators), which adjusted and corrected small details to bring drawings closer to the Edelmann originals, as well as maintain a consistency of line and technique.

With most of the Halas and Batchelor team reunited at the TVC building in Knightway House, the lunchtime sessions at the Dog and Duck picked up again. The pub's landlord and his dog, Scrumpy, found their way into the *Yellow Submarine* opening photo-animation sequence. The creative process continued without let up. Extraordinary when, as David Elvin recalls, 'We were regularly drinking three or four pints at lunchtime.' As the music played loud into the night in the trace and paint department, the artists and animators felt they were at the epicentre of fashion and creativity. The Beatles themselves showed little interest in the project, investing their time in the *Magical Mystery Tour* film, by then in post-production in an editing suite across Soho.

The eleven month production timeline for *Yellow Submarine*, together with limitations on budget and an often bewildering complexity of concept, direction, script (or lack of) and innovation at each stage, kept the project completion at risk for almost its entire duration. Clean-up was the one phase where there could be no short cuts. Repetitive and highly pressurised, it demanded intense concentration and extraordinary attention to detail. Animator Malcolm Draper remembers Lewis telling him that, along with Mike Stuart and Anne Jolliffe, they were the only ones who could really draw the Beatles' characters to the required standard. Draper believes Lewis created one of the film's posters. 'I know Heinz Edelmann did one of them, but I'm sure Ted designed another one.'

Another of Lewis's former colleagues from the Halas and Batchelor days, Gil Potter, had been employed as a layout artist and assistant to one of the two *Yellow Submarine* directors, Jack Stokes. Invited to Gil and Doreen Potter's home, a seventeenth century thatched cottage in the picturesque village of Wicken Bonhunt in rural Essex, Ted and Jo fell in love with the uncomplicated charm of the place. Potter remembers Lewis coming for the weekend. 'I said, "You're doing alright, if you see a place why not buy one?" Within a couple of weeks I rang him up and said he should get down here, because one of the cottages was for sale.' Lewis bought Erme Cottage towards the end of 1967. According to Jo, Harry Lewis thought it was a hovel and said so. She concedes it probably did look a little rundown and was in need of renovation.

With Lewis a stone's throw from Gil Potter's Clarke Cottage – the village pub, the Coach and Horses was between them – their friendship became closer. Gil remembers, 'I used to cross the road and Ted walked up and we'd meet in the pub, and so we got talking more, and of course we both worked in London so we used to travel up together. Ted didn't drive so I used to drive us both to the station and in the evening drive back again.'

As Lewis left London behind, the move placed him further from the friendships with which he'd grown up. Mike Shucksmith had married, although they kept in touch; by now John Dickinson was firmly ensconced in Barton as a general practitioner, and there was little contact with the other Riverbank Boys for whom work and family were overriding interests. Lewis's own world revolved around Jo, his work on *Yellow Submarine* and his writing. Tom Barling wasn't surprised to see Lewis leave London. 'He was clearly split. He liked London, but I think in a way he was frightened of it.' There was another reason for leaving: Jo was pregnant. With a new baby due the following year, Lewis and Jo were determined to provide a secure and stable home. Wicken seemed an ideal place to bring up children. Before leaving, Lewis caught up with Juliet Raahauge. She remembers they met for a drink a couple of times. 'It was very odd. He asked me if he could borrow some money. He was working on *Yellow Submarine* and I thought he should be earning much more than me. It was friendly. He told me about Jo, how he'd fallen in love.'

With around 200 residents, village life in Wicken had something of the simplicity of a bygone age. At the bakery, if no one was around, customers took their bread and left the money on the counter. The Coach and Horses still counted a sprinkling of rustic eccentrics and domino-playing old timers among its regulars. The downside was the landlord, Dave Kinnear, who would habitually bar customers for minor indiscretions or a word out of turn. The ban never seemed to last long and most regulars knew to keep a low profile for a few days then return quietly, by which time the misdemeanour would be forgotten. One regular was Frank Monk, a local oddjob man. Wearing his shirt open in all weathers to reveal a brass chain around his neck which had become green with corrosion, Monk dominated the public bar. When he'd been chicken-plucking or turkey-killing, he'd arrive at the pub covered in blood and feathers. He would also habitually refer to the local policeman, Constable Dicky Bright, as a 'button man'.

Lewis was a reluctant commuter, but settled into a routine of early starts, taking the train from Audley End Station into Liverpool Street, then travelling by tube into the West End. TVC's offices were a short walk through Soho. He worked until lunch, drank, worked, and slept off the lunchtime beer on the way home to Wicken on the train or as a passenger in Gil Potter's car. Most evenings, he would spend time with Jo or drinking at the Coach and Horses. Although Jo doesn't recall their time at Wicken being one of excess, or of Lewis drinking more than was usual, a scene of sorts developed around the *Yellow Submarine* crew. At weekends there were parties, usually at the Potters' cottage. Artists, animators and filmmakers made the trip to Wicken. Affairs began, were consummated, climaxed and came to an end during the film's production.

While the pub was the main meeting place for locals, there was also a transient population of teachers and students at the residential education centre located in the village. Funded by Essex County Council and delivering courses in what was loosely termed 'Liberal Studies', Barri Hooper was the long-term warden at Wicken House. He and Lewis struck up a friendship after Lewis had come to the pub one evening with a telltale bulge in his jacket. Hooper joked, was he 'packing a piece'? It turned out to be a toy Colt pistol. Lewis had been trying to replicate the experience of carrying a weapon, feeling the weight in his jacket and testing to see whether it would be noticed. Hooper, a former Royal Air Force armament mechanic, had carried his interest in firearms into civilian life. He found Lewis a willing listener, hungry for details about weapons and their capabilities. 'I told him he'd need a holster for something like that and certainly not an imitation Colt. The barrel was too long for a start.'

On Hooper's nights off he would drink with Lewis and Gil Potter until closing time. Afterwards, they'd go back to Wicken House for more drinks and a game of snooker in the basement games room. Potting fifteen reds and colours after a few pints and whiskies took some time and it wasn't unknown for sessions to last half the night, often interrupted by arguments over the score in which Lewis would accuse the others of moving the counter along when his back was turned. Hooper remembers he'd become incensed, slamming his cue on the table. 'I'd say, "Come on, it's only a game." And he'd say, "No, if you do a thing, you do it properly".'

When Hooper came across a collection of second hand *Police Journal* magazines detailing true crime cases and methods used in their detection, he and Lewis shared long conversations about real life crimes. Sitting in the public bar at the Coach, Hooper set out hypothetical scenarios based on cases in the journals and challenged Lewis to work out the solutions. A memorable case involved two men holding a conversation in an open field with the nearest cover 200 yards away. When one of the men is shot dead with a pistol, the other is naturally the chief suspect, but no weapon is found. Hooper asked, was it possible to shoot someone with a pistol from a distance of over 200 yards? Lewis thought not, but the case file suggested it was possible *if* you had the right weapon. Hooper showed Lewis a decommissioned Mauser pistol he'd recently bought. When I spoke to Hooper at his house in Newport, a few miles from Wicken Bonhunt, he produced the Mauser and laid it on the table. It was heavy in my hand, a solid weight, incapable of firing, but still somehow carrying a threat. The rear sight was calibrated to a wildly optimistic thousand metres. Originally, he explained, it would have had a wooden stock that could be attached, effectively giving it the stability of a rifle. Based on available evidence, the police in the true crime case had assumed the assassin's weapon was a rifle; meanwhile the perpetrator had his pistol in a backpack and was long gone. For a while, Lewis borrowed the Mauser and lived with it alongside the toy Colt and a dagger on his desk in the Erme Cottage annex, a well appointed wooden cabin that he had taken over as a writing studio.

At a party at Clarke Cottage one evening, Lewis noticed what he took to be an ornamental Beretta handgun Gil had mounted on the wall. Hooper remembers they'd all had a lot to drink when Lewis took the gun down. 'Ted was pointing this gun at me. I told him you should never point a gun at anybody. He said it wasn't loaded, but when we had a look it was. If he'd pulled the trigger, I'd have been shot.' The weapon, an early model 6.35 calibre Beretta Jetfire, had no safety catch. Having narrowly avoided being shot, Hooper explained to Lewis that, in spite of its lack of punch, the Beretta would be the ideal assassin's gun at close range, because it could be carried undetected. (It had been Ian Fleming's original choice of firearm for James Bond, later replaced with a Walther PPK.) Hooper had the distinct impression Lewis was working out specific scenes. After watching a film fight in which a tough guy's jacket was pulled down over his arms rendering him unable to retaliate, Lewis insisted they test the theory. They replicated the scene in the Coach and Horse public bar one evening. It was possible, they discovered, but relatively easy for the protagonist to pull his arms out.

With TVC's offices in Soho Square and nearby Dean Street, and the habitual drinking culture amongst artists and animators on *Yellow Submarine*, Lewis became a recognised face on the Soho scene around this time. Nick Hague had lived and worked in Soho since the early 1960s. Starting out as an actor, he began directing in television and, by the mid 60s, was working for Associated Rediffusion, later setting up his own production company in Hanway Street, then Wardour Street. He got to know Lewis through a mutual association with the actors' agent, Peter Crouch:

'Peter, who I knew very well, had an office next door to the Dog and Duck. He was a very heavy drinker and he used to spend much of his day in the pub. I'd join him for a drink and that's how I met Ted initially. He and Peter were quite good buddies. Ted drank in the Coach and Horses in Greek Street, too. He used to pop into the French House and I remember him coming down to Gerry's with Peter a couple of times.'

Gerry's Club, originally on Shaftesbury Avenue, had been opened in 1955 by the actor, Gerald Campion, best known for playing Billy Bunter on BBC Television. By the mid 60s it was a regular haunt for those in film, television and media and was used by certain members of the press on the understanding that nothing they witnessed there would find its way into the papers. Nick Hague remembers Gerry's attracted 'an awful lot of people who were in the limelight, but who didn't want their story published – actors who liked a drink or six, that kind of thing'. The reporting embargo also appealed to players in London's underworld:

'There's no question about that at all. A lot of East End boys used to drift in and out of Soho and socialise and Gerry's Club was the place where a lot of it used to happen – mixing with actors and directors and theatre folk, and film and television folk. I don't think there's any doubt that if those were the kinds of circles Ted was drinking in, he'd have encountered the East End boys. They were difficult to avoid.'

For Lewis, the contrast between family life in rural Wicken and the frantic hustle of Soho could hardly have been plainer. Filmmakers, writers and advertising executives rubbed shoulders, drank together and cut deals in the same pubs as Berwick Street market traders, small time chancers, bag-men, pornographers and protection racketeers. Tom Barling remembers introducing Lewis to his own underworld connections, but says that he didn't usually stick around. 'They were scary guys if they didn't know you. You had to get to know them before they'd trust you.' *Yellow Submarine* production administrator, Norman Kauffman, remembers Kray associates threatening local shopkeepers. The Krays and, before them, Jack Spot's gang and the Maltese gangs had extorted money from Soho businesses for decades. There wasn't a lot you could do about it and the police weren't always sympathetic. Interviewed for the book *Getting it Straight* some years later, former Kray gang member, Freddie Foreman, recalled the Premier Club in Little Newport Street as the place to 'do a deal with the Old Bill'. Kauffman remembers the violence came close to home one evening when a young woman was murdered on the doorstep of TVC's Dean Street offices.

In Gerry's and The French Pub, on the streets and in the clubs, Lewis was observing, listening, and making notes for stories and characters to take back to his writing studio. In 1971 he would speak about the underworld origins that inspired *Jack's Return Home*, including an account of a chance meeting with Michael Tink, an old friend from Barton Grammar School now working as a tout for a Soho strip joint:

'I was walking through Soho, in London, one afternoon, when a strip club barker stepped in front of me and began his spiel trying to persuade me to enter the club. We simultaneously recognised one another as being old schoolfriends! It turned out he had a regular job but was earning extra money by doing this. I met his girlfriend, who was a stripper, and through them gradually got to know several underworld criminal types.

'I mixed with them freely and never let on that I was a writer. In time they accepted me as "one of the crowd" and I learnt an enormous amount about the economic structure of crime, gangs, blue movies, gambling clubs, who had just beaten up who, and so on.

'I learnt about crime syndicates with tie ups in the north of England. A lot of the big time crooks are based in London, but many prefer to run their crime operations in the provincial cities. They would rather be big fish in small ponds than relatively small time in London.

Jack Carter is based on two or three different people I met in those days. He's tough, vicious, ruthless, but like so many criminals, he has a great family feeling.'

Whether Lewis's exposure to the London underworld came through a series of detailed but distant observations in the streets of Soho and a crowded Dog and Duck, or personal introductions to Tom Barling's old East End mates over pints and stiff whiskies in pubs, or on visits to West End clubs like Gerry's with Peter Crouch, or through semi-integration and acceptance thanks to Mike Tink and his stripper girlfriend's dubious contacts, he was intent on devising a story whose central character was a criminal, a hard man who'd be at ease in the streets of Soho. For that to be convincing the character would need real substance and that meant bringing him into his own world.

In tracing the evolution of Jack Carter and the development of what was to become *Jack's Return Home*, there are countless sources and influences. Lewis crafted conscious and subconscious fragments of lived experience, history, anecdote and fiction into his story, drawing inspiration from as far back as EC comics and B-movie gangster flicks. A single clear cut realisation of what he might be able to achieve came in February 1968 with the release of the film, *Point Blank*. Directed by John Boorman, starring Lee Marvin, and adapted from the 1962 novel, *The Hunter*, by Donald Westlake (Westlake used the pen name, Richard Stark), *Point Blank* starred Marvin as Walker, an amoral protagonist hellbent on revenge with little thought for himself and none at all for those he places in harm's way. Jo remembers they saw it together and, not surprisingly, Lewis loved it.

Speaking about the origins of Walker, originally named Parker in the novel, Westlake said, 'I gave him none of the softness you're supposed to give a series character, and no band of sidekicks to chat with, because he was going to pound through one book and goodbye'. As it turned out, his editor would persuade him otherwise, but the nihilistic disregard of a one-way-ticket antihero remains crucial to the story and clearly sparked something in Lewis. In his ruthless pursuit of those who betrayed and left him for dead, Walker confronts his wife, a few low grade hoods and middle-ranking mafia bosses (including one named Fred Carter) on his way to an unforgettable showdown on Alcatraz Island. Typically, Marvin invests Walker with relentless, brooding intensity, the threat of violence in every step.

Point Blank was one of a handful of films that included another Lewis favourite, *Bonnie and Clyde* – Tom Barling remembers they were drunk when they saw it and thought it a comedy – which shifted the limits of acceptability in terms of the degree of violence a mainstream audience could be exposed to. Marvin's performance in *Point Blank* led the field. It encouraged Lewis to express similar conviction with depictions of violence in his own writing.

He picked up the threads of ideas he'd been collecting and, with Marvin's Walker in mind, began writing what would become *Jack's Return Home*. Jo remembers him working on the manuscript at weekends. 'I couldn't wait to type each new page. I'd snatch them from him as soon as they were finished.' Lewis was adamant that nothing should be changed. He would read the typed versions and ask Jo's opinion, but never rewrite. 'He thought it would suffer if it was overworked, if it wasn't spontaneous.' Gil Potter was sometimes enlisted for a second opinion. 'Ted was never confident, he needed criticism before he showed it to anyone else.'

With the final animated sequences of *Yellow Submarine* segueing into the Beatles' half-hearted live end section, the psychedelic fairytale reached its uneven conclusion in summer 1968. Lewis's clean-up team was left to work on the film's final scenes, pulling a string of long days and all-nighters to get the work finished with money running out and people leaving the production. Chris Miles recalls they'd had a significant amount of work to complete and no certainty where funds were coming from – at one point John Coates and George Dunning hid reels of the completed film to ensure the project couldn't be taken from them. Lewis was one of the last freelance artists to leave *Yellow Submarine*. The film premiered at the London Pavilion in Piccadilly Circus on 17 July 1968. A little over a week later, on 29 July, Jo gave birth to a daughter, Nancy.

Towards the end of his time with TVC, Lewis was asked to assist in the development of a cartoon series in Germany. It was five weeks work, mainly in London, but also involving some travel. Norman Kauffman remembers being surprised at what he read as Lewis's unworldliness: 'They'd given him the air ticket and he asked me what he had to do. I asked him which airline he was flying with. He told me it was "Luftwaffe".'

Within weeks, Lewis found himself working in animation once again, this time employed by the BBC as designer and animator on *Zokko!*, a new format show described by its producers as a 'weekly comic for children – electronic style'. *Zokko!* ran between 1968–70 and was entirely characteristic of its time, with the BBC attempting to embrace new creative freedoms in children's programming. Presented by *Mr Zokko!*, a speaking pinball machine whose Radiophonic Workshop voice fascinated some children and terrified others, the show moved between a series of short features, intending to replicate the fast-read flick through of a cartoon strip or teen magazine. It was, as vintage television aficionado, TJ Worthington, writes, 'perplexing… a combination of inhouse animation, stock footage, pop music, and a small amount of specially shot light entertainment material, all cut together using "pop art" editing effects and graphical design'.

Beginning its first 13 week run on 31 October 1968, *Zokko!* retains a place in television history as the first BBC TV children's programme to air on a Saturday morning. As well as using library footage, much of the animated material was created by the BBC team. Malcolm Draper, Lewis's friend and colleague from the Halas and TVC days, worked as an animator. 'We got about 50 pounds a week for that as well. You couldn't turn it down.'

On Tuesday 4 March 1969, the Kray twins, their older brother Charlie, and associates including Tony and Christopher Lambrianou, Freddie Foreman, John Barrie, Ronald Bender and Cornelius Whitehead were found guilty after what was then the longest murder trial in British criminal history. The judge, Justice Melford Stevenson, postponed sentencing until the following morning. The accused returned to court in a convoy of police vans and motorcycle escorts. This was the underworld presented as entertainment. One reporter likened the sensation of being at the trial to 'sitting right inside a superior thriller'. Reggie Kray had asked if James Bond would be appearing and at one point, according to his defence counsel, Ronnie had been 'convulsing himself with laughter'.

In all probability, Lewis completed the draft of *Jack's Return Home* around this time. Containing few of the self-conscious literary flourishes of his first novel, it was vividly and determinedly non-metropolitan, the work of a writer finding his own voice. Padded prose was superseded by an altogether more muscular style. In terse, stripped sentences, he balanced atmosphere, character and story with note-perfect execution. He was out on his own, writing on the fringes of English crime fiction which, at the time, generally meant PD James or Ruth Rendell, or others with a direct line to golden age murder stories. The noir novel was overwhelmingly regarded as an American or a French medium.

It's not to say there weren't good crime novels, tense thrillers or gritty underworld stories. But reading British novels which might be considered contemporaries, particularly those which transferred from page to screen – James Barlow's *The Burden of Proof* (1968), filmed as *Villain*, and James Mitchell's Callan novel *A Magnum for Schneider* (1969) (later published as *Red*

File for Callan) come to mind – as well-written and absorbing as they are, they don't have the depth, the edge, the intensity, the honesty or the innovation of language of *Jack's Return Home*. No wonder Lewis wasn't keen to revise the early draft; had he thought too much about themes of exploitative sex, graphic violence or language written as spoken, that nagging self-doubt might have persuaded him to draw back. Rather, it is in place from the first sentence as we meet Carter heading for his connection at Doncaster on a wet October Thursday afternoon. Lewis wrote 'The rain rained.' Noun and verb inseparable. Jack Carter is what he does, and what he does is as inevitable as rain.

Questioning what makes *Jack's Return Home* the most important British crime novel of its era and the inspiration for one of the greatest British crime films ever made, inevitably you look to the character of Jack Carter. At which point it's difficult not to dial up a stock image of Michael Caine in a midnight blue mohair suit and Aquascutum raincoat, pints in thin glasses, Gitanes cigarettes, Ford Cortinas and big men out of shape. But to fully understand the unique place Carter has in the evolution of British crime writing, it's important to place him in context as Lewis originally intended. An ultra-real small town enforcer, violent, sadistic, irretrievably flawed, shouldering the burden of guilt; one of us maybe, if we dare to think it, taken a wrong turn, corrupted and unflinching. While he's not entirely without precedent, emerging from the roll call of irredeemably damned fictional villains that begins with Bill Sikes and gives us, among others, Kersh's Harry Fabian and Greene's Pinkie Brown, Jack Carter's consuming determination for revenge and his inability to be reasoned with exceeds every other lawless, amoral protagonist who'd been before. His appeal owes much to the traits Patricia Highsmith ascribes to the 'sleuth hero'; able, she wrote, to 'beat women, be brutal and sexually unscrupulous' knowing the 'public will still cheer them on because they are chasing "something worse than themselves, presumably"'. In Carter's case, for much of the novel, that's only just true. Lewis makes it plain that Carter is a psychopath, a misogynist, a torturer and killer; yet he challenges us not to identify with him as he grinds, beats and bruises through his manifestly personal crusade.

The story is straightforward. In terms of structure, it resembles a classic 'outsider' Western: Jack Carter, a fixer and enforcer in the employ of London gangsters, the Kray/Richardson-like Fletcher brothers, returns to his home town for the funeral of his brother, Frank. He suspects Frank, who never touched hard liquor, but was found drunk on whisky and dead at the wheel of his car, has been murdered. Thursday through to Sunday, Jack pursues the truth about the circumstances of Frank's death. The loner villain turned detective, antagonising associates and adversaries, refusing to stop, even when notice to cease and desist reaches him from the Fletchers.

Making Scunthorpe (unnamed), the surrounding towns and villages and the northern Lincolnshire landscape integral to the story was a masterstroke. Lewis brought characters from his Soho observations and gave them licence to wander the rain-washed streets, dead end alleys and riverside wastelands of his youth. In a vision of the industrial north untouched by London's swinging pop culture and faux hippy mysticism, he saw beyond the optimism and free love sloganeering of the age and committed to a compelling vision of the place he knew. It begins with Carter's entry to Scunthorpe by train, a journey Lewis had made on countless occasions. Set apart from the main text, the description of the heat, smoke and blast furnace glow hanging over this nameless rained-on town reads like a voiceover. Lewis shifts from Jack Carter's dominant first person voice to the second person to describe a 'Disney version of the Dawn of Creation'. Dawn of creation or descent into hell. No post-war British crime novel had opened with such a bold, panoramic statement of a place you'd never visited and probably never would.

Scunthorpe's sense of dislocation and geographical anonymity is crucial. Far from swinging London, the town's sole concession to fashionable modernity is a shop called 'Hurdy Gurdy' which, Jack observes, sells 'poove clothes and military uniforms' and had once been Rowson's the grocers. An incongruous splash of King's Road colour amongst the browns, greys and beiges that bring to mind Larkin's 'grim head-scarved wives'. Teenagers hanging around outside Scunthorpe Baths in 'open neck shirts and Walker Brothers' haircuts' are conspicuously behind the times, as if a watery version of the swinging sixties is only now spilling into the provinces as the decade closes.

Jack Carter arrives with the air of a man whose experience of London's clubs and clip joints, and the status afforded by working for the Fletchers, make him a cut above his local adversaries. Yet, before long, he reverts to the creed of the small town enforcer, losing himself in tight, terraced streets he knows well. Here, Lewis uses a succession of nearly, but not quite, street names and place names: Lindum Street becomes Linden Street; Jackson Road becomes Jackson Street, the Carters' family home a short distance from the outskirts of town and the Wolds beyond.

Scunthorpe is a grey rainswept version of the classic one-street frontier town. There is no hiding place. On the edge sits the dilapidated house Albert Swift runs as a brothel. We meet Greer – chain-smoking, hair in curlers – and two grubby kids, both girls. They're all glued to the television. The emphysemic Swift, Jack's one-time mentor, for whom he served a spell in prison, slumps in his chair, too old and sick for work. He's married Lucille, Greer's sister, a prostitute, and takes a cut of her earnings. There's a baby in a carrycot on the kitchen table, unattended as Lucille is having sex with an off-shift steelworker in the back bedroom. When one of the two small girls rushes to open the door for the punter on his way out, shrieking goodbyes and grinning as Greer and Lucille lose themselves in the pages of a mail order catalogue, the suggestion is that the child, too, will be earning a similar living before long. Lewis has a gift for the seedy, the bleak observances of an underclass existence. No one here needs reminding that they're peripheral, disposable.

More than once, Lewis spoke in interviews of how he'd tried to give Jack Carter a 'family feeling'. Whether this relates to his niece, Doreen, or his brother – present throughout the novel in a sequence of reminiscences – these relationships, never less than complex, are essential to understanding his motivations. Frank, we learn, was hard working and dourly conventional. A man not unlike Harry Lewis. As Jack moves through what was once their family home with Frank's open coffin in the front room, his brother's life is reduced to a collection of possessions, many of which, it's fair to assume, had been Lewis's own at one time or another: pulp western novels by Max Brand and JT Edson; spy thrillers by Alistair MacLean and Ian Fleming; Winston Churchill's and Guy Gibson's war memoirs; sports books by Bobby Charlton and Bill Bowes; records of brass bands, a handful of middling jazz LPs, a Vaughan Williams record and, notably, a Tony Hancock comedy album. The effort that Frank had put into making good around the house – newish wallpaper, carpets and shelves and boxed-in television cabinets with a space for the *Radio* and *TV Times* – needles Jack, perhaps because of its sheer ordinariness. By comparison, Frank's own room is drably austere with its iron frame bed, pre-war tallboy and wardrobe. Jack stubs out his cigarette on the linoleum. At the back of the wardrobe, he finds the shotgun they'd scrimped to buy between them as kids, each taking a turn to carry it to the river to shoot.

To begin with, then, Lewis paints Carter's desire for revenge as a familial obligation; justice meted out because that's the way things must be: what you do to mine, I do to you. Jack's status demands that the murder of his brother be avenged, but Lewis reveals his need to settle the score is fuelled equally by guilt. In the years he's been away, he has felt little other than contempt for his brother. He reminisces how, as kids, Frank made him feel ashamed after 'penny a wank' sessions with Valerie Marshbanks. Later, he recalls the billiard hall face-off when, as teenagers, they encounter a younger, tougher Albert Swift and his gang. Jack is shamed by his brother's refusal to fight Swift after a head butt gives him a bloody nose. He fronts up, knowing he'll take a beating, as if somehow that will compensate. When Frank staunches the flow of blood with a clean handkerchief, Jack finds it repellent, a sign of weakness. It marks the beginning of his descent into criminality and the souring of the brothers' relationship.

Worse still is Jack's self-loathing at conceiving a child with Muriel, his brother's plain-looking, mucky minded wife-to-be, the result of a drunken fuck on the front room carpet, shortly before they were married. He describes how Muriel wrote to Frank after he'd discovered her affair with a Pakistani neighbour and she'd left. She claims Doreen is Jack's daughter, not his. Frank simply and quietly tells Jack that he never wants to see him again. It is the last time they speak.

Jack visits the place on 'top road' where Frank's car had crashed. In reality, this is the A1077 Winterton Road near

Dragonby, running across the Wolds from Barton-upon-Humber, through the villages of South Ferriby and Winterton, twisting steeply into Scunthorpe. Jack reminisces about Frank and their ride to 'Back Hill' as kids, describing the town, the Wolds, the river beyond, and the sky that was 'wider than any other sky could be'. There, as they lay on their backs in sunshine, Frank had daydreamed of playing drums in a jazz band like Gene Krupa. America was the Promised Land. Freedom an open road, a drape suit and a shirt worn without a tie 'like Richard Widmark'. Returning to town, Jack's American reverie is confronted by the kitsch reality of ersatz ranch-style houses in the affluent suburbs.

Thread by thread, Lewis unpicks the relationship between the brothers. It would be the first of a series of close, usually interdependent, connections between men that he would write. It's evident that Frank's notions of right and wrong are at the heart of Jack's internal struggle; they share an inclination to shut out unpalatable truths, compartmentalising thought and feeling. Now, back home in Scunthorpe, with memories rekindled and his brother dead, fuelled by whisky, bitterness and revenge, Jack is unravelling.

None of the principal characters Lewis writes about in *Jack's Return Home* is honest, least of all with themselves. To varying degrees, all suffer from the corrosive effects of lying, of lies compounding lies, of the habit of manipulation and the paranoia it feeds. Truth is a device deployed to conceal greater untruth. Everybody smiles a smile which isn't a smile; laughter betrays a deeper knowing. When Jack meets Margaret, the prostitute with whom Frank had a relationship, she smiles in a way that makes Jack think he's missed something. The landlady's smile, had it surfaced, he knows could only have been sarcastic; the barman, Keith, gives a grotesque half smile at Carter's suggestion that Frank committed suicide. The initial verbal sparring between Jack and Eric Paice produces a virtual symphony of smiles, Eric giving 'the biggest smile ever' as Carter tries to find out who he's working for. When Jack tracks him to Cyril Kinnear's casino, Lewis writes a perfectly pitched old chums together routine over a game of poker that barely conceals the enmity between them.

Carter is an inveterate user of people, particularly women. Encountering Edna Garfoot, his prospective middle aged landlady for the weekend, he sums her up on the basis of whether or not she'll be up for sex, largely, it seems, determined by the colour of her underwear. He's polite, almost charming, in order to get what he wants. He uses Keith, the young barman, playing on the lad's naivety. With the help of a few large scotches, Jack strings him along on the promise of a few quid and the chance to help find out what happened to Frank without making him aware of the risk attached. In the wake of the beating Keith receives, Jack offers money. Lies and exploitation are part of his code. What happens to Keith is of little consequence.

Carter's path to retribution leaves behind a trail of damaged lives. The more he drinks – and he drinks a lot – the more he struggles to keep his paranoia in check. Where he finds those who might be friends, he uses, then alienates, them. His intimacy with his landlady, Edna, is because she is disposable, an older woman he no more cares for than the barman who pours his pint. That said, she is unique among the women in *Jack's Return Home* in that she offers a glimmer of resistance. Returning to his lodgings following his ill-informed confrontation with Cliff Brumby, Jack encounters Edna, roughed up by Thorpe's men. She accuses him of murdering the wrong man – assuming correctly that killing Brumby had been his intention – and reminds him how easily he was duped. At first his response is offhand, then silent; she mocks him and he loses his temper. She hits him and he embraces her forcefully, pinning her arms underneath her whilst massaging the bruise on her breast that Thorpe's boys have given her. Whatever resistance she had shown is subdued in Carter's intimate pain and pleasure foreplay.

Lewis raises the stakes with the Saturday morning arrival of Peter the Dutchman and Con McCarty, sent by the Fletchers from London to bring Carter back. Interrupting Jack and Edna's morning fuck, a naked Carter grabs the shotgun. Con and Peter mug their way through the 'you know you won't use it'/'the gun he means' lines. A twisted Bethnal Green incarnation of Hemingway's assassins in *The Killers*, Con is affable, but a killer nonetheless; Peter, a sadistic homosexual with a reputation for taking pleasure in hurting women.

In contrast with the easy conquest of Edna Garfoot, Jack's libido fails with Brumby and Kinnear's more glamorous confidante, his 'fairy Godmother', Glenda. After a few large scotches, a degree of flirting and blue movie wordplay, when Glenda goes down on him, he can't respond. Compared with his control over Edna Garfoot, impotence with Glenda is significant. Lewis seems to be pointing the finger at the root of his character's contempt for women and perhaps his own. The scene, pivotal in the drama which follows, suggests a deeper insight into Carter's motivations. Glenda's response to his poor performance is to lead Jack to the bedroom where a film projector is set up to play porn movies. The bedroom colour scheme is hotter – a deep orange carpet and red silk counterpane, floor to ceiling mirrors and a plain white wall which functions as a projector screen. Glenda screens 'Schoolgirl Wanks', a shambolic cipher of a blue movie; more importantly, Jack witnesses Doreen being made to go down on Albert Swift and take a spanking from Glenda. Jack drags Glenda to the bathroom, wrapped in the silk counterpane, and repeatedly pushes her under the bathwater. He threatens to cut her with the knife he's taken from Con McCarty until she tells him all she knows about the set-up for the film, who had involved Doreen and why.

Jack goes after Albert Swift, a Saturday afternoon pursuit that begins as Eddie Waring commentates on a Hull Kingston Rovers and St Helens rugby league match on the television. It's hard to imagine a more resolutely 'northern' chase, more specifically a Scunthorpe chase. When Albert runs towards the steelworks' western entrance on Brigg Road, he's running for the town's industrial heart. Carter keeps pace as Albert falters, falls, picks himself up and runs again. Lewis describes the narrow gauge railway and the pans transporting molten furnace waste. Carter corners Albert. He comes clean, explaining that it was Cliff Brumby who'd wanted Doreen 'pulled', that they hadn't known her father was Jack's brother. Albert's protestations and pleadings fall on deaf ears. When Carter stabs him twice, then stands back to watch him die, you sense it's as much for what he did to humiliate Frank in the billiard hall all those years before as for Doreen and the film. The violence is close, unflinching.

Similarly, when Peter takes Doreen hostage, she watches in horror as Jack, effecting a rescue, beats him until his fists are 'slippery' with blood. She rejects him, adamant that she won't go with him to South Africa, and we see her for the abused, confused and vulnerable young woman she has undoubtedly become. Later, Jack drives to where she is staying with a friend with the intention of giving her money, but is thwarted by the presence of the police. It seems Doreen is being cared for, making her the only character to come out of the novel with any hope for the future.

Carter's affair and planned getaway to South Africa with Gerald Fletcher's wife, Audrey, always seems delusional. As does his conviction that Gerald won't find out about the affair with so many people in the know, most of whom Jack antagonises in one way or another. When Con McCarty tells him they've told Gerald about the affair, Carter knows Audrey will be beaten up, possibly cut and disfigured. His stomach turns at the prospect. Attempts to reach her fail. Calling contacts in London, he discovers that Gerald has done 'the worst' and arranged for the doctor, 'Camm', to treat Audrey to keep her away from hospital. Carter refuses to persuade her to escape to South Africa and wait for him, instructing Maurice to tell her he'll follow and make her believe it's the truth. The implication is that he has no intention of remaining with her. He has ceased to care about anything but revenge.

Lewis brings Jack Carter to the banks of the River Humber for the novel's final scenes. This is the real 'home' of the title, author and character sharing a childhood playground. A place of escape: Jack and Frank from their father's beatings; Lewis from grammar school taunts, bullying teachers and a repressive home life. This is the final 'return'. Lewis slows the rhythm of the prose, reflecting the river's steady ebb and flow, measured steps towards a reckoning. The Humber mud ripples with dawn colours. Carter takes in the brickworks' walls, briar and elderberry growing wild, the roofless shells of the tileries, the remains of a burned-out landing stage, kilns and vats full of old bricks and rainwater. He reminisces about childhood games of tracking and hunting.

Whether Carter's hubris means he believes himself invincible, indispensable, or is beyond caring, his judgement is distorted by revenge. Earlier he has proven himself an effective streetfighter, dishing out a beating to Thorpe's men. Up against Eric Paice one-to-one on home ground by the river, Carter is off guard. He catches up with Eric and, at gunpoint, forces him to drink from the bottle of scotch he's brought, just as Eric had with Frank. But in his moment of victory, Carter is careless. Eric stabs him. The blood pumps out 'much too quickly'. Eric picks up the shotgun to finish Carter off. In a rain-sodden, blood and mud soaked irony, when he pulls the trigger, it explodes in his face, killing him instantly. Con McCarty arrives to find Carter bleeding; he walks away, leaving him to die. Finally, for Jack, 'there is nothing, nothing at all'.

Lewis's initial belief in the novel was dealt a blow when his agent, John Johnson, refused to handle the manuscript. He thought it too violent. As Jo recalls, the rejection came as a shock. 'At the time, we had no money. That's when Toby came along.' Persuaded to seek a second opinion, Lewis sent a section of the manuscript to literary agent Toby Eady.

A relative newcomer to the London literary scene, Eady had originally worked in banking before becoming an agent in 1966. Branching out on his own, he set up Toby Eady Associates as an independent agency in 1968 and found himself inspired by emerging cultural ideas and changes in the way language was being used, particularly evident on stage at The Royal Court. 'You had that wonderful man, Devine, changing what was on every month. And to stand at something like that was two shillings and sixpence. Half the audience would walk out because they were so offended. It wasn't conventional theatre, but as an agent, you knew everything was being challenged.'

Although from vastly different backgrounds – Eady, son of the novelist, Mary Wesley, had attended Summerfields preparatory school, boarding school, and Oxford – he and Lewis shared a similar contempt for formal education. Learning by rote and beatings from teachers were as commonplace at Summerfields as a dressing down and a slap from Norman Goddard at Barton

Grammar. Interviewed by Danny Danziger for the *Independent* in 1994, Eady explained how, after the first three weeks settling in period, new boys had been fair game. 'The minute the three weeks were over, I was beaten. There wasn't a reason: I was beaten as an example to the other boys.' In common with Lewis, school had taught him to 'hide what he really felt'.

I met Eady at the end of 2009 in his office at Orme Court, the same offices in which Jo had once typed letters for Associated London Scripts. An imperious presence, he sat behind a large desk uncluttered by anything resembling technology. I spoke with his associate about Lewis and my plans for the book. After what felt like a long time, Eady entered the conversation, speaking in general terms about London in the 1960s and the background to *Jack's Return Home* in the days when underworld figures shared gaming tables with members of the aristocracy and cabinet ministers. He spoke guardedly about his friendship with Lewis, referring to the author's 'darkness' and the way it had informed his writing. I asked about their first meeting. He recalled that Lewis had shown him the school exercise books with the first few handwritten chapters of *Jack's Return Home* and, within a matter of weeks, had written the rest of the book.

Jo remembered it differently. 'It didn't happen like that. I typed it. I can remember Ted was very single-minded about that book. He went into the studio and he wrote. A thousand words a day was his goal and I'd type it. It was quick. When Toby came along, I think Ted told him he'd only got this small amount written, but really he'd got far more.'

It isn't difficult to see why Eady was enthusiastic about *Jack's Return Home*. No one had written a British gangster novel as relevant, hard-hitting and thoroughly authentic. It had pace and anger; it was relentless, a fusion of hard-boiled crime storytelling and the language and register of the best northern

English fiction. It had Jack Carter, a grinding, sardonic, flawed and thoroughly ruthless protagonist – the singular vision of its cine-literate author. Nevertheless, Eady had difficulties placing *Jack's Return Home* with editors whose expectations of the crime novel seemed to begin and end with the country house murders of a previous age. 'Publishers wouldn't touch it because of the language. It was considered ungrammatical.' Eventually, he pitched the book to Peter Day, editor at Michael Joseph, the company which had published Gerald Kersh's *Night and the City* in 1938 – one of the books which, along with *Brighton Rock* and James Curtis's *They Drive by Night*, both published in 1938, had come closest to establishing a British noir tradition. Indeed, Curtis's brooding 'Lone-Wolf' killer might be a precursor of Lewis's embittered antiheroes. Thirty years on, in 1969, Peter Day was having to contend with a reader's report on Lewis which said 'he couldn't write English'. Interviewed years later, Day acknowledged the university educated publishers' readers weren't ready for a novelist who 'writes as he speaks'.

Lewis was devastated by the early criticism, but Eady persisted. 'We read it aloud to the editors. It was Ted's language and you couldn't muck about with it.' Day was won round and Michael Joseph agreed to publish. Eady secured Lewis a generous £6,000 advance for paperback, American and German rights. Peter Day travelled to Wicken Bonhunt for the weekend, and he and Lewis edited the book into shape.

Jack's Return Home was published in hardback by Michael Joseph on 9 March 1970. The front cover image was another 'designed by Ted Lewis'. Gil Potter (becoming the first man to appear as Jack Carter) is photographed wearing his own leather coat, a borrowed trilby hat and carrying a shotgun. On the morning I visited Wicken Bonhunt, with Barri Hooper as tour guide, he recalled how Lewis and Gil Potter had walked

155

round the village searching for the 'right wall' on which to stage the photograph. He couldn't remember which it was, although there were one or two potential candidates. I pulled back the overgrown ivy half-expecting to reveal faded white lettering.

Jack's Return Home turned Lewis's life around before it had reached the bookshop shelves. Under the title, 'A Cracking Novel That Almost Died the Death', Graham Lord's *Sunday Express* review, published on 8 March 1970, tells the story of the book's initial rejection and troubled journey into print. Describing a 'fast, earthy and violent, but also extremely well written' revenge thriller, Lord pays tribute to Lewis's cinematic style which, he says, 'makes compulsive reading'. He continues, 'so is the case, you may say, with 100 other crime novels. But Mr Lewis scores not only with his story but the way he has written it. His ear for dialogue and his feeling for atmosphere are both remarkable. He conveys exactly the tight frustration of a small English town ...' Ted Lewis, he concludes, 'is a name to watch'. Interviewed for the piece, Lewis once again tells the story of his own criminal associations and the realism he sought to convey:

'When I was working on *Yellow Submarine* I got to know people on the fringe of the underworld – in protection and vice rackets – which gave me the idea for the book. Even after the recent trials like those of the Richardsons and Krays, people find it very difficult to believe that others can behave this way. I've tried to make it real. Perhaps in a novel it's easier to make the public understand it.'

No one seems to have asked about the title. Consciously or otherwise, when Lewis named the novel *Jack's Return Home* he was borrowing from the 1958 *Hancock's Half Hour* episode. Listening to Hattie Jacques's opening lament as Jack's mother –

'Tis thirteen years since our son, Jack, left this house to seek his fortune in the colonies, I wonder what has become of him …' – it seems a wry nod to Lewis himself, perhaps a playful allusion to Bertha. It might also have been a tribute to Tony Hancock who had committed suicide in June 1968. Hancock had been notoriously self-critical, tormented by alcohol and marriage problems. Interviewed for *Q* magazine in 1989, Spike Milligan said of Hancock that 'He ended up on his own. I thought, he's got rid of everybody else, he's going to get rid of himself and he did.'

Looking back, it's almost impossible to understate both Lewis's achievement in writing *Jack's Return Home* and its subsequent impact on crime fiction. It was brave and ambitious, an expression of instinct crafted from a lifetime of pulp fiction, movie influences and real life observations. *Jack's Return Home* had a depth which belied its status as a populist crime novel. It was on a par with its American forerunners for exactly that reason. It threw a light on the social, cultural and political in a way which other British writers hadn't managed to pull off, at least not with anything like the same conviction or authenticity.

Lewis's initial motivation might well have been the need to pay the mortgage and support Jo, Nancy and Sally, the couple's second daughter having been born on 2 April 1970; but this was the novel he needed to write for so many other reasons. One after another he navigates autobiographical reference points: Brumby, a village outside Scunthorpe; Eric Paice, the writer of *The Avengers* and *Dixon of Dock Green*; Kinnear, the landlord of the Coach and Horses in Wicken Bonhunt; Doreen, married to his friend Gil Potter; Eddie Appleyard 'a local', a member of an old Barton family. Representatives of Lewis's world are reimagined and cast in the one inhabited by Jack Carter.

When asked about his methods in a 1969 interview, he was unapologetic:

> 'You have to be ruthless. When you write you are drawing on your own emotions and relationships, your family and friends – and if this means you are exploiting people, well, it has to be done. My wife has come to terms with this now, I think – but my parents, for example, still find it painful to be "used".'

Lewis and his contemporaries had ridden the post-war cultural escalator. They had the advantages and opportunities of grammar school and higher education. For the most part, the art school crowd escaped the white-collar humdrum of day jobs which would have been their lot a generation earlier. In Jack Carter's burning disillusionment and confused sense of self and belonging, Lewis blurred the boundaries between his own and his character's experience. *Jack's Return Home* served as revenge for the rejection and humiliation endured in the town he left behind. The part of himself that would be Jack Carter poured onto the page, most memorably in the scene at Kinnear's Casino, complete with its 'British B-feature' décor. In one of the novel's most revealing passages, Carter casts his contemptuous eye over the 'farmers, garage proprietors, owners of chains of cafes, electrical contractors, builders, and quarry owners'. These were Harry Lewis's masonic brothers and their families, the small businessmen, and their 'terrible offspring' with 'ex-grammar school girlfriends'. His greatest scorn is reserved for their wives 'sick to their stomachs with jealousy of someone or something'. He concludes they were 'the kind of people who made me know I was right'. It's a withering critique of the post-war generation and their provincial, materialist aspirations, as if to say: you had all this opportunity and *this* is what you chose to do with it. Interviewed by Brian Doyle, Lewis admitted that he'd put something of himself, or himself as he might have been, into the work. He claimed this was incidental, his subconscious at play:

'I had to imagine how it would be if I was involved in the same happenings that Carter was. So whether or not a lot of deep, subconscious leanings and desires came out in the character, I don't know. Maybe there's some of Carter in me – and some of me in Carter. Perhaps, deep down, I would like to have been a tough, masterful thug like Carter. But I think I'm happier as I am.'

The question that no one asked was the degree to which he'd invested himself in the character of Frank Carter. Those 'deep, subconscious leanings' might just as equally have created parallels between him and Frank as between him and Jack. The truth of which seems strikingly obvious in hindsight with Frank Carter forced to drink whisky to soften him up before he is killed.

What makes *Jack's Return Home* the greatest British crime novel of its era, the place where British noir begins, isn't simply that it was more extreme in its observations, darker, more violent, earthier, and more grounded in reality than its predecessors and contemporaries. Or that Jack Carter is the definitive antihero, the ultimate outsider, a hitherto unrepentant sinner faced with his Maker. Neither is it that Lewis achieved such a note-perfect synthesis of American hardboiled and British social realism that there was no longer a distinction. It's that *Jack's Return Home* was all of those things. It was literary, cinematic, and psychological. It was unique, fully formed. A stone cold crime classic.

6

Is there a Mr Carter
in the Room?
1970–1971

INTERVIEWED FOR THE *LINCOLNSHIRE TIMES* IN February 1970, Lewis spoke about the recent completion of animation work on the final series of *Zokko!* His friend and fellow animator on the programme, Malcolm Draper, was living in Islington with his girlfriend at the time. Early one weekend morning they heard the doorbell. 'It was Ted, really excited. I invited him in and asked, what was the matter? He said, "I just sold the rights to *Jack's Return Home* to MGM." My God, he was happy.'

The review of *Jack's Return Home* that appeared in the *Manchester Evening News* on 3 March 1970 remarked on the book's 'tang of life'. The following week's *Sunday Express* review recognised Lewis's Jack Carter as 'a man who deserves little of the reader's sympathy but still gets it'. That raw sense of a lived reality, and a character with the potency to transfer to the screen, had also appealed to film producer Michael Klinger. His son, Tony, then working for his father's company, remembers they had been on the lookout for good thriller material when the book arrived in November 1969. 'You get offered a lot when you're a production company; unfortunately 99% is trash. We needed something edgier, something that reflected a different sensibility, a toughness.'

For Michael Klinger, looking for something home grown, gritty and honest for a British crime thriller, *Jack's Return Home* was right on the money. When the manuscript arrived, Tony Klinger remembers he and his father and others in the office took a few pages each. 'We read it, then passed it on to the next person. We were so excited that we made the offer almost immediately. Before the last person had finished reading, we got through to whoever was doing the deal from Ted's end and the offer was in.' Michael Klinger acquired the rights to *Jack's Return Home* for £10,000. For him, it was more than a good crime thriller with a brutally compelling protagonist. With the Richardson and Kray court cases and the details which emerged from them present in the novel, Klinger recognised the potential to feed off public interest to make a film with far greater depth than a run-of-the-mill British crime caper. 'It was about a whole bunch of things that were really interesting to us,' says Tony Klinger. 'You need that if you have any pretence of making something that's more meaningful than just another piece of rubbish. We liked that it wasn't about redemption.'

Michael Klinger knew more than most about Jack Carter's world. Soho born and bred, Jewish, the son of a Polish tailor, he was smart, intellectual, and streetwise. Working as an engineering draughtsman in a munitions factory during the war, afterwards he turned his hand to a variety of short-lived jobs assembling toasters, making and selling children's clothes and, in the summer months, selling ice creams and hot dogs to holidaymakers on the Isle of Wight. Returning to Soho, he made his initial foray into business, via a spell working on the street markets, by purchasing a former bohemian club, The Gargoyle. Borrowing his stake from the gloriously named Billy

Bolitho, Klinger and his first business partner, Jimmy Jacobs, opened the Nell Gwynne Revue in October 1957. With its mix of strip shows and blue comedians, the club's success led to a move into the 'glamour' film business, often featuring the strippers from the Nell Gwynne. Klinger opened the Compton Cinema Club in October 1960, a members only film theatre which screened a mix of European sex films and films banned by the British Board of Film Censors. With new business partner, Tony Tenser, he set up the company Compton-Tekli, importing European films and financing what Andrew Spicer and AT McKenna, in their study of Klinger, describe as a 'series of low budget "sexploitation" offerings'.

Interviewed for a *Sunday Times* article in January 1966, Klinger made clear his ambitions to work beyond the confines of Soho and the sex film industry. 'There's always this desire to have your name on something you know will live… there are good reasons to consolidate, but it's only by overreaching that you reach out at all.' He realised his ambition to a limited extent, working closely with director Roman Polanski in the production of *Repulsion* (1965), and again on Polanski's second film, *Cul-de-Sac* (1966). Klinger formed his own independent production company, Avton Films, in November 1966.

Tony Klinger recalls how his father had come up against the kind of men Lewis created in Jack Carter:

'He knew those people [the gangsters]. They came after him for protection money and he threw them out, except one lot, a police gang. You couldn't throw them out. They broke the waiter's arm. My dad got them arrested and sent down with the bloke threatening to kill us. You're going to react to that one way or another. Usually you don't have to worry when they start shouting that stuff, you worry when they don't, and you make sure that if they go down, they stay down, because they're going to come back and get you. That mentality, we understood. Working in Soho you learned to look after yourself.'

By the time he secured the rights to *Jack's Return Home*, Michael Klinger had established himself as a highly effective operator, backing a series of challenging film projects, usually with new creative talent to the fore. At a time when bringing American finance into a British film project had become more difficult – MGM had incurred significant losses in 1969 and undergone a programme of restructuring and rationalisation, including the closure of Borehamwood studios – Klinger's good working relationship with Robert Littman, newly appointed as MGM's Head of European Production, paid dividends. Through a combination of Littman's need to commission new films that could be made relatively cheaply, thereby satisfying financial conditions imposed by new MGM President James Aubrey, and quickly, in order to head off difficulties with British film unions angry at job losses and the closure of Borehamwood. He agreed to co-finance four films, one of which would be the, as yet untitled, *Get Carter*. It would be Klinger's first international film. Tony Klinger remembers meeting James Aubrey on a visit to the US:

'His nickname was the Smiling Cobra, which tells you everything you need to know. He was a very scary kind of man. He used to say, "Join my family, be one with us." His idea was the tough guy part, the John Osborne part, should be Edward G. Robinson, which went down like a lead balloon. At the dinner before they started filming, he said, "Why don't we get Steve McQueen in the Michael Caine role?" He didn't get his way and got very upset.'

It would not be the last time MGM executives pressed for American actors to take key roles. At one point, Telly Savalas, fresh from playing Blofeld in *On Her Majesty's Secret Service* and Big Joe in *Kelly's Heroes,* was proposed for the character of Cliff Brumby, a part that eventually went to Brian Mosley.

Klinger was under no illusions that Littman's position was precarious. His problems with drugs and alcohol added to the urgency around the production. 'I think Littman did cocaine, and Ted obviously had an alcohol problem,' says Tony Klinger. 'There were times it felt like we were the only straight people involved. It gave the thing an edge, a danger. This is a process which could take years, but from the moment we got the material to the moment the film was in the can was 37 weeks. 37 weeks is ridiculous and this wasn't our money. This was MGM's money.' Klinger negotiated a contract that gave him a free hand in casting and, importantly, choice of director. He had seen and liked Mike Hodges' crime thriller *Suspect*, made for Thames Television and broadcast in November 1969. He sent a copy of *Jack's Return Home* to Hodges on 27 January 1970, with a note inviting him to 'consider turning the book into a film that he might like to handle'.

Tony Klinger remembers Hodges being commissioned. 'We saw *Suspect* almost at the same time as finding the material.' For Hodges, the former documentary maker, arts programme maker and TV drama director, *Jack's Return Home* fitted his taste in literature perfectly. He was more than ready to work on a big screen thriller. 'Some years earlier I had realised the thriller – because it can so readily engage our curiosity – was a brilliant way to apply the scalpel to society.' Hodges' literary hero was Raymond Chandler. 'His autopsy of the US and LA in particular was my template. I'd already written, directed, and produced two thrillers for television – *Suspect* and *Rumour* – which led to my being offered *Get Carter*.'

In Jack Carter, Hodges recognised a character who, like himself, but for vastly different reasons, was incensed by the state of his country. 'It was a country that had taken two years of my life for National Service and, through some freak administrative accident, put me in the Royal Navy.' As a member of the lower deck on board HMS *Coquette*, an ocean-going minesweeper and later, HMS *Wave*, both attached to the Fishery Protection Squadron, Hodges sailed into every port on the east coast, seeing at first hand the unchecked deprivation of what he refers to as 'Hogarthian hellholes', towns barely changed since the nineteenth century.

Ten years after completing his national service, as a producer and director on the radical investigative television programme *World in Action*, Hodges met and observed representatives of the British establishment, the politicians, journalists, bishops, chief constables, and celebrities of the day. The experience shifted his focus 'from the destitution of Hogarth to the corruption of Juvenal'. From the 'underbelly' to the 'potbelly'. Despite Lewis having no explicitly political intention, when his book arrived out of the blue along with an offer to write and direct it as his first cinema film, Hodges connected fully with the bitter inequities he felt were underpinning the story. 'I remember being excited by the lean, hard writing style illuminating a Britain I recognised immediately. He was stamping heavily on those rose-coloured spectacles used to survey this "green and pleasant land". His isle, like mine, was more septic than sceptred.'

It's a matter of some debate as to why Lewis, who had wanted to adapt *Jack's Return Home* for the film's screenplay and was disappointed not to have been given the chance, wasn't considered. If a window of opportunity had existed at all, it must have been brief and there is no record of the idea being put to the film's producers. At the time, Lewis had no experience of writing for the screen and was soon overwhelmed by events and the speed at which they unfolded, as was everyone else involved in the production. It was the first time Hodges had adapted a novel and his initial draft adhered closely to Lewis's original text, but with Carter severely wounded at the outset, then recounting in a long flashback how he'd ended up alone and on the brink of death. It carried structural echoes of *Double Indemnity*, which Hodges admired greatly, but he knew it wasn't working:

'Maybe I thought the form too risky for my first feature. Instead I chose to tell the same story as a straightforward narrative, but with a lethal payoff. Carter is gunned down. The hitman is in place from the moment Jack decides to return home. The decision to break free from the novel's structure made me realise I had to go even further. It's the same with an actor having to interpret a role in terms of their own experiences. I had to do the same with the translation from novel to film. I had to make it my own.'

Later, Lewis would complain to friends about some of the decisions Hodges made, but at the time he seemed satisfied seeing his creation brought to life. Hodges made sure Lewis approved the changes between novel and script. In a foreword for the republished Soho Press edition of the novel in 2014, he described how he'd worked through what felt like a 'creeping disloyalty' to Lewis:

I latched onto this passage about ten paragraphs into Ted's story: *Doncaster Station. Gloomy wide windy areas of rails and platforms overhung with concrete and faint neon. Rain noiselessly emphasising the emptiness.*

Jack Carter changed trains at Doncaster. It was here that I psychologically decoupled myself from the novel. I decided not to have him change trains for a town with *no* name, as Ted did. I'd have him change trains for a town *with* a name, Newcastle-upon-Tyne. I had Jack move north into my territory, territory I knew. That way I didn't feel so guilty changing the direction of the novel's thrust and even its very texture. I was discovering that, when the novel is a good one, adapting it to a screenplay can be a curiously painful process.

Lewis's note-perfect descriptions of Scunthorpe and Grimsby resonated with Hodges. Memories of his time in the Royal Navy and the towns, cities and east coast port locations he'd experienced came to the fore. One was a cavernous sawdust-on-the-floor pub frequented by Hull fishermen called The Albert Hall – at the time he had no idea of Lewis's connections with the city. In fact, he knew little about Lewis and has no recollection of meeting him before filming began. Lewis spent time on the shoot, nominally as part of Michael Klinger's entourage, some of whom, according to Toby Eady, were themselves fringe underworld figures. Hodges' impressions of Lewis are shadowy. 'As far as I recollect we never sat down alone or had a drink together. He appeared on the set several times, but always with Klinger and his people. He seemed shy, overawed by the excitement of having a major star playing Jack Carter, as I was.'

By all accounts and in all aspects, it was a frenetic production. For Hodges, it was a first feature film with the added pressure of writing, rewriting, and directing a major box office star. For Michael Klinger, sensing the need to capitalise on Littman's support and MGM's funding, he'd taken a calculated gamble in casting a relatively inexperienced director. To have given a novice scriptwriter a say in the process would have multiplied the risk and Lewis's feeling that he was overlooked should be seen in that context. As Hodges says, 'It all happened so fast I had no time for second opinions, nor would I have welcomed them.'

Hodges' first major departure, given the importance of Scunthorpe in Lewis's story, was to shoot in Newcastle and North Shields, one of the ports he'd sailed into ten years earlier. He and Klinger drove north, touring the districts in and around Newcastle somewhat conspicuously in Klinger's white Cadillac. Hodges was affected by the visual drama of the scenery and spent time adapting the script to the locations he found. One of which had been the scene of the killing of Angus Sibbet two years earlier, referred to in the press as the 'One Armed Bandit Murder' or the 'Dolce Vita murder' after the Newcastle nightclub named in the case. With its story of London gangsters bringing their business to the north, it had much in common with Lewis's narrative and has often, wrongly, been cited as the inspiration for the novel. Sibbet, along with the two men convicted of his murder and sentenced to life imprisonment, Dennis Stafford and Michael Luvaglio, had moved north from London in the early 60s to work for Luvaglio's older brother, Vince Landa, who was supplying fruit machines to pubs and clubs. Thought to have been caught skimming from the proceeds, Sibbet's 'bullet-riddled' body had been found in his E-type Jaguar under Pesspool Railway Bridge at South Hetton in January 1967. *Daily Mirror* journalist, Revel Barker, spent time on the *Get Carter* set and remembers speaking to Lewis about Sibbet and the Dolce Vita murder. 'The hype was that *Get Carter* was based on a gangland murder in Tyneside, but Ted told me quite specifically that it wasn't. He said it was based on somebody he'd heard about who was a shady operator of amusement arcades in Scunthorpe and Cleethorpes.'

By the time Hodges began shooting, his research had given him a firm idea of the film's geography. The locations were concentrated in one area making the logistics of filming comparatively straightforward. For Lewis's Humber foreshore with its disused brickworks, crumbling kilns and remnants of a burned down landing stage, Hodges substituted the bleak vista of Blackhall and the colliery slag tipping into the North Sea. For the estates and terraces of Scunthorpe, he chose the dockside streets of Scotswood. Kinnear's seedy casino, 'White, low and ugly' was replaced by The Heights, the house formerly owned by Vince Landa at Hamsterley, County Durham. Cliff Brumby's 'ranch style' house at Burnham was the rented home of local entrepreneur and scrap metal millionaire, Charlie Newton, on the outskirts of Belmont, a newish suburb of Durham. Carter's charged meeting with Eric Paice moved from pub to racetrack. This transposing of scene after scene, aided by Lewis's obviously cinematic writing and meticulously thought-through plot, was fundamental to enabling Hodges to shoot at speed.

In later years, Lewis said he regretted the changed location, although his interview with Brian Doyle shows him in favour of the decision. 'The city in my story was an amalgamation of several places... but Newcastle is ideal as far as I'm concerned because I know it quite well anyway. When I used to arrive there on the train I used to think how visual and pictorially effective it was and why didn't people make films there instead of London or inside studios?'

Analysis of the adaptation of novel to screenplay, scene by scene, reveals the extent to which Lewis's writing is at the heart of *Get Carter*. The core of the plot is intact, along with most of the characters and, in several key scenes, the dialogue. Unsurprisingly, since Lewis had written with such unique

169

authenticity of voice and expression, Hodges keeps the punch of some of Lewis's one liners. Doreen always doused Eddie Appleyard for saying Frank had been a 'bloody good bloke'; Eric's eyes were always 'pissholes'; Old Harry, the disgruntled poker player, always thought that Kinnear was 'having him on'; and Cliff Brumby was always a 'big bloke'.

Looking closely at the film's most quoted (often misquoted) line, you see the shift in emphasis given by Hodges' sharpening of dialogue and intent. The line, or at least its rhythm and intent, could well originate with Mickey Spillane. In the novel *I, the Jury*, Mike Hammer roughs up a man named Kines. As Kines looks to fight back, Hammer says, 'Don't go playing man when you're only a boy. You're pretty big, but I'm three sizes bigger and a hell of a lot tougher and I'll beat the living daylights out of you if you try anything funny again. Now sit down over there.' Lewis's line – Jack Carter to Cliff Brumby – in *Jack's Return Home*, twists Spillane into something altogether pithier. 'Cliff, you're a big bloke – you're in good shape, but I know more than you do.' Hodges, with the advantage of Michael Caine and Brian Mosley shaping up in Brumby's living room telling us most of what we need to know visually, nails the line. 'You're a big man, but you're in bad shape. With me, it's a full time job. Now behave yourself.'

Casting Michael Caine, an actor whose south-of-the-river credentials were firmly established in the public imagination as Thames, not Tyne, and definitely not Humber, was the second major departure from *Jack's Return Home*. Lewis's Carter is a northern man with the voice and the resentments of a steel town antihero. If he hadn't turned to crime and left for London, he'd have doubtless earned his wage from the steelworks, watching Scunthorpe United on Saturday afternoons, pissing it up on Saturday night, and taking his week's holiday at Cleethorpes or Skegness.

Caine had his own ideas for Jack Carter and gave him a sharper, more stylish London swagger, which, in combination with some classic tailoring and an Aquascutum raincoat, places him apart from the mismatched locals. Caine's Carter is obsessional, modishly fastidious, dropping black bombers in the train toilets on his journey north. Any doubts Lewis might have had initially were dispelled; as far as he was concerned, Michael Caine was 'ideal casting'. 'When I wrote the book I never really had a clear visual idea of how Carter would look. I have now. He'd look like Caine.'

In truth, without Michael Caine's star billing, it is unlikely *Get Carter* would have been made. His presence was fundamental to MGM's financial backing. Hodges admits that Caine lent Jack Carter a glamour that was never in the novel, and one he hadn't envisaged when he decided to make the film. He senses a depth of humanity in Caine's portrayal. The regret in his eyes when Glenda, in the boot of the car, is tipped into the dock, and his glance at the family on the ferry signify a longing for unattainable normality. But these are fleeting concessions, easily missed, and barely enough to sway audience sympathies. Caine's Carter encourages audience identification through being cold, hard, calculating, determined, and sardonic. He demands respect. Lewis's Carter was seedier, misanthropic, more obviously twisted by guilt, and driven by resentment and revenge. Lewis's novel had given Hodges an exceptional, complex character and an uncompromising, truthful story with which to work. Hodges gave Caine a vision, a script and a backdrop which, though neither of them knew it, were the raw materials he needed to create a screen icon.

Other characters take their lead from the novel. Hendry's Eric Paice is as effete as Lewis's, holding his cigarette a certain way and with his hand in his jacket pocket 'like royalty'. The dialogue between them is perfectly pitched for a pair of players with history. Lewis invests in the backstory, justifying the animosity between them which Caine and Hendry carry into their performances. John Osborne, too, delivers Kinnear with the air of a man who knows he's the kingpin, just as Lewis had imagined him; indeed, the *Get Carter* card game in which 'Old Harry' loses his money is bet for bet, bluff for bluff, the scene he'd written in *Jack's Return Home*.

In the *Get Carter* on-location photographs, Lewis is pictured on the quayside, sitting with a portable typewriter on his knees, the fingers of his left hand shaped more as if for a piano chord than for typing – Lewis rarely, if ever, typed his own manuscripts. He wears a suede jacket and desert boots, hair fashionably over his collar, cigarette, as ever, clamped between his lips. In the mid-ground, Ian Hendry stands, his back to the camera with a photographer and two other men. In the background Klinger, Caine and Hodges are deep in discussion.

Chronicling each step in the production process from a distance, it's easy to see how *Get Carter* moved on from Lewis's novel. He must have sensed its relevance diminishing. Hodges has spoken about the 'intuitive white heat' of the production and admits he was flying by the seat of his pants. Speaking to him even now, you sense the single-minded determination to pursue his own vision. And of course, he was right. From the behind-glass opening in the Fletchers' penthouse to the final scene in which Jack Carter is shot and killed, Hodges measured the story to perfection. Lewis had ended *Jack's Return Home* with fade to black nothingness, allowing a faint note of ambiguity. *Get Carter*'s resolution was absolute. There could be no follow-up. Tony Klinger remembers begging his father to change the ending. 'I wanted to make a sequel of this film'.

Brian Doyle's interview for the *Get Carter* press pack describes

Lewis as a 'quiet, sandy-haired, slightly cherubic looking young man' who spoke softly and looked as though 'butter wouldn't melt in his mouth'. Lewis, he claimed, was 'a classic example of the iron twist in the velvet mug... a nice guy who writes graphically about nasty guys. And dolls. And thoroughly enjoys doing it.' Asked the question how much of his own background and personality he invests in his characters, Lewis explains, 'It's all a matter of projecting one's innermost fantasy personality into print.' He seems in thrall to the notion of the criminal underworld:

'I've always been attracted to that kind of environment which is perhaps one reason why *Jack's Return Home* is a realistic book. Jack Carter is like many of the criminals I met – he just can't see farther than the end of his nose. It's a characteristic of the small time crook. He acts first, thinks later. Like all the tough boys. If they do a job they don't think ahead to the jail stretch they might have to do if they're caught. They haven't the ability to see into the future. This is why they are so limited as people. They may have certain technical accomplishments – drive a fast car, break open a safe, punch somebody in the head – but they don't consider the consequences of their actions.'

Lewis sees this as the difference between the criminals he writes about and those from his own aspirational background:

'The latter plan ahead and have a goal; the former only plan to release their own immediate energies and make a quick profit, usually ending up in jail. Jack Carter's like that. He has plenty of common sense but not the imagination to make him frightened. He never panics. He has this Viking-like

173

quality of walking into something and taking it on its own terms. Whether it's a fight, a woman, or whatever. A more frightened man would think about what he was going to do and weigh up possibilities. But Carter's got this ability to walk through things and disregard everything else.'

For a British movie, *Get Carter* was unconventional and, as such, a calculated risk for the producers. Hodges depicts Jack's old house decaying like the city in which it stands. Albert Swift's murder is shot closely, coldly and brutally in the back yard of a bookies, retaining Lewis's 'You knew what I'd do, Albert' line. Carter is amoral, nihilistic and driven. Caine's experience with the gangster he claimed to have based Carter on, as told in his autobiography, suggests the lives of real life villains were more prosaic, perhaps closer to Lewis's original vision. When the man confronted Caine in a club, he complained that Carter wasn't a real person. 'Michael, you weren't married, you never had any kids and you had no responsibilities. You don't understand why we do things. I had to keep a wife and kids with no special skills.'

Caine seems to have had mixed feelings about the role. Brian Case has interviewed him on three occasions. Caine, the Billingsgate fish porter's son from the Elephant and Castle; Case, a policeman's son from Deptford. 'Caine told me *Get Carter* was difficult on occasions; he couldn't stand being out in the fucking rain. He insisted on having a car. He said he had no great affection for the film and was very surprised at its cult reputation, but glad to have it all the same.'

For most of the cast and crew, billeted in the Royal Station Hotel in Newcastle, there was a sense of togetherness. It was a notoriously boozy production. John Osborne had made alternative arrangements, staying out in the country and appearing on set when needed. Hodges, likewise, remained purposefully distant. 'My friend Richard Lester advised me, when filming on location, to always stay in a separate hotel to the unit. It was wise advice. Everybody wants the director's ear. As soon as you enter the foyer at the end of a day's shooting, cast and crew settle on you like piranha fish. They nibble you to death with questions. I took his advice.'

Alun Armstrong remembers Lewis being around from the beginning. Of a similar age, sharing a sense of humour, and with plenty of time on their hands, much of it spent kicking their heels in the hotel bar over a few vodka and tonics, they became great friends. 'He was remarkably good company,' remembers Armstrong. 'He'd done so many things in his life and to me as a young lad, I was terribly impressed by him. He was cool, he was funny and just very warm and friendly. Good at bringing people together and getting a party going.'

Armstrong had taken an indirect route to the role of Keith – his first major part in film or television – helped in no small way by a chance meeting and tip off from an old associate of Lewis's from the Hull jazz days, Neville Smith. In the course of their time together on the film shoot, Armstrong got to know Lewis well. Lewis told Armstrong that he'd become a novelist with the express intention of having his novel made into a film, so that he could get into films and become an actor. 'I was never sure if I believed it, but he told me that had been his abiding ambition. He wanted to be a film star.'

Armstrong also recalls an incident soon after the arrival of Ian Hendry in Newcastle:

'We were all in the bar of the Station Hotel – half eleven it would be, maybe twelve o'clock – ten of us, and Ian Hendry was telling wonderfully funny stories, being delightful, and everything was going swimmingly well. Ted was contributing and we were all having a laugh, and suddenly Ted sprang to his feet and pointed at Ian Hendry and said something like, "Don't you try that with me, sunshine. Because you're not going to get away with it with me. If that's what you think, you can go and fuck yourself." Then he stormed off and went to bed. We all just said, "What the fuck was that about?" There'd been no altercation. Nobody had said anything sarcastic. We were all just left open mouthed. And Ian Hendry said, "Where did that come from?"'

It was the first time Lewis had displayed such intense paranoia in company. It wouldn't be the last. In the coming years, when Armstrong visited Lewis at his home, the same kind of episode would happen again, seemingly out of nowhere. 'He would think somebody had said something derogatory, or insulting, or critical, and they hadn't. Or even it might have been the slightest hint of questioning his position or what he'd said with no intent to be derogatory to him, and he would have this extreme reaction and that'd be it, he'd disappear and you wouldn't see him for the rest of the night.'

Geraldine Moffat, cast as Glenda, had won her part off the back of television appearances in *Half Hour Story*, *Armchair Theatre* and *Play for Today* productions, particularly *Stella* and *Doreen* written by playwright Alun Owen. She steered clear of the late nights and drinking sessions. More often than not, she had to be up early to see Alan, the hairdresser, before going on set. She has clear memories of filming *Get Carter*, not least of which were the scenes in which Hodges recreated the homemade porn film. 'I was terrified of doing it. The only way I could get through it was to have a bottle of VP. I was swigging it and it was pretty much gone by the time we'd finished, all in this little room in a terraced house in Newcastle.' Hodges was acutely aware of the way his film and Lewis's novel depicted women, something Moffat had to contend with. 'Women are treated awfully, although I didn't think of it that way at the time, there wasn't the political awareness. They're used, and happy to be used. Some were tough, playing working class women from Newcastle, but it could only have been written by a man.' She recalls Lewis on set as being shy and seeming quite lost. Not surprising perhaps as he would have been no more than an interested spectator. 'There was,' she says, 'something sad about him. I couldn't put my finger on it, though I remember him giving me an autographed copy of his book, which I still have.'

Tony Klinger's memories of Lewis are less endearing, 'We were in a restaurant together having a meal with everybody and I'm pretty sure he was drunk, he was quite aggressive with my business partner, Mike Lytton. I think he thought we were gay, which we weren't. We were with some girls in Newcastle, and he wasn't very pleasant.' The next day, they met and chatted at one of the locations. Klinger's lasting impressions were coloured by meetings like these and his parting shot is perhaps the most insightful. 'There was a truth about him. He meant it, which made him awkward. I'm sure you've heard that from other people. It's like Polanski, he shreds you. I think people on that edge – and I put Ted on that edge – they don't only shred themselves, they shred everyone around them. It's hard to survive around people like that for a long period.'

There is a still image from the location shoot, this one in Scotswood Road outside Frank Carter's dilapidated terrace, looking down the hill with chimneys and docks in the background. In his definitive British Film Guide to *Get Carter*, Steve Chibnall has added a shooting schedule which suggests the photograph was taken a few days into filming, towards the end of July 1970. Caine is in character as Carter. In Carter's suit, with Carter's flinted stare into the lens. Lewis has his arms folded, leather jacket, collar up. He looks tired, still wearing the 'shagged out' look once observed so astutely by Neville Smith, but he has a half smile that says, 'I've made it.'

With *Get Carter* in production, Lewis, Jo and the girls continued to live comfortably at Erme Cottage. Gil Potter was a regular lunchtime drinking partner. 'Ted would ring me up and say, "Are you going for a drink?" We'd meet at the Coach; he'd have a couple of gin and tonics or a couple of halves of bitter, that Essex countryside thing, and then about one o'clock he'd say, "That's it, I'm going home." He'd disappear and I'd get stuck with whoever was there. I'd go home, and Ted would be out of his brains. He'd drink a bottle on his tod.'

Lewis had spoken about his routine in a 1969 interview, reprinted in *Crime Time* Magazine in 1997:

After breakfast I go into the dining room and spend half an hour or so devoting immense care to making up the fire. While I'm waiting for it to catch I sit and read the newspaper, and once I've got a beautiful blaze going – then I walk to my desk and write. It marks the transition between my domestic and my working life: the equivalent, if you like, of the commuter's journey to his office. But somehow I always manage to run out of cigarettes by about 11.30. That means I have to go out and buy some more. I pass a friend's cottage on the way (incidentally, he's an artist with much the same problem) so we go together and end up at the pub. And that's it till the afternoon.

Tom Barling suspected that, in spite of the book and the film, things weren't going well for Lewis and that drink was increasingly the root cause. 'When they lived in Belsize Park

they were happy, but when they moved to Wicken Bonhunt...
see, they weren't that kind of people. Don't drink alone, that's
the rule. Always has been.' He remembers telephoning the
house one morning. 'I said to Jo, is Ted there? After about five
minutes, she put him on and it didn't sound like him. It was
nine in the morning and I thought, you're pissed you bastard. I
could understand it from the night before, but it's sad.'

Towards the end of 1970, Lewis and Gil Potter worked on
some music, recording two tracks they had cut onto a 45 rpm
disc. One side was a romantic number with Lewis playing piano
on a song called *Christmas Isn't Christmas without You*; the
other side was called *Carter's Theme*. When we met, Gil had
unearthed a copy of the record. It was warped, badly scratched
and unplayable. He had no memory of whether Lewis intended
to submit the music to the producers. Lewis had suggested to
Alun Armstrong, who also had written a song – 'a sort of theme
song, like a James Bond theme, Shirley Bassey, something
moody' – that he take it to Michael Klinger. Unfortunately,
Armstrong's visit to Klinger's apartment coincided with a visit
from Roy Budd's manager. Budd had recently completed his
score for the film. Armstrong remembers, 'I had to play this
fucking record with Roy Budd's agent sat there glowering.'

The UK premiere of *Get Carter* took place on 10 March 1971 at
the Empire Leicester Square.

Michael Klinger had advertised the film on the sides of
London buses with the slogan 'Caine is Carter'. Any thoughts
Lewis had that success might have improved his standing
with his parents or in some way convinced Harry that writing
novels that people made into films was an acceptable way to
earn a living were soon dismissed. Gil Potter met Harry and
Bertha and sensed the awkwardness between them and their

son; he recalled a 'weird relationship' between Bertha and Lewis. 'I think this haunted the man. I think it was a very sad relationship. A father he couldn't get through to and a mother who was overpowering.' Gil goes further, forming the view that Lewis's issues with women had their roots in his relationship with Bertha. 'I don't think he liked women very much, which I think stems from his mother. But then I think he fought against his feelings for men.'

Lewis was deeply troubled by the relationship with his father. Jo remembers, 'It was as if Harry was always looking for something that was wrong. He thought that Ted should never have given up full-time work, that it was all too insecure.' The success of *Jack's Return Home* and the film hadn't changed things. It came to a head on the night of the *Get Carter* premiere in London. 'Ted's parents and my parents had been invited to a drinks party at Toby's flat,' recalls Jo, 'and that's when Harry said to Toby, when is he going to start writing something – whatever it was that he said, in Harry's opinion – *"good literature".*' Lewis was crushed by the comment. His writing was good. It was recognised as such and critically praised. He'd seized an opportunity beyond his father's comprehension, but in Harry's eyes, it wasn't, and never would be, real work.

When a second premiere was organised in Newcastle, Lewis was again invited. Michael Caine was unable to attend and made a short film. Ron Burnett remembers Lewis being tremendously proud of the film. He had, according to Ron, made 'big friends' with Ian Hendry – the initial friction presumably set aside – a renowned drinker who reputedly downed a bottle of whisky before lunch. Revel Barker remembers clearly that Lewis had said he was one of the few people who did talk to Hendry. 'He had a reputation as a difficult character. Ted told me he wasn't very popular with the rest of the cast and crew. Truth was I didn't see much of Hendry at all.' Ron recalls the story of the Newcastle premiere, as told by Lewis:

'They were all waiting in the wings. The MC called them all on one at a time – "Mr Ian Hendry" and he came on, took a bow, said a few words and went off. Then the MC announced – "The man who made it all possible, Ted Lewis." By then, Ted was so pissed, he managed to walk on stage, walked straight past this feller and off the other side.'

Jo was with Lewis in Newcastle and remembers the premiere entirely differently. In her memory, the evening passed without incident. It seemed Lewis was embellishing the myth.

Reviewed in the *Observer* newspaper on 14 March 1971, *Get Carter* was named the best commercial film of the week, but also 'the most morally dubious'. The reviewer objected to the lack of any standards other than those of 'what used to be called the jungle'. While accepting that it's impossible not to identify with Caine's antihero, he is disparaging of Carter's method. In particular the fact that, en route to his own death, he 'kills or screws anything that moves'. Forced to admit to 'complete and shameless enjoyment from beginning to end', he concludes that if *Love Story* (released the same week) 'is like a loaf of sliced bread, this is a bottle of neat gin swallowed before breakfast. It's intoxicating all right, but it'll do you no good.'

In May 1971, the film *Villain* went on general release. Based on James Barlow's 1968 novel, *Burden of Proof*, adapted by American, Al Lettieri (Lettieri would go on to play Virgil 'The Turk' Sollozo in *The Godfather*), and scripted by Dick Clement and Ian La Frenais, then best known as the writers of television comedy, *The Likely Lads*, the film was a depressingly unimaginative take on the British gangster movie. Richard

Burton's cockney gangster, Vic Dakin – homosexual, sadistic, working class, and devoted to his dear old mum – simply didn't ring true. It was as if Clement, La Frenais and Burton had picked up every cliché Caine had avoided. *Villain* lacked Michael Klinger's ambition and scope, Mike Hodges' vision, the landscape of the north east, and the powerful aesthetic created by *Get Carter* cinematographer, Wolfgang Suschitzky. *Villain* goes some way to establishing why *Get Carter* is such an exceptional film, ahead of its time, socially and politically astute, and thanks to Lewis's novel, grounded in truth.

Lewis continued to work on his next book. He explained his writing day, or at least another version of it, for Brian Doyle's press pack. 'I go into my studio at 9.30am, and sit there until 1.00pm, whether I write anything or not. I spend the afternoon with my family, then write again in the evening, if I feel like it. I aim to do 6,000 words a week.' He was, he said, writing a novel about a private detective who worked for a right-wing organisation and, at the same time, 'drafting a long novel based on his own schooldays and toying with the idea of writing another book about Jack Carter.' It would, he said, 'be an episode in his earlier career'.

Interviewed for the BBC Radio documentary *Lewis's Return Home* in 2012, Eady claimed that 'about 85 per cent of what became *Get Carter* is Ted Lewis'. Agent hyperbole aside, the modest credit in the film's title sequence, 'Based on the novel *Jack's Return Home* by Ted Lewis', hardly seems to do justice to Lewis's contribution. That said, Michael Klinger had paid £10,000 for the rights to *Jack's Return Home*, £3,000 more than the £7,000 Mike Hodges earned for writing the screenplay and directing the film, a disparity which Hodges hadn't realised until we discussed Lewis's book and his film in 2013. Whilst there is no way of knowing the exact amount Lewis pocketed, he had undoubtedly done well. Besides which, as a consequence of the film, he had every right to believe that, from now on, he would be a commercially successful author.

7

Plender
1971–1974

I N THE WAKE OF *GET CARTER*'s success, Eady secured what he
considered an 'unprecedented deal' for Lewis with Edmund
Fisher, then a young editor at Michael Joseph. Eady subsequently
told Jo that 'Fisher was a bit of a drunk and that's how Ted got
the book contract'. Fisher, a similar age to Lewis with a gift for
friendship and a taste for long, liquid lunches, was a charismatic
publishing executive with an instinctive feel for the market.
Unsurprisingly, given the success of Carter, he saw potential
in Lewis's writing. The deal guaranteed Lewis an advance of
around £5,000 for one book a year. It meant he hardly had to
write anything else, but in reality it gave him time and money
to drink. Gil Potter remembers, 'They'd give him five grand up
front to write something, but he'd have to live on that for the
next eight months or something. He'd show them an idea, but
that's all, and sometimes it wouldn't get done till the last minute,
so all he had to do was get through the money. Gradually it got
done, he *was* producing.' Lewis seemed no more confident in
his own work than he had been before the success of *Carter*.
'Sometimes he'd say, "Can you read this, what do you think?"

And I'd say there's bits that are a bit funny and he'd go, "They've just sent it all back." That got him down.'

He'd begun work on his next novel, *Plender,* soon after the publication of *Jack's Return Home* in 1970. A malevolent Humberside-set blackmail thriller, *Plender* was more provincially claustrophobic even than Carter. Where *Plender* excelled, and what Hodges had necessarily set aside in *Get Carter,* was in the internal, psychological struggle and troubled backstory of its main characters. Lewis gave full reign to the inner reflections of his two protagonists, Brian Plender and Peter Knott. In doing so, he returned to his theme of the past haunting the present. There were implicit, provocative statements about his own life; at times ironic, at others sincere, Lewis explores the notion that our sins will surely find us out.

The novel opens with Brian Plender surveying an unnamed provincial city – obviously Hull – from the window of his twelfth-floor office. He looks over the docks and the river below, following the lights of the ferry bringing his blackmail victim. He is a fixer in the pay of the 'Movement', a powerful right-wing cadre within the British establishment with which Plender has established a reputation as a blackmailer and honey trap operator. Plender describes the cityscape, zeroing in on shuffling shoppers late on a wet winter Saturday afternoon, with Larkinesque detail: the 'grey wet wind' screams up the estuary and dirty barges 'shift surlily on the greasy swell'. He is a malignant puppet master, manipulative, friendless and damaged. Pulling strings of plots in which he entangles his victims, Plender plans his conquests with enticingly placed small ads in the newspapers. The first we see arrive is the daughter of a prominent member of the Movement whose affair with a black activist has brought her to Plender's attention. His disdain for her grammar school background, her father's money, her bohemian student clothes and political activism is clear. Within the first few pages, Plender expresses his contempt for women, students, blacks, homosexuals and transsexuals.

On a visit to Peggy's, a gay bar in the seedier dockside streets of Hull which Plender uses to arrange pickups for clients and victims, he recognises former schoolmate, Peter Knott. Ostensibly a respectable photographer taking advertising shots for his father-in-law's mail order catalogue, in reality Knott uses his warehouse studio as a location for illicit affairs, exploring his repressed sexual fantasies. Knott picks up a girl called Eileen in the bar with a view to taking her back to his studio to pose for pornographic photos. Plender follows the couple to Knott's studio. Knott takes the photographs and seduces the girl. When Plender witnesses her fatal fall from the staircase leading to the studio and Knott's panic stricken attempts to cover up the death, he follows, engineering a collision between their cars, covering up the girl's death, disposing of the body and placing Knott in his debt. He begins a process of drawing Knott into his world of blackmail.

In Gerald Kersh's novel, *Night and the City*, the narrator delves into the psyche of sometime pimp Harry Fabian, a 'habitual liar' who likes to imagine his lies ring true. 'No miracle of belief can equal the childlike faith in the credulity of the people who listen to him; and so it comes to pass that he fools nobody as completely as he fools himself.' It's a description that applies to Peter Knott, desperate to protect himself from exposure. His track record of deception makes him easy prey for Plender. His wife suspects him of an affair; evidently he has been found out on a previous occasion, and the marriage is on the verge of disintegration. Not least, it transpires, because Kate Knott is unwilling to satisfy her husband's sexual preferences. Knott is someone for whom sexual conquest verges on compulsion, but in its aftermath he finds only dissatisfaction and self-loathing.

As the plot unfolds in flashbacks from Knott and Plender's adolescence, it becomes clear that the festering animosity between them is a consequence of their relationship at grammar school. Plender, the outsider, longs to belong to the friendship group of which Knott is a leading figure. Knott's humiliation of Plender has left deep psychological scars.

He draws Knott further into his employ, coercing him into photographing blackmail victims in compromising situations with prostitutes or as players in S&M scenes. Meanwhile, Plender feeds Kate Knott's suspicions around her husband's supposed affair, systematically destroying all he holds dear until an awkward attempt to seduce Kate Knott fails, exposing his real intent.

Events reach a climax with the revelation that Knott's father-in-law is a significant player in the Movement. Knott is persuaded by Kate to explain to her father that Plender has been blackmailing him. Plender realises that the pattern established throughout his schooldays is being repeated: he can never be accepted, only tolerated while he is useful. The Movement realise that with his files on them, Plender has become a liability. His flight from their hired assassins coincides with Knott's desperate final attempt to discover where Plender has disposed of Eileen's body. At the quarry where Plender and Knott played as kids, there is a shootout and Plender is killed.

Once again, Lewis is unafraid to chronicle something of his own life in his characters. He sets out his autobiographical stall early during the meeting between Knott and the girl, Eileen. Knott tells her he'd lived in London before returning north, that he'd been brought up in a small town on the other side of the river and gone to art school in the city. He adds that he wasn't short of money and was happily married. Names of places are recycled; old friends reappear. Plender phones a blackmail victim called 'Hopper' – Miles Hopper was a childhood friend of Lewis's who had been on the fringes of the Riverbank Boys. In later life a committed naturalist and a highly talented nature painter, as a boy he'd had something of a cruel streak, shooting birds at point blank range or blowing up frogs with fireworks. The name Plender is presumably borrowed from Plender Street, Camden NW1, a once insalubrious backstreet, part of the red light hinterland behind King's Cross Station.

Locations have easily identifiable real life equivalents. Humberside settings alternate between the north and south banks of the river. Peggy's Bar, the bohemian haunt for gay men, transsexuals and married men on the pull, is on Jackson Street – Hull's Jackson Street is close to the former fish docks. Knott's home in the village of 'Corella' is a thinly disguised Kirk Ella, an affluent outpost on the city's rural fringes, once home to Lewis's art school girlfriend, Juliet Raahauge. The Ferry Boat pub was in Winteringham, North Lincolnshire, and was a favourite out of town watering hole for the Barton lads. (It also makes an appearance at the conclusion of *All the Way Home and All the Night Through*.) Plender describes the town of Barton, renamed 'Brumby', as the place where he and Peter Knott once lived.

These blurred autobiographical boundaries influenced Lewis's writing of the relationships in the novel, particularly that between Peter and Kate Knott. Confiding in Plender, Kate says, 'I always said to myself that if he ever got involved, if he ever put what he had with me and the kids at risk, then I'd walk out on him… make him realise the lie by bringing him face to face with the truth by showing him what he'd chosen to risk being rid of.' There is a strong sense that these were words Jo had already spoken, or that Lewis was anticipating a future in which they would be.

In one flashback, the adolescent Knott mocks Plender for not being 'the right sort', setting him up for an imaginary date with a girl he knows Plender likes. Knott, his friends and the girl are hiding, watching Plender wait in vain. Later, there are homoerotic undercurrents between the two boys, culminating in Knott coercing Plender to take part in mutual masturbation in the gang's riverbank den. Plender describes how Knott 'took hold of me and began to do it. I didn't dare try and stop him in case he told his friends I was useless.' Plender is humiliated. 'Immediately I felt sicker and dirtier than I'd ever felt in my life. "Now you've got to do it to me," he said.'

The flashbacks offer at least a partial insight to Lewis's schooldays. Whilst none of Lewis's school friends recalled these kinds of experiences, there were individuals on the periphery of the Riverbank Boys as in any friendship group. Inevitably it follows there were adolescent alliances, short-lived affairs, rumours, fallings-out and rejections. Equally likely, as Jack and Frank Carter represented extreme aspects of Lewis's personality, the same applies here; Knott and Plender are both radical reimaginings of his character set in opposition. Lewis draws us back to these school experiences as Plender exerts tighter control over his former tormentor, taunting Knott by reciting the words to their school song, *Keep Faith*.

As a student, Lewis's politics had, along with most of his contemporaries, tended broadly towards the left. Like many of his generation there was support for the Ban the Bomb movement and CND, though he had no overt political affiliation. In conversations with Barri Hooper in the run up to the 1970 general election, he'd given the impression he was a committed socialist, making the point, forcefully on occasion, that the punters in his rural Essex pub knew nothing of the industrial north and the struggles of the working class. Hooper remembers, 'I'd say something and he'd say "No, that's wrong, you know nothing about these things, you're from the south; you've not seen the deprivation in the north."' Lewis's acute sense of class resentment was evident in *Jack's Return Home* and *Plender*. Hooper recalled an encounter with him in the Coach and Horses – at the time he would have been working on *Plender*. On election night, 18 June 1970, Hooper arrived to find Lewis in the bar with a local named Roy Rogers. 'Ted said, "You'll never guess who I voted for."' Given Lewis's attitude and his previous claims to working class roots, Hooper joked that perhaps he had voted 'fascist'. 'He went crazy, and told me to step outside. I said, "You've read too many novels, Ted." He said "Step out!" and stormed out of the pub, and old Roy Rogers said, "You'd better go out there."' Hooper followed Lewis outside, expecting to be pounced on:

'He was waiting round the corner. He said, "Make a bit of noise" and he put his shoulder to the door. So we make a bit of noise, as if we'd been fighting, and as we go back in, he shakes my hand and he says, "We're all men of honour." I never did know who he voted for and I never brought it up again. I don't know what he was doing, but it was as if he was setting up a scenario, something you'd see in a pub between two aggressive blokes.'

Rumours of a terrible fight outside the pub briefly became the talk of the village. In the years since, Hooper has thought of the incident, and wondered whether Lewis really had been offended and intended to fight, and once outside and had thought better of it, or had the whole thing been set up from start to finish?

With the Wicken education centre the focus for much of his

leisure time, Lewis was encountering radical views amongst visiting lecturers and teachers. There was a large number of African students and, given the dominant political tensions of the era, presumably there were politically active teaching staff at the centre. Clearly, this was a source of inspiration for the character of Mr Nboro, the African activist who appears in the early scenes of *Plender*. For clues as to the origins of the novel's right-wing themes, Lewis's ongoing friendship with Michael Tink seems the most likely source. Tink had been employed at the British Museum, presumably on security or administrative duties, and been sacked from his job after attending a series of National Front meetings. He hadn't been shy about expressing his views at work and it's likely he lost the job after his photograph had appeared in a national paper under a National Front banner. The story found its way back to Barton. According to Martin Turner, 'when the officials at the British Museum found out he was going to these National Front meetings, he was asked to leave. He used to come back and spout it all. I don't know if it affected Lew, but I know he admired Mike for the world he lived in, the thuggery of it all.' Tink later returned to Barton, picking up with old friends and joining the Conservatives.

Plender's devotion to the right-wing causes espoused by his employers seems more a matter of expedience than an absolute conviction, although a room with Nazi memorabilia revealed late in the story indicates a deeper affinity than he otherwise discloses. Wider concepts of conspiracy are fed into the novel as plot devices, but Lewis chooses not to explore or develop them further. As Plender doesn't meet face to face with any of the subversive establishment figures – their contacts are by telephone and we never witness his reactions – his motivations are not explained beyond his misanthropic and sadistic pleasure in the humiliation of others. This internalised approach narrows the novel's scope. With his cast of damaged characters, Lewis makes a virtue of a suffocating provincialism, repressed sexuality and questionable moralities.

Plender found Lewis, for the first time, having to compete with his own reputation and produce work that was the equal of *Carter*, the novel having been retitled and remarketed as a Pan paperback to tie in with the film, its cover a photograph of Michael Caine on Blackhall Beach. Stylistically, *Plender* was the first instance of Lewis breaking down narrative structures. Plender and Knott each narrate in the first person, sometimes in short half page scenes with flashes of thought or action, a single story event or revelation. Fracturing the narrative enabled Lewis to develop and accentuate points of tension between characters. He seemed to be writing with film adaptation in mind. Indeed, Mike Hodges remembers being sent a copy of the book, but turned it down:

'I wanted to change tack. You need to remember, *Carter* was my first feature. I'd never before seen any film of mine on the big screen and with an audience. The reaction and the experience of watching it shook me quite a lot. It was, quite properly, bleak and ruthless. Just as I had wanted it. But it was an arena I didn't want to go back to for a while.'

Hodges instead was keen to work on his own ideas, writing and directing the black comedy, *Pulp*, released in 1972, once again starring Michael Caine and produced by Michael Klinger – they had formed the Three Michaels production company in order to continue working together post Carter. Decamping to Malta for the shoot, it was as if they needed to breathe cleaner air. Lewis, on the other hand, committed himself to deeper, noir-inspired explorations. Something Toby Eady says was 'all Ted'.

Lewis had created a criminal class antihero in Jack Carter. You might not like him and you might be shocked by his violence, but you could at least appreciate his style and the single-mindedness with which he pursues his cause. The characters in *Plender* offer no such relief. They are almost entirely unlikeable, grubby suburbanites living with lies, guilt, humiliation and bitterness, trading on the weaknesses of others. Plender trades in Ripleyesque levels of manipulation. Patricia Highsmith had used Ripley to 'dismantle the cosiness of conventional crime writing'; Lewis's character continuum does something similar in an English provincial setting. Andrew Wilson's biography of Highsmith speaks of how she 'seduces the reader into identifying with Ripley until by the end our moral responses have been so invaginated, we are actively on the side of the killer'. True, perhaps, for Jack Carter, but with *Plender*, Lewis had no such aim, creating characters who challenged convention and couldn't care less whether you identified with them or not. All this makes *Plender* a classic noir novel. And, whilst there are varying ideas about what makes a story 'noir', taking Paul Duncan's definition in *Noir Fiction: Dark Highways* as a start point, that noir is about 'the weak-minded, the losers, the bottom-feeders, the obsessives, the compulsives, psychopaths', Lewis was instinctively a noir writer.

In *Jack's Return Home*, Jack Carter's craving for revenge is compounded when he views Doreen in a pornographic movie. In *Plender*, the sex industry comes under scrutiny through Plender's blackmail scams and Knott's pornographic photography. Lewis was intent on flipping the 1960s sexual revolution for a long cold 1970s look at its underside and the dislocation it creates. Life was a gas for would-be hippies and middle class suburb dwellers playing away, but Lewis's characters buy, sell and use sex as crutch and commodity, usually with consequences. When Plender and Knott come into contact with transsexual prostitute, Camille, she makes advances to Knott, insisting they've met before and implying he has made use of her services. Lewis may well have been an observer, recalling nights in Soho and the blue movie industry for details, but Eady has no doubt that his books were a means to explore his dark side. He spoke cryptically about an unpublished novel 'too dark, too sado-masochistic for me to agent' that 'went further than pornography'.

When *Plender* was published in November 1971, *The Times* review called it 'fresh and original'. Writing in the *Guardian*, Norman Shrapnel praised Lewis's writing; the story was 'traced with a rare delicacy of feeling'. The *London Evening News* promised 'excitements galore'. In truth, it doesn't seem to have been the huge commercial success Lewis might have anticipated. It lacked the irresistible drive of *Jack's Return Home* and, for the reading public, at least those in Britain, perhaps the appeal of Jack Carter's name on the cover.

In spite of the support of MGM in Europe, Michael Klinger had encountered huge problems convincing MGM in the United States to get behind *Get Carter*. It was never properly released, famously playing as a second feature with the Frank Sinatra movie, *Dirty Dingus Magee*. 'It's something which has stuck in my mind and I'm sure in Mike Hodges' mind for our whole lives,' says Tony Klinger, 'how you can get screwed in America. Apparently, we'd upset the people at MGM.' Klinger believes that Carter reflected too much of a British provincial reality for American tastes. 'They had gangsters that did terrible things, but not in quite the same way. There aren't the same cultural sensibilities; it's the context, how we captured the reality of where the real heavyweight gangsters were.' Ultimately, MGM were content to treat *Get Carter* as drive-in fodder; Spicer and McKenna's study of Klinger points out that 'MGM, with its Las Vegas owner, had its own reasons for promoting Frank Sinatra's film and seemed content to sacrifice Klinger's'.

Not that MGM had finished with *Get Carter*. Following the success of *Shaft*, released in July 1971, the company was keen to commission low budget blaxploitation crime films and saw the money making potential for a *Get Carter* remake. *Hit Man* was directed by George Armitage and starred Bernie Casey as Tyrone Tackett (Jack Carter) and Pamela Grier as 'sultry skin flick star' Gozelda (Glenda). Released in December 1972, it credits '*Jack's Return Home* by Ted Lewis' as the basis for the film, transposing the action to Los Angeles and changing the names of the characters. In spite of some bizarre plot twists – Gozelda meets a gory end, chased and mauled by tigers in a theme park – it is plainly based on Hodges' film, which angered both Hodges and Klinger, not least because *Hit Man* is such a third-rate copy. Lewis would later complain that he 'hadn't received a penny' for *Hit Man*.

With the relative success of *Jack's Return Home*, the recognition and the new deal with Michael Joseph, Lewis achieved a degree of financial security for the first time. When Ron and Judy Burnett visited Wicken Bonhunt, Judy remembers Lewis seemed to be doing well. The village preserved its sense of rural calm with occasional excitements and Lewis maintained a regular presence at the Coach and Horses.

Family life for the Lewises was comfortable, successful and relatively settled. Erme Cottage had been renovated; they had friends in Essex and were close enough to London for Lewis to travel and fulfil his business interests and maintain a presence in the places which mattered. Nick Hague remembers Lewis being around the Soho artistic community into the early 1970s. He had a broad circle of friends, some were his mates from Barton or Hull, others people he'd just met in the pub. For the most part, these were the people with whom he felt most comfortable.

As neither Lewis nor Jo had learned to drive, they were dependent on lifts, the local taxi service, or public transport for day to day domestic needs. Jo would take a taxi to nearby Saffron Walden to do the weekly shopping. Lewis had registered with an estate agent and had been vaguely looking at houses for sale. Returning from a shopping trip one morning, Jo found him waiting. 'He said, "We *have* to go and see this house. I've arranged for Mrs Ellis next door to have the girls and we're going to Suffolk to see it. I've organised the taxi, it'll be here in half an hour."' The taxi took them to Hill Farm, Kettleburgh, near Framlingham in the heart of rural Suffolk. Jo remembers 'The moment he saw it, he moved heaven and earth to get it.'

Previously owned by two brothers whose mutually antagonistic relationship had resulted in them effectively splitting the house in two, Hill Farm, a traditional Suffolk longhouse with a paddock and barn, was set in around three acres of land. It needed major renovation. Set back from a narrow country road, it was without mains water. Jo remembers there was an outside tank, uncovered and, judging by what they found floating in it, probably insanitary.

Gil Potter was concerned about the isolation of the new place and the pressure that would place on them both. He tried to persuade Lewis to stay in Wicken. Doreen Potter was worried they were closing themselves off from everything and everybody. 'I was losing a friend, and they had such a nice set-up at Wicken.'

Why did she think Lewis was so determined to leave? 'It might have been because he was getting too involved with people and he didn't want to. Maybe he thought if he got out there he could write more, or write better.' Jo was justifiably apprehensive at taking Nancy and Sally, then a year old, to a home without proper amenities, but Lewis's mind was made up. The family moved to Hill Farm. Lewis took on a sizeable mortgage, made possible, Jo says, 'because of the success of *Carter*'. With the farm several miles from the nearest town, Lewis and Jo learned to drive and bought a car, although neither had any idea how to maintain it, something which frustrated his father. 'Harry went potty,' Jo says, 'because Ted didn't think about putting oil in the car. Neither did I, but it was always that sort of thing Harry was looking for.'

Buying Hill Farm symbolised Lewis's need to prove something to his parents, particularly his father, although one imagines Harry can't have been too impressed with the state of the building. Eady says pointedly that Lewis had 'become the country gentleman'. More importantly, buying Hill Farm enabled Lewis to create a home for Nancy and Sally, complete with goats, a donkey and numerous cats – Nancy remembers him rescuing one frightened animal and bringing it back from the pub one bonfire night. There's no doubt the house meant a lot to him. Jo remembers putting the children to bed, seeing him standing at the gate at the top of Hill Farm's long drive, 'looking at the fields and loving it, absolutely loving it'.

Lewis was an ambitious writer, motivated to produce commercial fiction with depth and insight. He challenged contemporary expectations of form and function of the crime novel with a noir-inflected experimentalism. The relative lack of commercial success of *Plender* as the post-Carter novel, with alternate first person narratives and the absence of a likeable hero or relatable antihero, demanded more of the reader than a traditional thriller plot. Taken at face value, Lewis's next book, *Billy Rags*, appears more conventional, but is perhaps the most contentious of his novels.

In 1971, convicted armed robber and notorious prison escapee, John McVicar, then in the first year of a 26-year prison sentence for robbery and firearms offences committed whilst on the run, had written a deposition from his cell in the special wing of Brixton prison. Reportedly smuggled from Brixton by McVicar's lawyer, marked 'defence documents', the manuscript had been transcribed and edited by publisher, writer and academic, Goronwy Rees. As convicted prisoners were not permitted to write memoirs for publication or profit – McVicar told warders he was working on his defence for impending firearms charges – the plan was that it would be published, presumably under a pseudonym, and a portion of the advance provide an income for the woman with whom McVicar had been living prior to recapture. She was also the mother of his seven-year-old son, Russell. It would also be a means for McVicar, then entering a period of study and re-education, to begin to prepare for life outside prison.

The manuscript made the rounds of agents and publishers, in all probability stumbling on the Home Office no memoirs rule. Although it isn't clear who made the initial approach, Jo remembers Toby Eady dealt with the lawyer James Morton, acting on McVicar's behalf. Morton would later establish himself as a chronicler of London gangland with a string of underworld themed books and criminal memoirs, notably in co-authorship with Richardson gang enforcer Frankie Fraser. Their books included *Mad Frank's Underworld History of*

Britain, *Mad Frank's London* and *Mad Frank's Diary*. Received wisdom has it that Lewis read McVicar's manuscript and was keen to write a novel based on the story. There is a certain logic in Lewis, a skilled exponent of crime fiction, adept at incorporating autobiographical detail, fictionalising McVicar's true crime story. The resulting novel, *Billy Rags*, opens with an author's note:

> *This novel and its central character were originally inspired by certain actual events and by a real person. But it is a work of fiction: all the descriptions of prisons, convicts and their friends and relatives, prison officers and policemen are imaginary.*

Taken on those terms, Lewis's convincing first person narrative of career criminal and hard man Billy Cracken is an atmospheric and thoroughly engaging novel. Through a series of flashbacks, he traces Cracken's path from playground delinquency to the maximum security wing, via sexual experiences and the prostitution and suicide of his sister. Lewis creates a sympathetic portrait of Cracken, describing a man of intelligence and self-awareness for whom criminality had been a choice. So far, so Jack Carter. Cracken was also emotionally vulnerable. Admonished by his headmaster in a way that shames him, he resolves never again to allow anyone to 'reach' him. Autobiographically, it was a counterpoint to Lewis's own experience of school and the martinet Goddard. Lewis had chosen art and writing. Cracken is harder, more resolute, and enters a life of crime.

It's easy to see why Lewis was keen to associate with McVicar's story. He must have seen much of himself in the former grammar school boy, long distance runner, and perennial observer; educated, intelligent, but contemptuous of those spending their eight hours at work every day. Lewis invested characteristic bite into a Cracken backstory scene at a party at which he becomes drunk and aggressive; 'There's a shaft of excitement in my chest because this is the best part, the chatting, the recognition, the reinforcement of my feelings about myself. Later she'll just be any other bird, a release mechanism; someone I'll resent giving it to, and I'll dislike myself for being weak.'

Early in the novel, Cracken is the ringleader of a failed escape attempt at 'Burnham' prison. The would-be escapees make it onto a low roof, but their homemade grappling hook lacks the necessary weight to swing to a higher roof and freedom beyond. Cracken is responsible for the malfunctioning hook. After the failed breakout and subsequent rooftop stand-off, Cracken is transferred to 'Aston', based on HM Prison Durham, specifically the high security E-Wing, where many high profile inmates were incarcerated. At Aston, he encounters Walter Colman, a character based on Charlie Richardson. Cracken has little respect for Colman's status as a prison baron. Instead, he confronts the authorities and the prison system at every turn, sometimes to save face, other times because it's expected of him or just for the hell of it. Lewis's tone is more sympathetic than in *Jack's Return Home*, and less self-consciously scathing of human weakness than *Plender*.

When conditions on E-Wing deteriorate, the inmates plan a riot in order to protest. During the subsequent lockdown, Cracken reads the case file of a known sex offender – Lewis names him Hopper, once again recalling his former friend. In McVicar's true life version, the Hopper character is Moors murderer Ian Brady.

Desperate to escape Durham, Cracken plans a breakout, via a tunnel in the prison shower block. He makes detailed plans and preparations. Lewis ratchets the tension as the night of the escape bid nears with Walter Colman and his crony, Gearing, attempting to muscle in on the escape. Cracken's determination to exclude them from the final break fuels the suspense. He leads them on, then leaves them behind, escaping across the rooftops into the streets below. On the run, Cracken endures hunger, thirst and cold. He swims freezing rivers and runs barefoot along shingle railway lines to escape. Returning repeatedly to a public phone box to arrange a pickup, he eventually receives help and is driven back to London.

He remains at large, holed up in a poky flat with his girlfriend 'Sheila' and their son, 'Timmy'. Frustrated at exchanging one form of captivity for another, Cracken takes on a final job to raise the cash to go abroad. He is forced to deal with a new generation of tearaways, flash lads in leather and suede with identity bracelets, trendy haircuts and misplaced arrogance. They aren't the professionals Cracken is used to working with, but for the promise of a decent return he takes on the job. Predictably, the tearaways funk it, the robbery fails and Cracken is recaptured.

Billy Rags is a highly accomplished piece of storytelling. Scenes are tightly written, characters evocatively drawn. Lewis colours his prose with precise detail and sharply observed cultural references. Cracken is disdainful of would-be hard men 'trying their hardest to look like characters out of New York Confidential'; a barmaid has 'Platinum hair and Ruth Roman lips' – a reference to the American actress, best known for her role in Hitchcock's 1951 movie, *Strangers on a Train*. Also notable is an example of Lewis's stylistic innovation. In Cracken's flashback telling of a failed wages snatch, he creates a driving, repetitious rhythm: 'The police car sways into view, in front of the Wolseley. The Wolseley is moving towards the police car. The police car swings broadside on, leaving no room for the Wolseley to get by. The Wolseley reverses. Policemen pile out of the police car and chase after the reversing Wolseley. The Wolseley clouts the wages van...'

Years later, similar use of repetition would become a defining feature in the writing of noir novelist David Peace.

Away from his familiar Humberside landscapes, Lewis's writing in *Billy Rags* feels closer in tone to a traditional crime novel. Cracken is his most sympathetically drawn character to date, a hard man with a moral sense and capacity for sensitivity notably absent in previous Lewis protagonists. Contrast Cracken's description of Sheila as she sleeps, 'Dark auburn hair tumbled over her bare shoulders. Her breath was soft and slow. I could feel the warmth of it on my neck. I looked at her a long time before I looked away,' with Jack Carter's appraisal of his landlady; 'She wasn't bad. About forty, probably the right side of it, hair permed, squarish face, well powdered, big tits, open-necked blouse shoved tight into her skirt.'

John McVicar's own memoir *McVicar: By Himself* was published for the first time in 1974. In the foreword, McVicar explains the circumstances that prompted him to begin writing within a few days of his capture in November 1970. He says that, in editing the original manuscript, Goronwy Rees misinterpreted some of his 'prison scribblings'. He had struggled with a scarcity of paper and his cramped handwriting rendered some passages virtually unreadable. Rees had transcribed around 50,000 words. Supplemented by McVicar's own 'Instructions to Council' (sic), a lengthy explanation of his journey into crime, delivered by Malcolm Morris QC at his trial in 1971, this became the book *McVicar: By Himself.*

John McVicar and Ted Lewis were born within six months

of each other in 1940. They were both from working class families. McVicar was sentenced to eight years for armed robbery in 1965. He escaped from Parkhurst Prison in 1966. On his recapture he was sentenced to a further 15 years. In Chelmsford prison in 1967, McVicar led an escape attempt through a padlocked trapdoor to the roof of the prison. Here a poorly constructed grappling hook prevented the escape from going any further and the situation developed, first into a standoff with prison officers, then a rooftop protest. Clearly, the model for Billy Cracken's failed escape attempt from 'Burnham' at the opening of *Billy Rags*. The method of escape, geography and ultimately the failure of the grappling hook are identical, as are the characters. Chelmsford's Major Reece becomes, in Lewis's words, 'a comic book little governor called Captain Davies'.

When it becomes clear the escape has failed and the governor tries to persuade the prisoners to return to their cells, McVicar's co-escapee Martin O'Day eyes the truncheon-wielding prison officers: 'No trouble! What's he got a riot stick for then? You're going to cosh us up.' Compare with Billy Cracken's co-escapee Gordon Harris at the same point in Lewis's story: 'No trouble? What's he got a riot stick for, then? You're going to cosh us up, you bastards.'

There is barely a cigarette paper between Lewis's reimagining and McVicar's original text. When the escape attempt fails, McVicar says, 'It's bad enough losing when you think you've won, but it's even worse when you know you should have won.' Billy Cracken says, 'It's always hardest to lose when you think you've won.' McVicar's prison governor, Major Reece, says, 'It's no good lads. The place is surrounded by troops. Come in quickly and don't let's have any trouble.' Lewis's prison governor Captain Davies says, 'It's no good lads, the troops are surrounding the place. Come in quietly and don't let's have any trouble.'

McVicar recalls the reaction of fellow real life escapee, Freddie Simpson. 'Freddie Simpson said to no one in particular: "I can't believe it. I just can't believe it. I was sure we'd made it."' Lewis's line is identical, the character name unchanged: 'Freddie Simpson said to no one in particular: "I can't believe it. I can't believe it. I really thought we'd made it."' Event for event, character for character and, in some instances, phrase for phrase, the Burnham escape attempt follows McVicar's Chelmsford breakout. There are countless examples. Consistently and faithfully throughout, *Billy Rags* is inseparable from McVicar's story.

Published in February 1973, *Billy Rags* received a positive critical response. In the aftermath of the high profile criminal trials of the late 1960s, penal reform was a significant topic for discussion, the underlying arguments between retributivist and utilitarian systems of punishment played out in think-pieces and television debate. Lewis, once more, had arrived at a point of cultural importance and, with *Billy Rags*, made a mark. The book received attention from an unexpected source, an article in *The Spectator* magazine by Auberon Waugh under the title, 'Criminal Connection', published on 3 March 1973. Waugh applauds Lewis's 'nobility' in refusing to make Billy Cracken any less 'repulsive' than he would be in real life. He notes the rarity of the prison escape novel, contrasting the popularity of the post-war prison camp escapes with *Billy Rags*' career villains:

These are no clean-limbed British officers bouncing up and down on a wooden horse. They are not even 'political' prisoners, whose burglaries or whatever are the result of some innate rejection of the capitalist system. They are ordinary, run-of-the-mill criminal psychopaths and the sad truth is that they are extremely stupid, extremely unpleasant people.

Acknowledging Lewis's commitment to the reality of the subject matter to the detriment of the easier thrills of traditional thriller fiction, Waugh says, 'Obviously, it is to Mr Lewis's credit as an artist that his book is extremely depressing and distasteful... scenes of sodomy and violence are described as they happen, neither more nor less.' In conclusion, he describes it as a 'depressing book', which, he says, 'fails as a thriller through our lack of sympathy with its hero-victim; but it is well written and most instructive and should persuade a few careless householders to invest in a shotgun and a savage dog.'

McVicar was paroled in 1978. In 1980, his story was the subject of the feature film, *McVicar,* with Roger Daltrey in the title role. The screenplay, credited to McVicar and Tom Clegg, who also directed, was based on the book *McVicar: By Himself.* It opens with the disclaimer, 'The prison escape shown in this film is based on true fact. Certain other events and characters have been fictionalised.'

Lewis had always been drawn to people who carried the threat of violence. When I spoke to his art school friend, Keith Riseam, about Lewis's fascination with criminal classes and the real life gangsters he wrote about, he saw it as 'a kind of rebelliousness'. It was something Keith had experienced himself as an art teacher in Full Sutton prison. Among his students was Eddie Richardson. When I interviewed Keith in 2009, they were still in occasional contact. 'I have to ask myself, why do I keep in touch with Eddie? It's because he's charming and I think Ted was a bit like me, he liked the underworld. These people are devious, good at manipulation.' But Riseam believes Lewis's association with professional criminals changed something in him. 'He explored the side of him that he wanted to hide through his books, or used them as an outlet for a side of him he couldn't really handle.' Tom Barling believes Lewis's curiosity was rooted in his fear of criminal hard men, but he was shocked at the publication of *Billy Rags*:

'I hadn't seen him for a while, so I bought a copy and my heart turned over. It was a rip-off of John McVicar's story. And I thought, what have you done? If McVicar comes after you, you're a dead man. It's over. I met the agent and he said, "His [McVicar's] common law wife sent us his notebooks." And I said, "It's all in Ted's book, all he's done is changed the names." And he went white. I thought you silly boy, Ted. Either you know them, or you make it up. It's plagiarism, for Christ's sake.'

The stories are the same; that is beyond doubt. Had it been agreed that Lewis would act as a front for McVicar, using his time and talent for his and McVicar's mutual financial gain? Or had he taken more liberties with the original text than anyone imagined or, at the time, fully realised? He certainly applied the novelist's craft to the source material, layering in the textures and storytelling he'd shown so adeptly in *Jack's Return Home* and *Plender*, and there are sections which reveal his own ideas and preoccupations. Nevertheless, a close reading and comparison between *Billy Rags* and *McVicar: By Himself* can only conclude that Lewis's novel was not wholly 'imaginary' as claimed by the author's note. Far from it, his characters are identical, changing only the names and not always doing that; the locations are described in exactly the same terms; and his dramatisation of real events and dialogue paraphrases or copies much from McVicar's original deposition and his subsequent book.

For his 1992 *Arena* magazine article about Lewis, John Williams spoke to McVicar about Lewis's 'thinly-veiled account' of his life and prison breakouts. '"Yes," says McVicar, "he took my story and fictionalised it. I wrote a manuscript while I was in prison, it did the rounds of the publishers and Lewis must have lifted stuff from it."' Responding in the following edition of *Arena*, Jo vehemently refutes this version of events and any suggestion that Lewis 'lifted facts' from McVicar's deposition. She wrote, 'A deal was negotiated with James Morton and Toby Eady, Ted's agent. The percentage McVicar was to be paid was agreed before one word of *Billy Rags* was written.'

In May 2015, I was contacted by the celebrated photographer and chronicler of London street culture, Derek Ridgers. A long-time Lewis reader, Derek had a forty year old question that needed answering:

'When *Billy Rags* came out, I obtained it from the local library fairly quickly and probably read it within a few days. I thought it a great book but a little different to some of his others. At this time, John McVicar was still in prison. When *McVicar: By Himself* came out in 1974 there was a fair amount of publicity surrounding it and, of course, I read that one quickly as well. I was quite shocked insofar as they are so similar, in fact, almost the same. It was never mentioned in the reviews of McVicar's book.'

Derek wrote to the publishers and received an anodyne letter together with a sheaf of press cuttings. 'I forget exactly what the letter said but they certainly weren't admitting anything at all.' In the early 1980s, he did some work with McVicar. 'I asked him about it. He was a nice enough chap, but taciturn in the extreme and he didn't answer my question. Just ignored it. I didn't want to accuse him of anything and he wasn't the sort of bloke one pressed.' Ridgers speculates, 'It may well have been that Lewis got in with a few of McVicar's pals and they were persuasive. I don't mean threatening, but I've found gangsters and ex-gangsters to be charming, intelligent, charismatic and persuasive individuals, and there would always be a slight feeling that one was best advised not to disagree with them too vehemently.'

Whatever the precise terms of the deal, the question remains; why did Lewis feel the need to plagiarise McVicar's memoir? Because he needed the money? Because he was bereft of ideas of his own? Perhaps *Billy Rags* is evidence that Lewis, a writer who systematically and ruthlessly exploited his own experience in his work, had simply exhausted himself, or that his experiences at the time were too disturbing or difficult to write about.

It is unlikely Lewis wrote *Billy Rags* with the knowledge that John McVicar would publish his own version a year later, and it is unclear whether James Morton or anyone else was aware of this at the time the deal was agreed. But if *Billy Rags* was a means to exploit Lewis's name and reputation for money, or an experiment in true crime fiction, it would not be repeated.

The first indication that Lewis was working on a new Jack Carter novel came with the publication of a short story for *Men Only* magazine in November 1973. The Bumper Christmas edition of the top shelf, soft porn magazine featured an interview with Peter Sellers, a spoof review of a story claiming to be 'Charles Dickens's Only Erotic Masterpiece', and an article on 'Pipe Smoking with Eric Morecambe'. Cosily placed between full frontal nudes, ads for Raymond's Revue Bar and John Player Special cigarettes were two pieces of fiction. The first, 'Mr. Big', was an existential Mickey Spillane pastiche by Woody Allen.

'She wore a short skirt and a tight sweater and her figure described a set of parabolas that could cause a cardiac arrest in a yak.' Naming his characters 'Heather Butkiss', 'Kaiser Lupowitz', and 'Claire Rosenweig', a Vassar philosophy major searching for God – the eponymous 'Mr. Big' – Allen was on familiar ground.

So was 'Ted "Get Carter" Lewis', whose story 'Kings, Queens and Pawns', the strapline informed, 'plunges us once more into the sexually perverse and brutal jungle of Britain's underworld'. Howard Pemberton's softly drawn illustration accompanying the story depicts Jack Carter in blue open neck shirt and grey slacks on a couch close to a petite Audrey Fletcher in pink silk lingerie holding a knife to his side. The smoke from Jack's cigarette forms a ghostly naked male figure. The story opens with the line, 'I'm lying back in bed smoking and I say to Audrey, who I've just lit up in more ways than one, isn't it about time you had your nails cut?'

A slice of backstory for *Jack's Return Home* and subsequent Carter prequels, 'Kings, Queens and Pawns' revisits many of the characteristics that made the novel a success. Jack is recognisably Jack, resentful, amoral, violent, and governed by his relationships with women. The story finds him in Soho looking after the Fletchers' interests whilst conducting an affair with Gerald Fletcher's wife, Audrey, and helping himself to a little more on the side with Barbara, a 19-year-old erotic dancer at the Fletchers' nightclub. Appropriately, Lewis weaves threads of erotic fiction throughout the story; a scene in which Audrey phones Gerald whilst she and Jack play a sexually provocative game of dare and caress delicately references Michael Caine and Britt Ekland's *Get Carter* phone sex scene.

Jack's troubles multiply with Peter the Dutchman's entry to the Fletchers' inner circle, ostensibly to set up a security van robbery. Personally and professionally affronted, Jack's carefully maintained separation of affairs threatens to crumble around him.

'Kings, Queens and Pawns' enabled Lewis to revisit the impetuses and provocations which underpinned Jack Carter's eventual disillusion, and which culminate in the events in *Jack's Return Home*. His casual conquests, along with Audrey – a deadly serious one – make him vulnerable, a situation which Peter the Dutchman is quick to exploit. Their mutual loathing is explained, emanating from Jack's murder of Peter's former boyfriend. Peter revels in his sadistic handling of Jack's part-time squeeze, Barbara. Jack sees it coming, saying, 'I've seen that charm before and the crazy thing is I've seen women fall for it and regret it afterwards because when Peter can't pull a bloke he invites home a woman and takes it out on her by giving her lumps and bruises and worse.'

The story's opening scene would surface again, virtually complete and marginally more explicit, in *Jack Carter's Law*, suggesting the story was written with a second Carter novel already under way. It would be a full year between the Christmas edition of *Men Only* reaching the newsagents' shelves and the publication of *Jack Carter's Law*.

This was not a settled time for Lewis. He had effectively left a large part of his social life behind in Wicken and was, if anything, drinking more heavily. Fellow animator and friend from the *Yellow Submarine* days, David Elvin, had previously visited the Lewises at Wicken Bonhunt, and he and his family made the trip to Hill Farm. 'That place was bigger, more spacious. He had more money and he was drinking more than he was eating. I remember at breakfast, we had bacon and eggs and he had gin.' Mike Shucksmith had kept in contact and, on a visit to Framlingham, he and his long-term girlfriend, later his wife, gained an outsider's perspective on village life. 'I went out down the pub with Ed and there they were. One guy was a very talented artist and another woman – there was a gang of them – they were all alky, just what he didn't need, but I guess he'd found his level.' Shucksmith couldn't keep up. 'They'd meet up at half past ten in the morning. By eleven o'clock they were into their first round of drinks. I had the impression he was involved with one of the women. It was just sex, that's all it ever was with him. Bang, bang, thank you ma'am and back to the beloved. Jo didn't drink with him. She'd had the children then.'

The rigours of daily life, particularly the drinking, began to affect Jo. 'If he wasn't writing, we were living the sort of social life that was unbelievable. I got to the stage where I was thinking, if I can't beat him, join him. And I started drinking.' Every weekend there would be visitors, friends and others invited to the farm. 'It didn't last very long – I realised this was not a good way to be going on. Alun Armstrong was down several weekends with his wife, Sue, and I think he could see the way it was going and he stopped coming.' Armstrong's memory is sketchy, but he remembers each time he visited there would be an episode, a row of some sort. Lewis would be generous, thoughtful, making sure his guests were looked after. 'He had this very eclectic, broad spectrum of friends. There'd be guys coming to the house, people that he knew who lived locally, that they'd got friendly with and he would help them.' To all intents and purposes, he was the successful, urbane writer with his drink and cigarette in hand with his beautiful wife and children living in this lovely house. Armstrong says 'the reality was he wasn't living the dream at all, he was living a bloody nightmare of his own characters. He didn't have to think it up too much, he just drew on his own experience and stretched it.'

The television script *Thirteen Women* sees Lewis telling the story of a weekend visit by Mary Treece. The ages of the two children, 'Polly' and 'Daisy', are six and four, which points to the events taking place in autumn 1974. The full cast of Framlingham characters appear in all their intense, brooding, soap operatic glory. Victor Graves is having an affair with Diana Swales, the 'slightly plummy' horsy woman whose grey mare is named 'Minerva'; Vic's wife, Sally, might or might not be having an affair with Diana's husband, Malcolm. Entering the fray are neurotic Kate Greaves, her three children, her gay boyfriend, Alan, 'a sort of non-functioning gigolo-in-residence', and artist 'John Easton', driving his battered Triumph Spitfire. That October weekend's events place the remarkably unruffled Mary at the centre of a degeneration into booze-fuelled acrimony, from which only she and the children emerge blameless. When one of the souvenir dolls in Russian costume Mary brings the girls is accidentally left by the fire, Lewis invests the metaphor with a sense of their vulnerability. 'Throughout the night the heat from the inglenook has acted on the cellophane so that it has fused irreversibly with the costume of the doll itself. Complete ruination.'

When Polly and Daisy are playing at mummy and daddy, pretending to drink with an empty bottle and wine glasses, their conversation littered with 'Of course, darling' and 'Is that enough, darling?' Lewis leaves no doubt that he is aware of the damaging consequences of their seemingly continuous drinking sessions.

Jo would regularly come home from doing the school run and find him sitting at the table drinking with a friend or neighbour. Drinks bills were mounting. Lewis was struggling to meet the needs of maintaining Hill Farm and, it seems, to cope with the necessity of writing. Jo remembers, 'We had this incredible bank manager in London and Ted would go and see him so he'd allow us an overdraft. When the bank manager changed, the sky fell in.' Letters began to arrive. Lewis refused to see the bank manager and Jo made the journey to London. 'I had to tell the bank manager, this is what's happening, this is what we've got coming in. Until that point, I had no idea of how dire our financial situation had become.'

Lewis had made attempts to limit or cut down his drinking, at least he'd said he had. On one occasion he claimed he hadn't been drinking at all, but when his old friend Alan Smith visited for the weekend, Jo remembers, 'They were going out for a drink and I said, "Look, Ted isn't drinking, so don't encourage him." And Alan came back and said, "He is drinking, he's drinking vodka."' Much of the time Jo couldn't tell. 'I was very naive about Ted's drinking for a long, long time. Until it became really bad.'

The really bad came to a head at the end of 1974. Jo is reluctant to discuss details of the events that led up to her decision to leave, only that she had felt certain making the break would force him to confront where he'd brought himself, and the impact of his drinking and the behaviour that accompanied it on those he loved. Jo knew she dare not tell him she was going. 'I met the children from school and confided in a friend that I was going to my mother's with the girls and leaving Ted. When Ted got home from wherever he was and was totally drunk, he phoned Toby and threatened suicide.' Eady took the threat seriously and phoned the local police. They drove out to the house and, for his own safety, Lewis was sectioned and committed to St Audry's, a psychiatric hospital at Melton, some ten miles from Framlingham.

It is impossible to know what happened to Lewis in St Audry's. Only that he remained there for at least a week, later confiding his shock at finding himself committed. St Audry's is an imposing structure, its façade redolent of the archetypal

Victorian asylum. Whether there is any truth in Lewis's subsequent claim that he had been placed in a straitjacket is debatable. He seems to have spent his time observing all that was going on around him, reading people, deepening his mistrust of the psychiatric staff and confirming, in his own mind at least, that he knew more than they did. Throughout his time in St Audry's, Jo maintained contact. 'I talked to him in that week; he phoned me at my mother's. I got a court injunction to get back into the house, because it was so traumatic and I wanted to normalise the girls' lives. Sally had only just started school. She must have been nearly five.'

In 1970, when Lewis had written a scene in which the *Plender* character Peter Knott anticipates his wife leaving him, he wrote, 'To be on my own, now, would be unthinkable. The madness would spread through me and then there was no telling what would happen.' What happened was that Hill Farm was sold and Jo went about settling the family finances, paying off Hill Farm debts and ensuring Lewis had as little of the business and its attendant pressures to deal with as possible.

'There was just enough for me to put a small deposit down on a house in Monks Eleigh with the girls. All the bills were paid, except for an oil bill, which was about 300 and something pounds. The solicitor advised me to write to the oil company and tell them that so much would be paid off monthly, only a small amount. That was the only debt Ted had personally, because I knew the debts were weighing him down as well.'

In the midst of the chaos, November 1974 saw the hardback publication of *Jack Carter's Law*, a prequel to *Jack's Return Home* and the first time Lewis had returned to Carter in novel form. Featuring a handful of scenes from the 'Kings, Queens and

Pawns' short story, it was a punchy no-nonsense crime novel, distinctly Lewis, drawing us in through Jack Carter's first-person, present tense narration as he seeks out an informant in the Fletchers' organisation. Taking place mainly in London – a mention of the 1970 World Cup in Mexico suggests the events of the novel take place in the run-up to Christmas 1970, referencing the *Get Carter* film timeframe rather than the 1960s implied by *Jack's Return Home* – Jack's troubleshooting for the Fletcher brothers brings him up against a cast of crooks and crooked cops in the pay of the Colemans, Walter and Eddie, gangster brothers loosely based on Charlie and Eddie Richardson, a partial recycling from *Billy Rags*.

Writing a Jack Carter novel made clear commercial sense. Lewis was under severe financial pressure and, if new ideas were hard to find, it can't have taken a great deal of persuasion that Carter was the answer. Going back may have seemed like a retrograde step, but Lewis would have been drawn to working with a cast of characters he knew well, and whose voices were already established. Jo remembers he seemed to be reaching for something; what that was, she wasn't sure. She certainly didn't think he'd find it in Carter. 'I hated the fact that he was going back to Carter. I thought that was the wrong thing to do.'

Toby Eady recalls the distinguished publisher and editor Sonny Mehta asking, why had he allowed Carter to be killed in the first place? 'I said, "I didn't, but Ted did. It was finished, he was never going to write another one." Mehta said, "He could have written Carter, Carter, Carter." And I said, "Yes, but that's not his [Lewis's] character."' Eady remembers the writing process as anything but straightforward. 'The end of the year would be nigh and Ted wouldn't have written anything, and he would come and stay at my flat, and I'd lock him in and say,

"You can have a bottle of gin when you've done X, Y and Z each day." And he would.' As ever, Lewis wrote longhand in exercise books, annotating with doodles and captioned cartoons. The manuscript was typed with few, if any, subsequent alterations. Other times Eady tried to dry out Lewis, keeping a case of Mars Bars at his flat 'for the sugar'. Eventually, he says, Lewis would 'just get fed up with being on the wagon and go on a bender'.

Jack Carter's Law is among Lewis's most accomplished and complete pieces of crime fiction. The Sphere paperback added the bold back cover heading 'Bloody Christmas!' and boasted 'brutal realism, crackling tension and naked violence'. It wasn't kidding. Opening with a typically evocative piece of scene-setting, Lewis alludes to his own back catalogue, describing Plender Street as 'empty and lifeless except for the toffee papers and the newspapers and the fag packets'. Meanwhile, Jack Carter sits in his car and waits.

Jack Carter's Law plays out in a series of scenes in smoke-filled cars, rooms in drab terraced houses, dimly lit underworld nightclubs and seedy bars set apart from the workaday world. Until its final few pages, it is a book of astutely observed, almost fetishised interiors. Time and again Jack returns to the Fletchers' ostentatiously appointed penthouse apartment, featuring a sunken area with its 'all Swedish' furnishings and curtains 'that make a noise like paper money when you draw them'.

Blue movies and the people who make them are a key component of *Jack Carter's Law*. Lewis writes knowledgeably of the set-up: one man to operate the camera, one to pull the girls and package and deliver the goods to the Fletchers, all under the cover of a legitimate production company dedicated to making commercials. He draws heavily on knowledge of the semi-legitimate zones between the film and television world and pornography rackets – perhaps knowledge gleaned from conversations with Michael Klinger's associates. As he had in *Plender*, Lewis revels in exploring the marginal nooks and crannies of gay and transsexual life. Away from the public glare the 'queens' and 'slags' mix with underworld enforcers and pornographers, and the best place to find out what's really going on is Maurice's Bar.

Although there are references to Jack's and, by extension, Lewis's northern upbringing, one involving 'The asthmatic… who always sat beside me at Saturday morning pictures repeating the American phrases that glided from the screen,' there are strong southern inflections of voice that distinguish Carter in 1974 from the brusque Scunthorpe vintage of *Jack's Return Home*. Jack encounters Lesley, sometime walk-on TV actress and girlfriend of corrupt copper Hume. They meet at the Fletchers' club, 'Arabella's Stable', a loosely reimagined version of the Krays' Notting Hill club, Esmerelda's Barn. Lesley, he guesses correctly, is from Grimsby. Later, after a run-in with Hume, Jack drives her home. She asks how he was so sure about Grimsby:

'Because I'm from Scunthorpe.'
'Scunthorpe?'
'That's right.'
'You don't sound like it.'
'Well, that's the difference between you and me then, isn't it?'

Deprovincialised, Jack is somewhere between the Scunthorpe hardcase Lewis created in *Jack's Return Home* and the stylish Savile Row representation of *Get Carter*. As the story plays out, Lewis explores Carter's fallibility. The notion that he and Audrey will make sufficient cash to get away from the Fletchers and do so under their noses is exposed as delusional, particularly as

Jack plays fast and loose, risking all for a session with Lesley, tied to the bed with her own tights before he 'goes to work' on her. Consistently misreading the situation in which he finds himself, the final discovery of sexually compromising photographs of Hume which have been in Lesley's possession throughout, and which Carter can use as leverage to relieve pressure on himself and the Fletchers, comes by accident. Con McCarty is quick to remind him, 'This is really one for the *Guinness Book of Records*, this one. Jack the Lad. Shacked up with all we need to sort the situation and he doesn't fucking know it.'

The subsequent US edition of *Jack Carter's Law*, published by Knopf in 1975, would be retitled *Jack Carter and the Law*. The translation misses one essential reading of the title, that in Jack's world, his 'law' refers to the corrupt police he employs as well as the underworld 'law' he imposes and on which he hands out punishment.

Searching for original press reviews of *Jack Carter's Law* proved to be a largely fruitless task; they are absent from the original paperback edition which might have included them. Even Bertha Lewis's old scrapbook in which she had glued newspaper clippings of her son's early reviews has a space where *Jack Carter's Law* cuttings might have been. One surviving review from the *Carroll Daily Times Herald*, 'Iowa Book Shelf' section, drily summarises the plot, praises the author's creation of a 'realistic background of the London criminal element', but concludes that the book is flawed by 'explicit scenes of sexuality and overuse of four-letter words'. R Choate concludes, the book is good, but 'not recommended for those with squeamish stomachs'.

For the foreword to the 2014 edition of *Jack Carter's Law*, crime author Max Allan Collins wrote that it was 'tougher and more uncompromising than its famous predecessor'. He has a point. In London, Jack is up against some serious opposition which places Thorpey, Albert Swift and the Scunthorpe boyos in the shade. Only for the climax does he leave London, trailing a desperate Walter Coleman to the frozen fields of rural Suffolk for a killing in the surroundings of Hill Farm.

8

Prisoner
1975–1979

FROM MANCHESTER SHIPPING CLERK TO SERVICE in the Royal Air Force and 30 years as manager of Elsham Lime Works, Harry Lewis had always provided for his family. A respected member of the Barton business community, he was known as a quiet, modest man who smoked his fags, liked a pint or two, and enjoyed working in his garden and watching Manchester United on the telly. His son, by the time he was 30 years old, had achieved the kind of success and earned the kind of money which Harry, had he thought about such things, would have dismissed as fanciful. Now, at the age of 34, Ted Lewis was returning to Barton to live under his parents' roof. Recently discharged from a psychiatric unit, virtually penniless, almost certainly an alcoholic, with a failing marriage and daughters he adored left behind in Suffolk, there was nothing positive in the decision to move back home.

Those closest to Lewis are in no doubt coming back to Barton brought with it a sense of failure, made worse because he'd effectively compartmentalised his life. Now everybody knew the extent to which things were unravelling. He wasn't looking well, appearing gaunt and haggard. When he ran into Martin Turner, his old friend barely recognised him. 'He'd done that much drinking, he'd changed. He spoke to me and I had to think, *who's this?* It took a moment before I realised.'

Nick Turner admits he might have seen more of Lewis had it not been for the reputation that preceded him. 'I was busy, occupied full time with my own circle and it didn't include Ted. I would have wanted him to be a part of it for his sake, but not with what he was doing.' There's more than a dash of understatement when John Dickinson says it wasn't a happy time. In truth, Barton responded with indifference. 'He picked up with some old mates, but no one in the street would have known. He wasn't viewed as a great writer. He came back because he had nowhere to go.'

Dickinson did more than anyone to reintegrate Lewis, introducing him to his group of friends. The difference in him hadn't seemed so obvious in Framlingham, but back in Barton, Dickinson could see he was drinking far too much and the impact it was having on his health. 'It was difficult, but I did talk to him about it. The problem was, apart from the odd jazz club, if you wanted to go out, you'd go to the pub.' Lewis seemed to have lost any sense of optimism. 'He was sad that he wasn't seeing his kids. I used to say, "Get yourself sorted out and then you can get a relationship with your children." And he'd say yes, wouldn't he? And he'd be off in the Swan or wherever.' Alan Dickinson met him for a few drinks in Barton; they started in the Volunteer Arms:

'He was essentially the same person, but life had given him a few knocks. On the other side, he was very successful, so you got the two extremes. He was upset about the divorce, but then it was his own stupid fault that it came about. He couldn't understand how people couldn't accept his way of life to a degree, probably his brain was in his trousers at times. I don't think he could resist the temptation. He was always upset about it afterwards, but he still went ahead and did it.'

Booze had always been Lewis's way of overcoming shyness and bolstering confidence; now it played an essential role in loosening his inhibitions sufficiently to write. It's difficult to say for certain when social drinking drifted into alcohol dependence and addiction but, at some point between 1971 and 1974, alcoholism took a firm hold. There's no doubt Lewis knew he was trapped in a cycle of dependency for some time before others realised. Jo maintains it was as a result of the stress of mortgage payments on Hill Farm and the pressure of having to write the next book, always striving to live up to the success of *Get Carter*. Interviewing Lewis's friends, colleagues and associates, you realise the story was similar for countless graduates of the 1960s and 70s drinking culture prevalent in advertising, media and the arts. Gil Potter had drink problems, as did Keith Riseam. Neville Smith, who'd adapted his own novel for the cult British detective film, *Gumshoe*, released almost at the same time as *Get Carter*, found himself in a similar situation to Lewis. Brian Case paints a vivid picture of his friend's struggles with success. 'It looked good, but it knocked Neville off his feet, to the extent that he had to go into an alcoholics' ward. I can see how that can happen – too much success too quickly – like a pie in the fucking face. Obviously, Ted's decline took longer. It's hard when you've done it once and you don't again.'

And that was the point: Lewis couldn't seem to do it again. For friends like David Elvin, observing at a distance, the decline was difficult to fathom. 'I really couldn't understand it. He just wobbled. He had the writing, the TV work, but he faded. I lost contact with him when he moved back up north. Someone said to me, "Don't bother going to see Ted, he's not worth seeing at the moment."'

Lewis maintained contact with Jo and the girls. They spent the Christmas after the separation together, relaxed in each other's company for the first time in a long time. Jo remembers Harry and Bertha's absence came as something of a welcome relief. 'We never, ever – and I did used to resent this sometimes – we never had a Christmas, we never had an Easter, a Whitsun, a two week summer holiday without them. They were there all the time. At Hill Farm we'd be sitting by the window and they'd walk by and Ted would joke, "Here come doom and gloom."'

Living in the remote Suffolk village of Monks Eleigh, Jo was dependent on her car, a Mini. 'On one occasion, Ted came to see the girls. I wasn't working and he said, "Can I borrow the car for the weekend, I want to see Gil and Doreen?"' She hadn't realised he'd be drinking and driving. 'He was a shocking driver anyway. He turned a corner, the car went into somebody's garden and he didn't dare tell me.' Gil Potter phoned to explain about the accident. Jo was devastated. 'My car was a lifeline. I ended up having to get a job at a local factory because there was transport that stopped outside the house.' Doreen Potter remembers that weekend as the last time she and Gil saw Lewis. 'He asked if he could stay with us. He'd been up to see his parents and written off Jo's Mini. So he stayed for one night. He had a bottle in his pocket when he arrived. When I went to clear his room up there was the empty bottle.' For Doreen, it made it easier to understand the divorce. 'He was a very complicated man, difficult to live with. He had moods as well. I think Jo suffered a lot with him. When the divorce came, that didn't help him, and it didn't help him not seeing the kids.'

Lewis's second story for *Men Only* was published in March 1975. 'With This Song, Baby, It Don't Matter' is a violent and bloody tale of sex, drugs and betrayal. Stretching the bounds of credulity, the 'trek around Europe, a few deaths, more than a little intrigue and one very cool blonde' is entirely in keeping with the successful *Men Only* formula. In terms of its geography, the story was based on a trip Lewis and a group of friends had made to the south of France. Gil Potter's memory is of 'eight blokes, four in each car. A day down, a day back, a week there. Not many solids. It was total madness. We'd go over to Calais, put the cars on the ferry and straight to the bar.' The Potters moved to the Camargue around this time, living in the small city of Manduel for over 20 years.

'With This Song' opens with sometime private investigator and debt collector, Brian Armstrong, driving south on the raised stretch of autoroute through Lyons, musing that it is like 'being on a conveyor belt in the upper reaches of Hell'. Armstrong relates the circumstances of the trip and the task he has been commissioned to carry out, explaining that his paymaster, 'Toby', painted as a gullible, love-struck playboy, has sent him to keep an eye on his fiancée, 'Lesley', whom he suspects of being unfaithful with the mysterious 'Max'. On arrival, Armstrong encounters Lesley who, in Lewis's hands, becomes the archetypal *Men Only* 1970s fantasy stunner. His half-hearted interrogation is interrupted by the appearance of Max, evidently and stereotypically a gay man, with a white poodle and a 'half-caste' boy called René in tow. Armstrong and Lesley drive to a bar in Nîmes to get drunk. When they return, having picked up a local lad, Jean Pierre, Lesley invites Armstrong to bed. He considers his moral obligations to Toby, before concluding, 'I was pissed and I wanted to.' When Max and René return, Lesley follows them to the bedroom. Armstrong searches her car, discovering a stash of heroin she is smuggling for Max. In the morning, Toby arrives as planned. Armstrong fills him in on the details. Toby beats Max into unconsciousness, shoots the poodle, then dashes the dog's 'quivering and screeching' body against a stone wall. After a not altogether convincing reconciliation with Lesley, she drives them away with Armstrong following in his own car. He sees them stop to get rid of the drugs then, a few miles down the road, watches helpless as their car accelerates, veering across the lanes into the path of an oncoming tanker. The car explodes, killing Toby and Lesley in a 'sheet of flame'.

It's difficult not to read 'With This Song, Baby, It Don't Matter', at least on one level, as a blackly comic tale at Toby Eady's expense. For some time, Lewis had given friends the impression he felt let down, suggesting there were promises made that were undelivered. What they were, beyond wanting more money and greater recognition, isn't clear. Eady was spending more time in America, but maintains Lewis was well served. 'We looked after him, this agency did, particularly Nicola Boyle, because I was living in America then and going and coming back and forth, but he sort of cut off from everyone.'

On one occasion, shortly after his return to Barton, Lewis encountered his former headmaster, Norman Goddard, on the Humber ferry. Goddard made a comment about how gratifying it was to see one of his old students doing so well. Lewis could find nothing to say in response. If there was any doubt that the incident with Goddard continued to affect him, it was confirmed with its prominence in the 1975 novel, *The Rabbit*. The humiliation he'd endured, its injustice and consequences, continued to play on his mind, and coming home didn't make it any easier.

225

Initially, *The Rabbit* had been part of the burst of creativity that followed art school, the subsequent move to the West Country and then London. In late 1974, presumably in the wake of his return to Barton, encouraged by Toby Eady, Lewis returned to the drafts of the story, supplementing, updating and refining the narrative. Almost 20 years on from the events of summer 1956, he revisited his adolescence with frankness, omitting few of even the most uncomfortable details. He recalled the fights he'd picked, and invariably lost, that had reduced him to tears; the girls to whom he was cruel; the friends with whom he got drunk and fell out; the nature of the town, its people and the surrounding landscape. He brought fresh potency to the characters and conflicts of his youth through art student Victor Graves' story of a summer vacation flinting at the quarry managed by his father.

A comparison between the 1966 short story and the 1975 novel reveals how the intervening years had honed Victor Graves' outsider credentials. Lewis must have been reconciled to the fact that it would always be this way. There is additional bite and depth in the novel as Victor reacts against his parents' prudishness, his father getting undressed only 'after the light was out'. He reflects on the shame of his own sexual awakenings, discovered 'playing doctors' at the age of seven.

Central to the novel is Victor's awkward struggle for acceptance with the quarry labourer, Clacker, with whom he is paired at work. As the boss's college boy son, he is set apart. When Victor and his friends drive to a pub in an outlying village, they encounter Clacker and his mates, one of whom, Keith Phillips, had been in his class at school and witnessed the incident with the headmaster. (Lewis did have a friend at school named Keith Phillips, known as 'Glegger' or 'Clegger'. According to those who remember Phillips, he is painted rather unfairly here.) In *The Rabbit*, Phillips has never allowed Victor to forget the experience, which Lewis retells, locating the events in a classroom:

> The memory of the Headmaster slapping my face and the rush of piss shattering on to the classroom floor, uncontrollable because of my illness weakened bladder, the faces of the class as I staggered out of the classroom, the awed voices I'd heard discussing what had happened while I'd stayed locked in the toilets till everyone had gone home, the gauntlet I'd had to run at school the next day, the living down I'd had to do until the very last day at school.

Lewis's writing of Victor's painful, often self-inflicted, decline makes *The Rabbit* the antithesis of countless summer coming-of-age narratives. It might not have been what Michael Joseph expected from their gangster noir author. It was out of place in the contemporary market. 'They thought they were getting the guy who wrote *Carter* and, true to form, Ted delivered *The Rabbit*,' says Eady. Nevertheless, its earthy brutality and acuteness of observation made it one of Lewis's most accomplished pieces of writing.

In June 1975, three months before publication of *The Rabbit*, Harry Lewis died. He had been suffering from lung cancer, retiring from work a little over a year earlier. *The Rabbit* has the distinction of being the only Lewis novel to feature a dedication: 'for Harry Lewis'. Ostensibly a mark of respect – Lewis didn't otherwise bother with book dedications – the reasons for this one are far from clear, particularly given the novel's unsympathetic insights into Victor's home life and the mutually antagonistic relationship with his father. Jo's perspective is that the book suggests an affection between father and son. 'The thing that made me laugh out loud when I reread *The Rabbit* was the irritation with his father, and Harry would irritate him, deliberately sometimes.'

On an evening out with his father and Uncle Eddie, Victor is embarrassed by put-downs directed at him by Norman, a character they meet in the town's Constitutional Club. Victor's father gives Norman a 'what-can-you-expect kind of grin'. While the insult appears trivial, Victor finds it impossible to contain his anger at his father's failure to speak in his defence. He feels he has no option but to stand up for himself, realising, too late, that by rising to the bait, he has played into Norman's hands.

Old conflicts between father and son had inevitably been reawakened by Lewis's coming home at a time of ill health. Barbara Hewson believes Lewis wrote *The Rabbit* 'to show what he [Harry] was like'. There are those who believe Harry had resented Bertha's close relationship with her son, and that Lewis had been upset by his father's relationships with other women. 'The whole town knew it. It was hard for Bertha, but she had to accept it; there were reasons. Divorce was out of the question.' It is disquieting to think that Lewis chose the end of his father's life to lay bare the differences between them, although he must have known his father would never read the book.

Eady remembers *The Rabbit* sold particularly well on publication, in spite of a largely indifferent critical response. The review in the *New Statesman* on 19 September said disparagingly that the novel was 'all a bit of a ramble'. It acknowledged the 'convincingly reported talk of proles in the Scunthorpe hinterland and the chillingly accurate account of adolescent sexuality'. It was as if Lewis was wilfully out of time, revisiting the territory of Sillitoe, Storey and Braine. The cover claimed Lewis as 'author of GET CARTER', but the rural noir of *The Rabbit* bore no relation to the gangster novel, less still the film. The *New Statesman* reviewer concluded that, if you cared to 'wince along memory lane with shots of the Star flick-house manager bawling out troublemakers ('Seat yourselves in the proper manner') or the local 'erbert going in for coitus interruptus with a scrubber called Jean in Plaskett's coalyard, then Ted Lewis is your only man.' The *Guardian* review at least recognised the novel's virtues of pace, characterisation and local detail, all of which made it 'worth reading'. Taking a potshot at the blurb's description of the novel '"climaxing with... powerfully graphic scenes of sexual confrontation"', the reviewer suggests the writer 'hasn't read much recently'.

Taken as a whole, the reviews are disdainful of Lewis's working class, non-metropolitan narrative. As if the subject had been exhausted, a hangover from the previous decade. But rereading *The Rabbit*, there's a sense Lewis was exploring more profound tensions he and others of the grammar school generation were experiencing in escaping their roots. Education meant you would always be mistrusted, unaccepted by the working class; neither were you welcomed by the class to which you were supposed to aspire. Lewis knows there can be no way back; achieving your ambitions was no guarantee of acceptance. In 1956, Victor can still think of himself as 'the only one who had got away'. In 1975, the snared rabbit struggling hopelessly against Clacker's wire noose is an expression of Lewis's struggle to free himself from the constraints of his upbringing. He could no more embolden Victor to put the rabbit out of its misery in 1956 when the event took place, 1966 when he first wrote about it, or 1975 when its meaning resonated more starkly. 'I knelt down and tried to release the snare but I couldn't find the noose because every time I touched the wire the rabbit wriggled, like madness itself.'

In May 1975, Lewis signed with AC Theatrical and Cinema (ACTAC), an agency specialising in representing film and television writers. ACTAC would act for Lewis on issues relating to television and radio work in association with Toby Eady Associates Ltd, which would maintain control over Lewis's other writing.

With the agent Judy Daish working on his behalf, Lewis agreed his first commission for the BBC: a 50 minute script for the long running police drama *Z Cars*. A typewritten note on the commissioning brief from series producer Roderick Graham states that, 'As far as we know Ted Lewis has not written for television but is a successful novelist, one of his novels having been made into a feature film.' Lewis received the standard fee of £750 for the script, provisionally entitled *Prisoner*.

Z Cars had been the prototype gritty police drama on British television, bringing social realism to weekly crime stories located in the fictional Newtown, notionally on Merseyside. Devised by Troy Kennedy Martin and first broadcast in 1962, it had broken new ground as a hard-hitting, northern, issue-based drama, with realistic depictions of police officers at work and in domestic settings. Criticised by the Police Federation for depicting police characters with drink and gambling problems, and as perpetrators of domestic abuse, it set a sharp counterpoint to the affable and, by then, anachronistic beat coppering of BBC stalwart George Dixon and *Dixon of Dock Green*. Where Dixon was cosy, *Z Cars* packed a punch, using real life casebook stories to deal with contemporary issues.

Troy Kennedy Martin had developed the show with the help of documentary makers Elwyn Jones and Robert Barr. Its writers and directors were pioneers of British television drama, bringing working class language and experiences into millions of living rooms. Many would go on to direct landmark productions of *The Wednesday Play* and *Play for Today*; a handful moved into cinema, notably Ridley Scott and Ken Loach, who cut his teeth on uncompromising *Z Cars* episodes such as *Profit By Their Example* (1964).

By the mid 1970s, however, *Z Cars* had lost the vitality of earlier series. Its pre-eminence had been overtaken by harder hitting shows like Thames Television's *The Sweeney*. First screened in January 1975, *The Sweeney's* depiction of contemporary crime, policing and street violence owed a considerable debt to *Get Carter*. Naming its main Flying Squad characters DI Jack Regan and DS George Carter suggests someone had made the connection, although the show's originator, Ian Kennedy Martin, brother of *Z Cars* creator, Troy, has denied it was intentional. 'We would have seen it [*Get Carter*], but I don't think it affected *The Sweeney*.' He does concede that the show's writers, particularly Trevor Preston, may have been more influenced. (Preston would later collaborate with Mike Hodges, receiving a writing credit for his 2003 film, *I'll Sleep When I'm Dead*.) The parallels were evident to Lewis, especially as the first episode of the first series of *The Sweeney* featured Ian Hendry as Dave Brooker, a no nonsense villain, second in command of a violent criminal gang. There were technical similarities too: *The Sweeney* used a fast rehearse and record method; actors taking the script, rehearsing once in situ on set, then going for a take.

Although Lewis would have been better placed and more naturally inclined to write for the hard men of *The Sweeney*, he was in need of a credible route into television when *Z Cars* came calling. Produced by Roderick Graham and script edited by Graham Williams, Lewis found himself writing story and dialogue for characters he had not created; nevertheless, *Prisoner* featured characteristic autobiographical traits. It tells the story of prison escapee Billy Catlin, played by Keith Barron, a petty criminal who has escaped from prison one month short of his parole date. Holed up out-of-hours in an off licence, he coshes one of the show's regulars, Constable Alec Quilley, and takes him hostage. Catlin handcuffs Quilley to a storeroom rack, surrounded by cases of booze, cigarettes and Golden Wonder crisps. *Prisoner* director Derrick Goodwin remembers Lewis and the episode well. 'We spent many hours together getting the script in good shape. I was only recently out of the theatre as a director and Ted seemed to be a little puzzled by that, but we got on fine.'

In early drafts, Lewis's script had been over-elaborate, detailing shots and camera angles. With Goodwin and Graham Williams collaborating, Lewis delivered a tight, powerful script. Catlin's references to life in prison owed much to the source material Lewis had shaped for *Billy Rags*. He enlightens Quilley about life inside:

CATLIN: I'll tell you what it meant. It meant a stinking sweat from the billet above twelve hours a night. It meant staring at the brickwork to take your mind off what's beyond it. It meant trying to remember what your girlfriend's face is like. It meant staying out of the hands of the screaming puffs but at the same time not being able to get away from what they're up to... it meant thinking about nice boys like you as put me there.

In an atmosphere of mounting claustrophobia, *Prisoner* also alludes to Lewis's time in St Audry's Hospital, as a remorseful Catlin remembers, 'She always came to see me... I'd ask her, is it still the same?' As Catlin swigs from a bottle of whisky, his relationship with Quilley deteriorates. 'What was great about

Ted's script,' says Goodwin, 'was that it was more or less a two hander and that's always a challenge, and also very interesting as it reveals the characters much more than car chases and the usual cop shows.'

A feeble escape attempt by Quilley ends with Catlin, now drunk and unhinged, threatening him with a broken bottle. Quilley taunts Catlin, accusing him of being too drunk to finish him off, telling him he hasn't got the guts to go through with it. Lewis gives Quilley arguably the script's most insightful line. 'Soon as you leave here, the dream's over. It's back to reality. No more scotch to make the fantasy seem fact. It's all over.' Catlin grabs Quilley by the collar, forcing the whisky bottle against his lips and making him drink. Some goes down his throat, most over his uniform. He rolls onto his side trying not to be sick.

In the final scene, Catlin, in an 'alcoholic sweat', walks the streets on his way to Norma's flat. Police cars screech to a halt and Catlin is surrounded by uniformed officers. He begs in vain to be allowed to see Norma before being arrested. The officers lift him from his knees and put him in the back of a police car. For all his bravado, Catlin is wretched; a hopeless, self-destructive drunk. He stares through the car window, plaintively singing the words to Buddy Holly's *Oh Boy* to himself.

As Lewis rejoined the Barton social scene in the spring of 1975, he became a regular at parties within a circle that included a sprinkling of old friends. Among the new crowd were local artist Jill Baxter and her husband, mutual friends of the Dickinsons, whose children were members of the same cub pack. For them, Lewis was an unknown quantity. Jill remembers, 'We thought it'd be quite interesting because we'd get to meet the guy that everyone had talked about all this time.' After a few drinks, Lewis held court, telling stories and making people laugh. 'He was obviously quite *weathered*,' says Jill. 'It was clear that he was a drinker. He had that slightly swollen look to his face.'

Later, they met at a house party. People were dancing to Carly Simon's *You're So Vain*. 'Ted turned to me and said, "I see they're playing your song then." Obviously it was one of his chat-up lines – insult her and she'll become interested, that was his thing. He offered to lend me a book or something. I went round and his mum was there, and we had a chat.' Soon afterwards they began seeing each other clandestinely. They discussed moving away from Barton, but decided it couldn't possibly work, that it would be too unsettling for Jill's children. 'We were kind of on and off, should we do it or shouldn't we? In the end we knew we just had to.' The relationship was intense from the outset. 'That's the way he was and that's the way he liked things, but it's difficult to sustain, terribly difficult. I wouldn't go through that again for anything.'

John Dickinson felt his friend had let him down. 'I wasn't terribly happy about that, mainly because of the kids, they were at a vulnerable age.' He wasn't the only one to voice concerns. Lewis called Jo and told her he'd met someone; that she had three boys and he was thinking of moving in with her, what should he do? 'I said, "You've got two daughters. You've got massive responsibility." I hadn't got a car, I was working in a factory and I couldn't understand Jill taking three young boys into that situation.'

But Lewis's mind was made up. He found them a large bungalow at Theddlethorpe, near the seaside town of Mablethorpe on the Lincolnshire coast, an hour's drive from Barton. Isolated, with wide skies and mile after mile of sand dunes and the sea within easy walking distance, Jill remembers the bungalow, one of two set back from the main road into Mablethorpe. 'It had a large hall with glass doors – I think someone had been going to build a staircase up into the loft. To the right there was a large sitting room with a bay window that went down nearly to the floor, and a fireplace, and then there was a smallish kitchen, two or three bedrooms.' To minimise disruption to the boys' school year, it was decided that they'd wait until term ended in July before moving.

The children settled, seeing their father most weekends; but almost as soon as they began living together, Jill was faced with the worst of Lewis's insecurities. 'He would analyse everything. You couldn't make an innocent remark without him questioning it. "Why did you say that?" And "What did you mean by that?" It's hard to live with because sometimes you don't mean anything at all.' She acknowledges their happiness was short-lived. 'I was feeling really happy that we were together; probably in my naïve, idealistic way I thought it was all going to be lovely, and then realised it wasn't.' Lewis seemed resigned to the eventual letdown. 'He had that, it's all going to go bad, because it's wrong, way of thinking.'

If Lewis had moved to Theddlethorpe looking for somewhere to lose himself, he succeeded in doing precisely the opposite, finding himself drawn deeper into a self-destructive spiral. Visiting Theddlethorpe, it's not hard to see why. The wind whips relentlessly off the North Sea across a vast beach. The landscape is bleak and featureless. Mablethorpe out of season is the epitome of a worn and weary seaside town, shabby and poetic in equal measure. In winter, it feels like the end of the world.

Although Lewis was probably unaware, Theddlethorpe already had literary significance, featuring prominently in DH Lawrence's novel *Sons and Lovers*. As the nineteenth century railways had opened up direct routes to the seaside, each town or city decamped en masse, colonising a section of coast.

Workers and their families from Nottingham and Leicester had traditionally travelled to Mablethorpe. For Lawrence's Paul Morel and Clara, it was Theddlethorpe. Lawrence wrote, 'In the spring they went together to the seaside. They had rooms in a little cottage near Theddlethorpe, and lived as man and wife.' In the semi-autobiographical account of Lawrence's conflicted home life – the relationship with his father with whom he cannot see eye to eye, the mother who dotes on him, and the lovers who shaped his early years – the similarities with Lewis are inescapable.

Lewis got on well with Jill's sons. They played board games and he introduced them to the films of the Marx Brothers, which they adored. During the football season, they'd watch *Match of the Day*, sitting on the sofa sharing between them the enormous red and white Manchester United scarf Bertha had knitted.

Lewis was soon well known by the Theddlethorpe locals, playing darts in the King's Head, becoming friendly with the landlord and the local solicitor who seemed impressed by the writer in their midst. Less so the taxi driver who frequently drove him home and whom he rarely paid. Jill remembers going in for a lunchtime pint. 'We were both quite good at darts so there was a bit of competition between us. I think he liked being challenged.' Other times, usually late at night when he'd been drinking, Lewis contrived reasons for an argument, stirring himself to anger. Sometimes the exchanges became violent and Jill would be forced to fight her corner. 'I just had this sense of submission, because I couldn't do anything. If he lashed out, I would lash back.' Lewis was jealous of her past, anything that didn't involve him. 'I'd tell him he was being unfair, that it was irrelevant, and what about him? Was he so free of his past that he could go on about me? Then he'd say, "Perhaps you'd better get back to your husband, to your *perfect* husband who isn't flawed like I am." I never criticised Ted at all, he did that to himself.' When things became too bad, Jill remembers running out of the house. 'If the children were away for the weekend, I'd go down the road and sit on a wall until I was ready to go back. It was a horrible time really. There were highs when we were laughing and just having a great time, then there were lows that were just deeper than deep.' Typically, after one of these episodes, by the time Jill went home, Lewis would have fallen asleep. Sometimes he found reserves of energy that kept him going long into the night. She would lock herself in the spare bedroom. In the morning he would be contrite, ashamed. On one occasion, he tore off a dress Jill was wearing, which he had bought her, and threw it on the fire. 'Afterwards, he said, "Why am I doing this to you when you've been so good to me?"'

Lewis had been drinking hard since his art school days and showed no signs of stopping. He was increasingly losing control. On one occasion, Jo asked would he look after Nancy and Sally during the school holidays? 'I had to keep this bloody awful job and I rang him to ask if he could come for half term so that I could go to work.' Lewis arrived in Monks Eleigh on the Friday night. He saw Nancy and Sally tucked up in bed, then went to the pub. Later, Jo heard a terrible row outside. She was incensed; they'd only just moved to the area:

'Ted was in the phone box having a colossal row with Jill. I got him out and I was really angry and said to him, "You can't ruin our lives here. Nobody knows anything about us." And he was so drunk that I had to ring Bob, who lived in Felixstowe, and tell him to come and please take Ted back. Bob drove him home to Theddlethorpe the following morning.'

Prisoner was screened on BBC1 on 19 January 1976. It was high drama for a show that went out at twenty past seven on a Monday evening. Lewis was already working on a second *Z Cars* episode, *Juvenile*.

Lewis developed a bond with many of the people he worked with on *Z Cars* and was particularly close to Graham Williams, his script editor. Williams was also a heavy drinker. For some time, he had been working on a concept for a series of one-off plays themed around a contemporary reading of GK Chesterton's *The Club of Queer Trades*, a series of stories about the members of 'an eccentric and Bohemian Club', the condition of membership of which lies in the candidate having 'invented the method by which he earns his living'. The members were not to be purveyors of the 'mere application or variation of an existing trade', and the trade must also be a 'genuine commercial source of income, the support of its inventor'. Early in 1976, Williams was given the go ahead as executive producer to commission scripts for the new series to be called *The Zodiac Factor*.

The series concept underwent further development, presumably with Lewis involved. He was being considered as one of the writers at the initial stage and it seems clear the *Queer Trades* idea had been discussed at length during conversations Lewis and Williams had whilst working on *Prisoner*. Williams had *Plender* in mind. He sent the novel out to BBC readers for comments under the misspelled heading 'PLUNDER', adding that he was hopeful for its 'inclusion in the Zodiac programme, with Lewis adapting'.

As a blackmailer setting up honey traps in gay clubs, by turns manipulative, nasty, violent and frequently in the pay of shadowy right-wing politicians, Brian Plender was an ideal candidate for membership of a contemporary Club of Queer Trades. The BBC commissioning brief went out in June 1976 with the intention to screen each of the 12 plays under a generic title sequence, produced, transmitted and sold overseas as *The Zodiac Factor.*

Lewis worked on the script at the bungalow in Theddlethorpe or at the bar of the King's Head throughout the summer of 1976, writing drafts that were sent, or taken by Lewis if he could get a lift, to a secretary in Lincoln for typing. His writing continued to be the one thing he could, on occasion, be optimistic about and he was happy with the work he produced. There remained, however, a simmering resentment, particularly about *The Sweeney*, which Jill remembers him watching. 'They've taken all my fucking ideas' was a familiar refrain on Monday nights at 9pm. 'He was furious about them using *Jack* Regan and George *Carter*. He felt it was obvious and it made him cross.'

Life settled into a pattern, with Lewis eating little, drinking slowly through the day, and then building up at night. Jill remembers each day had low points. 'He'd be miserable around four o'clock in the afternoon before the pubs opened and just sit around in his chair, staring at the telly. Then the first drink, six o'clock down the pub again and he was fine.' He made occasional trips to London, but found the convoluted train journey interminable. He seemed especially uneasy when he had meetings with his publishers, or at the BBC. Consequently, he drank more. On one occasion, an invitation arrived for the *Z Cars* wrap party. Jill accompanied Lewis to the distinctly glamour-free affair in a draughty school hall in west London. There was a table with buffet and drinks, but they spent most of the time with *Z Cars* actor James Ellis and his wife. To the viewing public, Ellis's much loved character, Bert Lynch, was the series' moral centre, providing continuity between 1960s and 1970s incarnations. In truth, he'd had his own problems with drink. Lewis wanted to know how he had coped.

At the party, Lewis was witty and engaging, but he had been drinking heavily. The trip is remembered in 'Mrs Lewis's diary', an occasional journal Jill had begun to keep for her own amusement. Inspired by the *Private Eye* spoof diary of Mary Wilson, wife of then Prime Minister Harold Wilson, between the lines of Jill's pastiche of Mrs Wilson's prim prose and bad poetry, there is, she admits, a frank and faithful account of their lives together. Lewis thought it was funny. 'It was true, it was about our lives.'

She jokes about their plan to stay with 'nice Mr Dumplings' – as yet unaware of their intentions – 'as we can't risk his being off on urgent business to Alaska, like the last six times we asked to be put up'. Missing the train, waiting six hours at Market Rasen, then 40 minutes at Newark in a waiting room 'full of morons and young conservatives', Lewis opened the wine they'd bought for their host. There are more drinks on the train and a pub crawl which leaves them worse for wear before arriving at the party:

> I can't say I enjoyed it tremendously – perhaps because Edward got the idea it was the 'Sweeney' party and became rather aggressive. Indeed, he had to be forcibly removed in the end, fighting and yelling: "Haven't you got <u>any</u> original ideas, you bastards!" The poor partygoers looked most agitated. Bert Lynch even woke up momentarily. What with that, and throwing up over the food table and yelling "Stuff Z Victor one!!" at the producer, I feel he may be jeopardising his chances of writing more scripts.

After a failed attempt to hail a cab in Acton High Street, Jill describes Lewis, patently worse for wear, taking his frustrations out on the staff and customers at the 'Mambasi Take-away'. As usual, I ate my sausage and chips and Edward threw his against the nearest wall.' She finishes the entry with a description of a phone call from Jo on their arrival home. 'His ex-wife has now phoned and I answered by saying he was out, to which she replied, "Where *is* he then?!" She seems to be becoming increasingly angry and I think I am starting to understand why.'

Behind the humour, the episode is indicative of the kind of chaos into which Lewis's life was descending. Alcohol fuelled unpredictability, often ending in argument and occasionally a 'punch-up'. On one occasion he became angry with a friend who he felt wasn't treating his wife very well. Things came to a head at a party at the bungalow. 'Ted just punched him and knocked him through the front door. They were okay afterwards. Geoff said, "I shouldn't have been treating Maureen like that, you're quite right."'

Often he was overcome with remorse, knowing his life was out of control and unable to help himself. 'He would cry about things sometimes. Really, really cry and say, "I've messed up my girls' lives, I've messed up your life." He'd be really upset. If I tried to console him, he'd say, "Shut up, what do you know about it? What can you possibly know about what I'm feeling?" He'd be angry you were trying to understand. Once he got a letter from Nancy and it was really sweet, because she was obviously missing her dad and it upset me a little. He said, "What are you crying for? You don't know what it's like."'

Published by Michael Joseph in June 1976, *Boldt* marked a significant departure for Lewis. Boldt is a member of a corrupt police department in an unnamed American city which his brother, a presidential candidate, is planning to visit during a forthcoming election campaign. While checking security for the visit, Boldt finds out that one of the country's top hitmen

241

has checked into the town's best hotel, and then uncovers a connection between him, the Mafia and the local police.

Even by the standards Lewis had already set, *Boldt* made a feature of pulpish reductive sex, racist characters, misogyny and overwrought homosexual and black stereotypes. Borrowing from the reactionary extremes of the later *Dirty Harry* films for its tone – it feels as though this could be New York or San Francisco – *Boldt* is a short step from pastiche. Lewis, by his own admission, had never visited America and admitted that *Boldt* was a response to watching the deluge of US cop shows on British TV. *Ironside, Kojak, Cannon, Shaft, Starsky and Hutch, The Streets of San Francisco* all had regular slots in the first half of the decade. Lewis had never been afraid of writing men who were bastards, but with Boldt and his partner Murdock he took the signature tropes of an orthodox hardnose cop to extremes.

While acknowledging the racism, sexism and homophobia are impossible to ignore, or to accept, it's possible that *Boldt* was written as Lewis's riposte to MGM's blaxploitation reimagining of *Get Carter*. A thoroughly nasty revenge job. There's no doubt he was bitter about the film and Mike Hodges has spoken in unfavourable terms about the deal which saw his film gutted, reimagined and, in his view, cheapened. With *Boldt*, Lewis turns the tables. There's a suggestion of wordplay in the title: *Bold T*. Otherwise, with its silent 'd', it seems an odd spelling. This was Lewis testing himself against modern American crime fiction writers, possibly inspired by Douglas Fairbairn's 1973 macho thriller *Shoot*. In attempting to cover unfamiliar ground and dragging out 1970s cop show clichés, Lewis sacrificed the most powerful elements of his writing, that of the sense of people living real lives in believable worlds. His interpretation of American English is only partially successful, patched over in places with false notes and banalities.

Nevertheless, *Boldt* received a sprinkling of positive reviews. *The Scotsman* acknowledged the introduction of the 'genuinely tough new US cop partnership of Boldt and Murdock', and said the book was 'Good value from Mr Lewis'. The *Daily Record* concluded that the novel featured 'wit, cynicism and steamy sex in a powerful mix'. John Roberts in the *Derby Evening Telegraph* applauded a story 'as uncompromisingly blunt as the title'. The *Times Literary Supplement*, published on 23 July, was more considered, acknowledging Lewis's aim in shifting focus from British gangsters and places he knew well to American cops. 'Ted Lewis has taken on Mickey Spillane on the latter's home ground and has gone the full distance with him. The pace is as fast, the sex as explicit, the action as brutal and the characters as vicious as anything in the original. But the novel has lost the individual note of Ted Lewis's earlier works.'

By the time *Boldt* was published, Lewis's creative focus had shifted further towards writing for television. It's likely he began writing the *Thirteen Women* script around this time. Possibly as an attempt to place the experience of Framlingham and Hill Farm in some kind of context, and to revisit the debt he owed Henry and Mary Treece. There is no record in the BBC archive of it having been commissioned, so presumably it was written to pitch to BBC producers. It's interesting to speculate on what they'd have made of Lewis's social satire of a darkly comic, proto-*Abigail's Party* for the rural arts and drinking classes.

Lewis delivered the *Plender* script for *The Zodiac Factor* at the end of September. The manuscript was faithful to the novel, each scene described with visual and aural clues. The opening sees Plender, in a scene reminiscent of the opening of *Get*

Carter, viewed behind glass. Behind him, two men dish out a savage beating to a third. Plender is detached, indifferent to the violence taking place a few feet away. Lewis, retaining the novel's autobiographical undercurrents in a series of flashbacks, depicts themes of pornography, sex, deviance, deception and blackmail unambiguously. It would have been a radical piece of television had it satisfied BBC censorship rules and made it to production. Peter Knott's regular visits to Peggy's gay bar, Camille the 'drag artiste' and the underlying sordidness of Plender and Knott's pornographic world were, in terms of television drama, ahead of their time.

As a novelist, Lewis had formidable visual craft. At his best he wrote lean, focused scenes with tough imaginative dialogue. But the *Plender* script is overlong, written as if only for reading, rather than as a basis for dramatic presentation. Unable to remove himself as author of the source novel, *Plender* is the clearest evidence that Lewis would have struggled to write a feature length script for *Jack's Return Home* in 1970 without considerable latitude from Klinger, Caine and Hodges. Impractical if not impossible, given the pressures of production.

By the end of 1976, Lewis's relationship with Jill was all but over. Once again broke, he confessed to Jill they'd been living on loans he had no hope of paying back. He declared bankruptcy in order to begin again, riding out the stigma attached to being insolvent, accepting it as part of the inevitability of living his chosen lifestyle. Jill admits she had to take a deep breath and begin her life again with nothing. She applied to social services and received money to feed her children for a week. 'I got a waitressing job in Mablethorpe. My solicitor said I was better off staying in the bungalow even though I couldn't afford the rent. You were allowed to do that for six months.' They met once more while Jill was still at Theddlethorpe. A mutual friend was throwing a party and Lewis took a taxi from Barton determined to see her:

'My friend Janet, who knew what Ted was like, said, "I think you'd better go upstairs to one of the bedrooms if you need to talk." So we went up and he was really drunk and it just got really, really bad. I actually managed to drag him into the bathroom – he was getting quite violent – I dragged him into the bathroom and put him into the bath and turned the taps on. I came downstairs and said to Janet, "I've put Ted in the bath and turned the bloody taps on him!"'

They realised Lewis was dangerously drunk and called an ambulance. He was taken to hospital, at times incoherent and, in more antagonistic moments, telling the nurses to 'fuck off!' 'In the end, Janet drove me to the hospital and he calmed down a bit. I stayed with him the rest of the night.' Lewis went home to Barton and Jill tried to rebuild her life, taking out an injunction to prevent Lewis from seeing her. 'I knew it was never going to get anywhere if we carried on. I found another place, at Marsh Chapel, nearer to Grimsby. I couldn't take any more. I don't think he had any notion of what loving somebody really was, that it wasn't just falling in love, it was caring afterwards and I don't think he had any idea of that at all.'

In the years following the *Get Carter* film release, Lewis came to despair of achieving similar success. When he returned to Jack Carter once more, it was almost certainly motivated by money. *Jack Carter and the Mafia Pigeon*, published in May 1977, is the least successful Carter novel. Arguably, it is Lewis's most insubstantial piece of writing, achieving barely more than fulfilling his Michael Joseph contract for a book in 1977. On publication there was little fanfare and there are no records of contemporary reviews. Nor, does it seem, was there much of an effort to create publicity.

The lacklustre handling carried into the presentation of the text itself. The novel patently needed an editor's and a proofreader's eye. Toby Eady's claim in a 2009 BBC Radio interview that Lewis was the only writer he ever handled who 'hardly needed editing' falls flat with *Mafia Pigeon*. The book cries out for input from someone willing to tackle its deficiencies. Perhaps Michael Joseph were simply satisfied that Lewis had produced a manuscript. Clearly, no one thought it worth reading closely. Aside from structural and narrative weaknesses, there are numerous proofing and typesetting mistakes; parts of the text are missing; words are misspelled or wrongly typed, suggesting Lewis's secretary had misread his original handwritten draft. In the few samples of Lewis's handwriting in BBC documents, there is a clear deterioration around this time. Either way, it seems no one gave it that much attention.

Jack Carter is the novel's narrator. Given its not entirely clear place in Jack's timeline, *Mafia Pigeon* notionally precedes *Jack's Return Home*. It builds on the narrative threads of *Jack Carter's Law*, including the relationship with Audrey and the antipathy between Jack, Peter the Dutchman and Con McCarty, once again arriving to rescue the plot in the final act. But it's almost inconceivable that the character is the same cold killer of 1969 vintage. His voice, littered with mockney dialogue, is more Michael Caine as Charlie Croker than original Jack Carter.

The novel sees Jack despatched to Majorca by the Fletcher Brothers, ostensibly to take two weeks holiday at their villa outside Palma. On arrival he finds himself babysitting

D'Antoni, a former Mafia operative hiding out under the Fletchers' protection. The villa is housekept by ex-con Wally Lomas, retained by the Fletchers to handle their distribution of pornographic movies from Majorca. Via a swathe of backstory, exposition and pages of static dialogue, Jack discovers the true nature of the trip.

Lewis constructs a series of stereotypes: the Brits abroad brothers from Dagenham with matching Ford bomber jackets and frigid wives; the boozing Spanish cab driver; and Wally Lomas, the cringing 'sewer rat' functionary, are never far from central casting. With the arrival of Wally's art student daughter, Tina, closely followed by Audrey, bringing orders from the Fletchers that Jack is to execute D'Antoni, the novel degenerates from bedroom hopping farce to its inevitable bleakly comic shootout. There are cheap shots at the expense of 'yanks' and 'cockneys'. Jack baulks at being called a 'cockney craphouse' – 'I was born in Lincolnshire, friend, not London'. The sex is joyless. Jack and Audrey's on/off affair amounts to mutual loathing, drunken fucking and beatings, often in the same act. When Carter refuses to do a 'topping job' on D'Antoni, Con and Pete arrive in Majorca to finish him. Matters come to a head at the villa at a late night screening of 'Schoolgirl Rape', one of the Fletchers' pornographic movies Wally stores in the basement. Audrey has brought the Dagenham boys back for a party. In a self-conscious imitation of *Jack's Return Home*, Wally realises that one of the film's female performers is his daughter.

Underpinning *Mafia Pigeon* is the basis of what might have made a good story. In its underlying theme of transatlantic linkups between 1960s London crime firms and the Mafia, the novel has its roots in real events. John Pearson's *The Profession of Violence* describes a meeting between the Kray twins and Mafia representatives in London as early as 1964. When Ronnie Kray travelled to the USA in 1968, Pearson writes, 'Tommy Cowley, one of the shrewdest members of the Firm, had decamped instantly to Majorca.' Later the Krays would hatch a plan to eliminate a Las Vegas gambler and club owner staying over in London as a way to impress their Mafia connections. *Mafia Pigeon* had tapped into the idea of 'hands across the ocean' relationships, but had done so with a novel reminiscent of a Confessions movie knockabout.

Rereading *Mafia Pigeon*, it's fair to assume that Lewis was thoroughly sick of Jack Carter. He needed the money and would have expected the Carter name to add to sales, but it feels like a book too far. *Jack's Return Home* had imbued Carter with a degree of dry wit. Here he is boorish, misanthropic and, frankly, a bit of a mug. The novel is a padded, pulpish throwaway that guaranteed Lewis would never be asked to write another Carter book, which begs the question, was that his intention? It concluded the deal with Michael Joseph. For the first time in almost a decade, Lewis was without a publisher.

Written by Ted Lewis, *Juvenile* was the final episode of *Z Cars'* twelfth season, broadcast on 5 July 1977, nestling in the schedule between *Sykes* and the *Nine O'Clock News*. The episode told the story of two teenage lads. English student 'Barry Hooper' lives comfortably with his family, listens to Elton John records, and has a steady girlfriend, Janet. 'Ronnie Burnett' is a ne'er-do-well. When he and Barry bump into each other in the record department of an electrical shop, they clearly know each other. As the *Radio Times* synopsis explains, 'While Barry Hooper was in the record shop either a shoplifting was attempted or it wasn't; he either saw it or he didn't; and either he was involved, or he wasn't. So he's either being very loyal to an old mate, or very, very cocky.'

The underlying message, repeated by PC Fred Render throughout the episode, is that the kids these days are 'frightened of nothing'. Hooper acts the innocent, apparently drawn into the criminal activity of his wayward friend, and Ronnie is arrested. Inspector Lynch recognises that Ronnie is being manipulated and attempts to persuade him to inform on his mate. Ronnie refuses.

With the newsagent 'Pop Doughty' and references to film and family, Lewis plundered his past for story and character, although here he creates an almost parallel universe in which character traits are the opposites of their namesakes. In spite of the arrival of Ronnie's mother at the police station, an archetypal working class woman with dyed hair, wearing an overall and smoking a cigarette, it's clear that Ronnie will be charged based on Barry's statement. It emerges that Barry is at the root of the trouble. His university bound, middle class exterior is an act; he dupes his parents and everyone else, boasting of his 'natural born brilliance'.

Juvenile doesn't have the sharpness of script of *Prisoner*; neither does it have the dramatic intensity of the central relationship between Billy Catlin and PC Quilley. The Barry Hooper of *Juvenile* is a Plender-in-waiting, a manipulative sociopath conscious that Ronnie Burnett, a working class lad easily manipulated, will be written off as a shoplifter and a thief, because that's what the police assume working class lads do. Barry knows his friend will go to prison while he and Janet will continue their scam.

At home again in Barton, Lewis was living with Bertha, waiting for the pubs to open. For a while, his local had been the White Swan on the corner of Butts Road and Fleetgate, run by former Hull FC rugby league centre three quarter Colin Ali – Ali later changed his name to Colin Mountain. When Ali wasn't around, Lewis began an affair with his wife, the pub's landlady. When Ali found out, he gave Lewis what one friend described as 'a bloody good hiding'. The bruises were visible for some time afterwards. Lewis started drinking in the Red Lion.

Shortly after morning opening time he'd take his place, usually at the end of the bar with a notebook. Some days he seemed in a world of his own, making it patently obvious he wanted his own company and a couple of quiet pints. Jack Compton had just left the army after 22 years. Between jobs for a few months towards the end of 1977, he spent his lunchtimes at the Red Lion. 'If Ted didn't want to talk to you, he'd acknowledge you and that was it, you couldn't get anything out of him at all. If he was in the mood and wanted to talk to you it was "Oh hello, Jack, how you doing?" He didn't so much have a conversation with you, he questioned you.' After a while, Lewis began to open up and the themes were familiar. 'He said, "I sold my book. I got robbed." He'd lost a lot of money out of it, he reckoned he didn't get what it was worth. Once he spoke about his ex-wife. He said, "It wasn't her fault, it was mine."' Often Lewis quizzed Jack about his time in the army. 'Everything was a question with him. I'd been to a lot of places and he wanted to know what it was like there, what happened there.' He told Jack he wanted to write something local again.

After Jack started work at Hall's Barton Ropery early in 1978, he saw Lewis less often. But when he did, he noticed a difference. Lewis had been living with a schoolteacher who lived on Priestgate. Jack lived a few doors down. 'I'd pick him up when he couldn't stand. Some nights he was really bad; drunk, crying and banging on her door to be let in and she wouldn't let him in. Then he'd try to walk off and he couldn't make it, there was this wall, it was only two or three feet high; he'd sit on it and fall off.' For the ex-soldier, no stranger to a night on the beer, witnessing Lewis's decline was shocking. 'It was terrible to see a bloke in such a state, cryin' and askin' for help, it was pitiful. He'd gone, he was in turmoil. I think Sue threw him out at the finish, she couldn't take it anymore.' It seemed to observers that Lewis was reaching a stage where he didn't need to drink to excess. Jack recalls, 'he'd have a pint or two in the pub at lunchtime, then go home, just topping himself up all the time. His mother went through absolute hell. "I live with me mother," he'd say, and that was it.'

Throughout this period, Jo did her best to ensure that Nancy and Sally had time with their father. They had little, if any, sense of the chaos of Lewis's life. When Jo took the girls to Barton to stay with their grandmother, somehow Bertha managed to ensure all was as it should be. Nancy has fond memories of 'Mr Kipling cakes and pots of tea, all laid out very nicely with doilies'. Bertha had cashed in her not inconsiderable accumulation of Embassy cigarette coupons for a silver tea service. Always made up, dressed smartly with a large handbag and court shoes. There were cabinets of fine china and ornamental cats. Nancy remembers an air of formality about the visits. 'She used to have these special Pyrex cups with ornate holders and she'd make us a milky coffee in these cups. Very fancy. It was wonderful for us, we felt like we were at a tea party.' By nature, Bertha was a worrier and having her son at home didn't make life any easier. 'She wouldn't relax,' says Nancy, 'even when she watched television, she'd sit up straight. There wouldn't be feet on a sofa or a footstool; she'd be sitting properly.'

Lewis entertained his girls, making up characters and telling stories. He'd send them beautifully illustrated birthday cards, usually featuring cats and comics he'd drawn, in which they were the characters. Nancy remembers one about a flying bed. 'It must have been in the days of *Bedknobs and Broomsticks* and we were the two girls in the flying bed going about having adventures.' When Sally showed an interest in ballet and began taking lessons, Lewis took the girls to see the Nutcracker at the Gaumont in Ipswich. 'There were elements of our childhood which he thought about and did things which he thought we would like.' Sally remembers a picture her father sent. 'It's sort of poster sized and it's of Frankenstein's monster with a haunted house in the background and me as a six-year-old in my nightdress just holding Frankenstein's hand and it says, "A little midnight walk." And I'm perfectly happy and smiley in the picture with my teddy under my arm.'

Often they spent time together by the river. Bertha made the girls' breakfast and Lewis would have his fried eggs on toast and a cup of tea, then take them to the Humber Estuary, a place he clearly loved. 'We'd talk about the river,' says Nancy:

'At that time the bridge was being constructed, and we would talk about this feat of engineering that was going into building the bridge, but it was just such a massive expanse of water. I just remember it was obviously quite a special place for him – somewhere he loved to go back to. He was funny and he'd make us laugh. He'd tell us funny stories, just make things up and we'd sit and listen.'

On occasion, Lewis took the girls into Scunthorpe. After home and the rolling fields of Suffolk, this was something different. 'We'd go into the arcades, or into these terrible cafes and have egg and chips. It was loud, exciting.'

Terms of the visits changed after Jo found out Lewis had been looking after the girls whilst drunk. As she told Paul Duncan in an interview for *Crime Time* in 1997, 'After about our second year of actual divorce, he was having the children at his mother's house. I found out that he was drunk in charge so the visits became more supervised. He would come up to Ipswich and stay in a hotel with his mother, then the children would go to see him. I had to make sure the children were safe, you see.'

By the time Lewis was commissioned to write a third *Z Cars* episode for what would be the show's final series in the summer of 1978, the producing and script editing team of Roderick Graham and Graham Williams had moved on. On *Driver*, Lewis worked with Simon Masters as script editor and Ron Craddock as producer.

This time script development was more problematic. On 6 April 1977, Masters wrote to Lewis expressing concern that he hadn't received a response to an earlier letter outlining 'various points' in Lewis's original draft. Craddock wrote to Masters on 25 May outlining further changes he wished to see, mainly in developing existing conflict within the police ranks and creating a more 'tidy ending'. Craddock writes that he has also taken out 'the odd swear word' and 'unnecessary camera direction'. On 9 June, Craddock wrote to Lewis with a copy of the *Driver* script he and Simon Masters had discussed, hoping that nothing more would need doing. BBC files include two pages of typed comments signed by Lewis, sharpening detail, with Craddock's annotated comments.

Unusually for *Z Cars*, whose episodes were mostly standalone, pressure for each script to weave several storylines towards a satisfactory conclusion for the final series meant a succession of changes to scripts. On 3 August, Simon Masters wrote to Ben Travers as Head of Copyright to inform him that, given further rewrites, which amounted to 25 pages of a 140-page script, the production team thought Lewis should be paid an additional fee. At the end of October, Masters wrote to Lewis to confirm final dialogue changes. He also wanted to let him know he had read the copy of *The Rabbit* Lewis had given him, that it was, in his opinion, a 'fine novel', and that he looked forward to ringing Lewis, as it had 'awakened in me things I should love to discuss'.

Masters effectively signed off the script for *Driver* in a letter to Lewis, dated 16 January 1978, in which he acknowledged that Lewis may have been 'saddened by things that have had to go'. He emphasised it had been 'purely a necessity of timing' and goes on to say, 'I love this script – always have – and greatly look forward to seeing it made.' Masters invited Lewis to director Terrence Williams' initial read through at the end of February and hoped he was able to make it, as Masters was to leave the BBC the following day.

Driver was the first episode in the final series of *Z Cars*, transmitted on 28 June 1978. The arrangement of the traditional theme, *Johnny Todd*, which had been given a lame cod-funk makeover for previous series, reprised the 1960s original. It was a good sign. Lewis was writing the kind of story at which he excelled. *Driver* was darker, grittier. The *Radio Times'* synopsis is typically Lewis: 'Even though Eddie Dancen is an ex-con, he and Quilley are next door to being mates. But Eddie has some information about a major crime and that can put a big strain on friendship.'

The story saw Eddie Dancen, now working as a cab driver, drawn into the world of George and Sammy Armstrong, brothers and underworld operators looking to defend their turf against a London gangster and purveyor of porn magazines and blue films, Joey Goldner. When the body of a dead villain is found in Newtown and investigations make the link to one of Eddie's fares – two dodgy customers 'from the smoke' – the ambitious Detective Inspector Madden orders Quilley, now transferred to CID and promoted to Detective Sergeant, to apply pressure. Quilley knows repeated contact with the police places Eddie in a precarious position. When Eddie's plea, 'I don't see, I don't want to see' falls on deaf ears, he turns to drink. Quilley's disillusion reaches new depths when he has to pull Eddie in for questioning a third time. DI Madden conceives a scheme to draw the Armstrongs into the open, letting them know Eddie has 'gone QE' (Queen's Evidence). He waits for the Armstrongs to act.

Driver set the tone for *Z Cars'* final series and the work that went into sharpening the script makes the most of Lewis's story. The writing is precise and the central characters more credible, particularly Quilley. Joining the series as a breezy beat copper in 1969, played by Douglas Fielding, Lewis invested him with a worldweariness and a neat line in sardonic asides. Between them, he and Eddie Dancen's everyman cabbie draw out the moral dilemma. In the final scenes, we see a frightened Eddie preparing to go on the run. He tells Quilley, 'It's either you or them, I don't know which is worse.' In the last shot, Eddie is alone, waiting on a bench in the dark, his suitcases by his side.

Taken in the round, Lewis's collected *Z Cars* episodes give an insight to the parts of his life that preoccupied him in the mid 1970s. *Prisoner* is the story of a frightened, lonely man, drowning in whisky and self-pity with a dark past and a darker future. *Juvenile* updates the tone of *The Rabbit* and revisits backstory scenes reminiscent of *Plender*. *Driver* sees Lewis refocusing on what he does best in the convincing portrayal of life on the fringes of the provincial underworld – the chewing up and spitting out of small men in the face of ruthless ambition.

The appointment of Lewis's friend, Graham Williams, as series producer for *Doctor Who* in 1977 came with the clear direction that he was to bring a lighter tone to the show after the successful, but ultimately controversial, stewardship of Philip Hinchcliffe and Robert Holmes as producer and script editor. Complaints from influential campaigner Mary Whitehouse that *Doctor Who* was unfit for children had brought to an end one of the programme's most successful periods. Williams' brief was to make the programme less violent and more humorous.

For what would become the sixteenth series of *Doctor Who*, Williams brought Anthony Read on board as script editor. Keen to make a series with a running theme, echoing the Saturday Morning cinema serials of their youth, they devised the concept of the Doctor's search for *The Key to Time*. 'We wanted to give it a serial element,' says Read, 'something that hadn't been done before. Creating a quest to run through an entire series appealed to us as adding that extra element.'

The idea of commissioning Lewis came from Williams who knew him from *Z Cars* and liked his writing. Read knew of Lewis's novels and admired his skills as a storyteller. The approach typified the producers' aim to broaden the scope of *Doctor Who* writers. 'We were bringing in new writers who had been successful in other fields or other areas of TV. I suspect that Graham and Ted had hit it off personally as two of a kind – both were heavy drinkers bordering on alcoholism.'

They called in Lewis for an initial chat at the end of 1977. The meeting went well. Read liked Lewis's 'dry northern humour' and his professional approach. Lewis was invited to write story outlines for four 25 minute episodes for the *Doctor Who* series, initially titled *The Doppelgangers*. Read and Williams had the idea of turning the Robin Hood story on its head. 'Graham thought Ted might be a good bet for such an approach, but it was more tricky than it sounds, because the general ethos of the series, like most drama, always favoured the rebel, with the authorities as the bad guys. We worked out a basic storyline with Ted, and he went off to develop it.'

Lewis submitted the outline, then a detailed breakdown. In Lewis's storyline, the Doctor and his assistant, Romana, would encounter Robin Hood in their search for the fourth segment of the key to time, but would discover that the 'hero' was, in truth, a sinister villain. On that basis, Willams formally commissioned Lewis to write the four part script for the series, now retitled *The Shield of Zarak*.

Read remembers that the main problem dramatically with Lewis's story was that Robin Hood inevitably became the central character and was fundamentally unsympathetic. 'This may have worked okay in *Get Carter*, where there are virtually no sympathetic characters, but it didn't work in *Doctor Who* terms, where you need to have a hero – apart from the Doctor himself, of course.'

Ron Burnett received a weekend visit from Lewis around this time. He had fallen for one of the production secretaries on *Doctor Who* and brought her to York to meet Ron and Judy. Ron's memory is that Lewis and the girl, a devout Christian, went for a walk by the river – Ron and Judy's home is a short walk from the city near the towpath of the River Ouse. 'Within 15 minutes she came back and asked when was the next train back to London?' Ron went outside and found Lewis 'sitting red faced under a tree, grumbling to himself'. After Lewis had gone home, Ron found an empty Martini bottle under the bed. He was still going to the bar, getting a round in and having 'a couple of snifters' while he was there. Still trying to keep it a secret. 'If we were having a meal,' says Ron, 'he'd very carefully just have one glass of wine, then drink afterwards'.

Through the summer of 1978, Lewis worked on at least one major rewrite of the *Doctor Who* script, looking to overcome the difficulties with tone and narrative, but in Read's opinion Lewis's story 'never really gelled'. It seems obvious in hindsight, but Lewis was the wrong writer for the show at the wrong time. He wasn't a particular fan of *Doctor Who* and found himself unable to capture the show's highly individual style. He was by no means alone. Other writers hit the same trouble. 'It's a strange, jokey, semi-sci-fi/science fantasy style which is extremely difficult to grasp,' says Read. Lewis's creative imagination worked in a different way and what emerged was not a *Doctor Who* script. 'It was just too tough and realistic. I don't remember the exact details, but we tried to steer him back onto the right track until we were forced to decide that it could not be rescued by any further rewrites.'

The script meetings took place in Read's office in Threshold House, an anonymous block of offices half a mile down the road from BBC Television Centre on Shepherd's Bush Green. At their final meeting, Read told Lewis they wouldn't be using the scripts:

> 'We parted on friendly terms, with me commiserating with him and accepting some of the blame for selling him a bum steer in the first place and not succeeding in guiding him out of the hole he had dug himself into, scriptwise. Nobody likes firing a writer, and on the few occasions I had to do it, I always did everything I could to soften the blow by explaining exactly why, and reassuring him or her that it didn't mean they were a bad writer, just that it hadn't worked this time.'

Read is at pains to point out that, contrary to some versions of events, he has no recollection of any problem over delivery dates and deadlines; neither was Lewis drunk at their final meeting and thrown out of the BBC. Graham Williams was in on their final decision and was equally sympathetic. 'Naturally,' says Read, 'Ted was a bit glum, but by no means suicidal, more resigned to the situation, though after a few drinks in the pub he probably became a touch bitter.' Lewis made his way to the Bush Hotel, their regular post-meeting watering hole, and spent some time in the bar loudly slagging off 'that bastard Tony Read'.

Because Lewis had put so much work into the scripts, Williams arranged for his fee to be paid. Issues with payment dragged into 1979. Lewis's financial dealings, never wholly conventional, had depended on maximising his BBC income. The UK tax regime was tough; many freelancers incorporated, forming companies to take advantage of lower rates of tax. The Channel Islands operated as a tax haven, but the only way to access funds was by going there in person, drawing out cash and bringing it back into the country in contravention of the currency exchange laws. Tony Read remembers Lewis, like many others, 'making regular trips to collect hard cash'. On one return trip from Jersey or Guernsey, Lewis carried 'a neat leather attaché case packed with bundles of banknotes'. As Read says, 'a real *Get Carter* touch'.

On 11 January, Williams wrote to Ben Travers, Assistant Head of Copyright, to outline the position regarding Lewis's final payment. He confirmed that episodes one, two and three were delivered but not accepted. There was no record of the fourth script. Williams' letter states that the decision not to proceed had been agreed mutually by Lewis and Anthony Read. Ben Travers wrote to Emmanuel Wax at ACTAC explaining that he had authorised a final payment for the rejected scripts. Rights to the work reverted to the author. Travers' letter has a handwritten note with a ring of finality: 'TED LEWIS – WRITE OFF'.

The myth which emerged around Lewis's non delivery of the

Doctor Who scripts, that he'd arrived at the final meeting drunk and been shown the door by Read and Williams, never working for the BBC again as a result, seems, in all likelihood, to have emanated from Lewis himself. At the time, producers and editors were largely autonomous, able to commission pretty well whoever they wanted, without restrictions, budgets permitting. 'There was never any blacklist,' says Read, 'or even a preferred list.' For Lewis, always highly self-critical, perhaps it was preferable to have been rejected for being drunk and unmanageable than to have been seen to fall short as a writer. Read isn't convinced a successful *Doctor Who* script would have had much effect on bringing Lewis's work to a new audience. 'It wouldn't have been an original, personal piece of work, simply part of a long running series.' That said, with viewing figures peaking at just over ten million for the series, it would have been a significant achievement.

In truth, this clouds the issue. Lewis was never a BBC writer in the traditional sense. As the television drama pioneers of the 1960s had moved into film, or earned the creative freedom to write and direct on their own terms, Lewis's brand of dark, deviant intensity was rare. Reading BBC correspondence between creative and executive staff about commissions, contracts and payments, reveals a structure which is intractably hierarchical, in which craft and creativity are subservient to the Corporation's public service ethos. That isn't to say that individual writers, directors, and producers weren't able to work against the grain, only that the appetite for breaking new ground, particularly in long running series, was measured and controlled. With *Z Cars*, particularly *Prisoner* and *Driver*, Lewis navigated a route through the process, creating a handful of the most sympathetic characters of his career; although, as some of the rewrite notes show, his language, tone, and novelistic structure meant that he was steered towards a safer middle ground, never wholly able to subsume his natural flair for noir. The *Doctor Who* format of the era wouldn't accommodate his ideas and Lewis could only compromise so far.

In 2011, I met Jonathan Holloway who had adapted and directed *Jack's Return Home* for the stage. The Red Shift Theatre Company production which toured extensively in 2005 was titled *Get Carter*, its source undeniably Lewis's novel, rather than Hodges' film. Holloway gave an insight into the way the film and TV business had worked in the 1970s, explaining the demarcation between the Oxbridge educated BBC establishment which, with a few exceptions, rejected anything they considered low or vulgar or difficult; and, in sharp contrast, those 'down in Soho' in the independent film and television industry who skirted the fringes of criminality – Michael Klinger's Soho blue movie connections are a case in point. ITV and the home grown film industry had long had links with the criminal fraternity, never more so than in the late 1960s and early 1970s. Holloway explained how the cars that picked you up – 'the transport' – tended to be owner/driver Mercedes 'driven by blokes you know have a past' and recalled the 1970s National Theatre strike, largely instigated by 'Bermondsey families which managed the backstage scene shifting'.

Lewis did good work for the BBC but, in essence, he was a writer whose instincts were independent, almost always testing the boundaries of what was acceptable. The BBC had demanded compromise and he had produced to the best of his ability. Perhaps there was a desire for the respectability that working for the BBC conferred, but it's easy to imagine how much better a writer he'd have been for a programme like *The Sweeney*, or writing original standalone crime dramas. It was his turf. He'd more or less created the blueprint.

9

GBH
1979–1982

AFTER THEDDLETHORPE AND JILL BAXTER, WITH the exception of a handful of short-lived affairs, Lewis lived with Bertha in her terraced house on Ferriby Road. By 1979, it was clear this was a permanent arrangement. 'At AA, they refer to it as doing a geographical,' says Keith Riseam – a reference to the alcoholic's longing for the comforts of home and familiar people and places. Lewis's routine revolved around writing and pub opening times. Lunchtimes and evenings he could be found drinking and playing darts in one or other of the Blue Bell, the Volunteer Arms, the George, the Red Lion or the Coach and Horses. If the mood took him, he'd knock out a tune on the piano, reportedly entertaining the locals on occasions with an impromptu rendition of the funeral march.

Among his circle of friends was Brian Jickles, a former quarry worker who had known Lewis as a young man. Jickles invited Lewis home for drinks after the pub. 'I know what the attraction was – the wife. Ted was involved with her. She ran off with a policeman in the end and left me with the three kids.' Lewis called several times a week to ask was he 'going for a jar?'

But it was never just one. After a pint, he would drink spirits, usually gin and bitter lemon, which he called the 'drink of the gods'. With his drinking mates there were few demands. Jickles says, 'if there was somebody you could take the piss out of, you would do.' In such easy company, Lewis was able to relax into that version of himself that was one of the lads, even if his accent set him apart.

He seemed interested in those people he'd known in his youth, asking what had happened to this person, or where had so-and-so ended up? When Jickles had problems with the Inland Revenue, he turned to Lewis for advice. 'I told him I'd got the taxman on my back, and they were coming for all my furniture. Ted said, "I'll buy it off you, if it's mine they can't take it."' Lewis bought the furniture. When the bailiffs arrived, he and Jickles were waiting. 'We had a piece of paper that said it had all been signed over to him for 20 quid – filing cabinets and desks and a standard lamp, odds and sods. Ted wasn't going to let them take it off me.'

Lewis's own financial situation wasn't a great deal better. The subject was a source of discussion with his doctor, John Ball, then a senior partner at the town's Central Surgery medical practice on George Street. Shortly afterwards, Dr Ball, an avid local historian and collector, put forward the idea that Lewis might like to make drawings of photographs he'd recently bought of Barton during its Victorian and Edwardian heyday. Lewis was glad of the commission and they agreed a fee of £100 for the 18 drawings.

His skills as an artist had never been in question. Usually that meant a short notice birthday card or caricatures of friends and locals in the pub. His numerous letters and cards to Nancy and Sally often included drawings and comic strips, and he'd recently sent Nancy a drawing from a children's cartoon he'd been working on called *Ackroyd's Yorkshire Dragon*. The Barton drawings were the first paid artwork he'd undertaken in years. Initially, progress was slow, a little too slow for Dr Ball's liking, but the work was detailed and demanding. The results confirmed Lewis had lost none of his ability. His fine pen and ink interpretations of the original photographs were typical of his best work. They recalled Barton's golden age, a characteristic Englishness, and said much about Lewis's affinity with the town and its people. Dr Ball later donated the drawings to Barton's Civic Society. They remain in storage, occasionally released for public display or exhibition.

Between commissioning and completion, Dr Ball had spoken with Tom Nicholson, manager of Hall's Barton Ropery, about Lewis's need for work. A Scot with a reputation for running a tight operation, Nicholson agreed to offer Lewis a position. The Ropery had been a fixture in the town for over 150 years; its mix of skilled and semi skilled workers often had family ties to the company, some of which could be traced back to the nineteenth century. The morning 'buzzer', a steam hooter, sounded out across Barton for clocking on time at the beginning of each working day; and the distinctive smell of Swedish tar, applied to waterproof ropes in much the same way as they'd been waterproofed since the Napoleonic Wars, carried on the breeze from Waterside. While it's safe to assume Tom Nicholson would have offered Lewis an administrative job, rather than the hard physical labour demanded of the men who worked on the ropewalks, he would certainly have struggled with the routine. Nothing more is recorded about his response, other than the offer was turned down. It seems Dr Ball had been unaware of the extent of Lewis's drinking when he offered him the commission and sought employment on his behalf. He maintains that Lewis hadn't been an alcoholic, and 'only drank a couple of pints at lunchtime to enable him to write'. A partial truth, no doubt; but if one or two drinks freed him to work, many more made him incapable of doing so. Drink inhibited his writing. It also made finishing a piece of work inordinately demanding. By the spring of 1979, Lewis had begun to show signs of serious ill health. There was little indication that he had the motivation to complete another book, let alone write anything as vital or ground breaking as the novel that would materialise.

In a stubbornly resistant market for crime fiction generally and an indifference towards Lewis's writing specifically – *Boldt* had failed to out-dirty Harry, and *Jack Carter and the Mafia Pigeon* barely bothered to conceal its cash-in-on-Carter rationale – the novel *GBH* found Lewis, perhaps for the first time since *The Rabbit*, writing on his own terms. He made sound decisions, the first of which was to bring the story home. It seemed to re-energise and reauthenticate his voice; making Grimsby, Theddlethorpe, Mablethorpe and the Lincolnshire coast his backdrop reawakened the instinctive feel for texture, landscape and atmosphere that had worked so effectively a decade earlier in *Jack's Return Home*. Exploring his own psychological and emotional disintegration in a crime novel was brave and inspired.

George Fowler is a London gangster and pornographer hiding under an assumed identity in a bungalow at Theddlethorpe on the Lincolnshire coast. The story alternates between present and flashback sections – 'THE SEA' and 'THE SMOKE' respectively. In the Smoke, someone on his firm has been skimming profits and he sets out to nail the offender. At the Sea, he is alone and abandoned, scarred by betrayal. He retreats into an interior world, confronting his past, dependent on drink and with an almost certain foreboding that he will not survive. Within this structure, Lewis sets up a series of oppositions, often in short, brutal scenes: then and now; drunk and sober; sane and insane; loved and bereaved. Smoke dissolves into Sea as Fowler reminisces about his wife, Jean, present only in memory through the Sea passages. Lewis invests a fearless autobiographical truth in Fowler's decline. Like Fowler, he was living more and more in his own mind.

Opening at night as a 'dry light wind ripples softly across the coastal plain... bound for the sand dunes and the shuddering brittle grass', the setting is purposely opaque, remote and unsettling. The location is the real life bungalow Lewis and Jill Baxter shared in 1975–76; however, the fictional version is designed to its owner's unique specifications, featuring a safe and under-garage cellar where Fowler stores boxes of pornographic movies. Fowler wanders aimlessly through the streets of Mablethorpe, drifting through an out-of-season purgatory of pub, café and arcade. Lewis perfectly captures the seediness of the place and its off-season cheapness. Nothing here is quite as it seems: the South Hotel faces north, and the town's faded grandeur is described in 'colours which are brilliant but never quite primary'.

Fowler reads the sports pages of the *Daily Express*. Spurs' impending relegation to the old Second Division places us in the spring of 1977. The story is derived from that period and the end of the relationships which, for Lewis, defined it. The assumption is that Jean Fowler is a cipher for Jill Baxter, and while there are similarities – Jill recognises some of the clothes in which Lewis dresses Jean as her own and there is, she acknowledges, a vague physical resemblance – she maintains the comparisons end there. She admits to never having finished the book. 'It wasn't for me.'

Taken at face value, the relationship between Fowler and Jean at the heart of *GBH* is a rarity for Lewis, existing outside the realm in which brutality, business and sex are one and the same. Their love is founded on murder, exploitation and mutual corruption, but it is love. Lewis gave the relationship an edge, exploring the darkness at the hearts of two deviant souls, sparing nothing in spelling out the consequences. Psychosexual thrills are so vividly taken to their limits, you'd be forgiven for thinking the author had experienced them on some level. In fiction, there were no safe words for Lewis who had once told Jill Baxter, 'There's nothing I haven't tried.'

An initial interrogation scene, with curtains drawn and blankets against the curtains to muffle sound and block out light, induces an erotic thrill in Fowler. He detects a whiff of Jean's perfume as she moves quietly to his side. The victim, a middle aged functionary, Arthur Phillips, is questioned, humiliated, and then tortured. Fowler uses the language of industrial dispute – unions, workers and conveners – in trying to find out which members of his firm have broken ranks. Arthur says he knows nothing. Fowler instructs his associate, Mickey Brice, to go to work. The scene, which shares aspects of events described in the Richardson brothers' and Frank Fraser's 1967 court case, is remembered by noir author, Jake Arnott. 'I was re-reading the part in *GBH*, where he's taking the guy's trousers down – you don't need any description of the nastiness – you *know* it's sordid, nasty.' The bucket of water and bare wires hanging from the light socket tell the rest. Phillips is tortured to death. In the aftermath, Fowler and Jean return to their penthouse apartment. Jean demands, 'Do it to me now.'

As drink and deepening paranoia govern Fowler's actions in the Sea scenes, he walks repeatedly along a path which leads, through gorse, marram grass and sand dunes, to an immense featureless beach used as an RAF gunnery range. Burned-out tanks and obsolete military trucks dotted around the beach are all that give the panorama any sense of scale; otherwise there is only a vast expanse of sand, a distant sea and seemingly infinite sky.

During a 1994 BBC interview, the poet Allen Ginsberg spoke of a 'hallucinatory' experience which resulted in an eight-month stay in a psychiatric hospital. Ginsberg attributed the breakdown, in part, to contemplation of 'the endlessness of the skies'. Spend time on the beach at Theddlethorpe and it's easy to imagine how Lewis's walks sparked similar shifts in perception and reflection. He used them to full effect, prompting Fowler's thought processes. 'As I walk towards the tank, I walk alongside the undisturbed footprints of my journey of the previous day, and the day before that, and as I walk the thoughts I have are the ones that remain from previous journeys, and will continue to haunt me.' The experience is dreamlike. The tank never seems to come closer. The sequence concludes with one of several passages in which Lewis's own voice emerges from behind that of his character. 'Consider a man like me and love,' he begins, then writes about the butcher who slaughters animals and the men responsible for Hiroshima who are loved; those who planted the bomb at the Abercorn rooms are capable of love. (The 1972 paramilitary attack on a Belfast city centre restaurant killed two diners and injured dozens more.) Finally, he questions his own love for Jean, why is she *the one*? He calls it 'obsession'. He recalls how Jean had been married, awaiting her errant husband to return to finalise a divorce. When Jean is reconciled with her husband, Fowler arranges a car crash and the husband is killed.

GBH is a savage valediction for that breed of smart suited working class gangster who had all but disappeared by the late 1970s; and, by association, had consigned the writer of novels about them to relative obscurity. The Richardsons and Krays had been in prison for nearly a decade, their firms scattered and their most telegenic lieutenants making a living by way of talk show appearances and hard case roles in film and television dramas. The Soho vice squad, once the infamous 'dirty squad', so-called for their propensity to take a share of the dirty money that followed blue movies through Soho and out to the provinces, had to a large extent been cleaned up. *GBH* offers a self-destructive coda for that generation.

Others were thinking on similar lines. In production as Lewis was writing, *The Long Good Friday* would prove to be as prescient as *Jack's Return Home* and *Get Carter* in its anticipation of a decade of pitiless self-interest. First shown at the London Film Festival in November 1980, it tells the story of London gangster Harold Shand, played by Bob Hoskins, later dubbed the 'cockney Edward G. Robinson' by *Newsweek* magazine. One of the old school, Shand is an East End guv'nor who runs a string of semi-legitimate enterprises. He's on the up, seeing himself as part of a new future; a freewheeling, small-scale capitalist, patriotically doing his bit for England and looking to the American Mafia to finance a deal to buy a tract of London docklands.

Barry Keeffe's script, originally titled *The Paddy Factor*, was directed by *Play for Today* stalwart John Mackenzie. As Klinger and Hodges had done a decade earlier, Keeffe and Mackenzie sought to make a gangster film of contemporary relevance. Hodges' examination of provincial corruption and criminality was superseded by a face-off between Thatcherite gangsterism and political extremism. *Get Carter* gave us Newcastle, pornography and the dodgy practices of Poulson and T. Dan Smith; *The Long Good Friday* anticipates a land grab and carve up of the old East End. Shand, though he doesn't know it, represents the past. The future is unfettered capitalism in the shape of the London Docklands Development Corporation and its City political connections. All of them outplayed by the cause of Irish Republicanism. Shand and George Fowler are similar, men of their time, impotent in a world in which they no longer function.

In the past, the gang boss was king. In *GBH*, the business of running Fowler's firm and managing the blue movie operation in his absence falls to the unscrupulous lawyer, Morville. It's fair to assume the character is a version of James Morton, the solicitor who'd brought the McVicar deposition to Toby Eady. Fowler sets out the details, the minutiae of the business of blue movies. He runs eighty four agents. Each agent has a thousand clients who pay £10 to renew a film once a month. Added to which, there's the law with a ten per cent take – in this case, the law is represented by a hardnosed careerist policeman, Parsons, who is angling for a seat on the board. Morville, to whom Fowler turns as his empire begins to show cracks, is a slick corporate shyster. That he betrays Fowler hints at the possibility that Lewis harboured similar feelings towards Morton, conceivably in relation to the *Billy Rags*/McVicar arrangement. Either way, Lewis seems to have been in the business of settling scores.

The introduction of Bertega, a high end operator dealing in more extreme pornography, gives Fowler the opportunity to draw Jean more deeply into his world. In one graphic scene, Bertega screens the snuff movie kidnap, torture and murder of an Italian industrialist. Expounding his theories on the place of the viewer of pornography, there is a distinct change of register, and another instance of the author's voice growing louder as Fowler's recedes. He writes, 'It is impossible to satiate the voyeur... he needs a continuation of innovatory corruptions and humiliations ...' Fowler accepts that he and anti-pornography campaigner Mary Whitehouse share common ground in that 'The process itself is corrupting: that is why she is in her business and I am in mine.' He concludes in almost Ballardian terms, citing the voyeurs of disaster, 'motorway pile ups', 'plane crashes', 'massacres' and 'public executions', that people are either corrupt or corruptible, and it is hypocritical to believe otherwise.

Lewis exerts a powerful narrative control in *GBH* that had been notably absent from *Boldt* and *Mafia Pigeon*. The Sea and Smoke stories converge and collide; threads of plots and cleverly worked subtexts, themes and motifs interweave and tie the story together. When Fowler has Jean's husband murdered, an innocent girl passenger in the car is also killed. Their bodies are burned beyond recognition. Later, when Fowler destroys tanks rolling across the landscape in an arcade game, there is no sense that it's any more than a way to kill time. Sometime afterwards, when he witnesses the death of a girl he has been following in a car crash on the Grimsby road, the psychological stakes are raised. Each step brings Fowler irrevocably towards his own reckoning.

Of all his novels, *GBH* most effectively makes the case for Ted Lewis as a great writer. More so even than *Jack's Return Home*. He writes with an acutely observed sense of time and place and, in Fowler's story, there lies an intuitive and insightful study of what is real and unreal; of fear, guilt, loss, and the corruptive power of violence, sex and pornography. Ending with a version of hell, fire and torment, it is as violent and final a conclusion imaginable.

In an echo of John Johnson's reaction to *Jack's Return Home*, the 'blackness' of the novel disturbed Toby Eady. 'I remember when I first read the manuscript of *GBH*, I said, you've got to meld this down a bit, because it's not going to get published. It's too claustrophobically violent in people's minds. I think he'd reached that point in his own life when he wrote the book.' It's something about which Nancy Lewis has given much thought. 'Physically he must have been in the worst condition when he wrote *GBH*, in the depths of alcoholism, it's astounding. In a way that's part of him, isn't it? You can't hide it.'

In February 1980, *GBH* was published straight to paperback by Sphere with minimal publicity and barely any subsequent attention from reviewers. It was the first of Lewis's novels not to be published in hardback. It seemed the time for Lewis's brand of crime fiction had passed. The book was not well handled in an editorial process which allowed errors to slip through; proofreading and typesetting oversights compounded factual mistakes: Lewis's description of the burned tank's blackened cannon as it 'points out to sea in a metallic parody of Drake's Childhood' is something of a false memory, perhaps a reference to something remembered from art school. Almost certainly Lewis is referring to Millais's *The Boyhood of Raleigh*. There are, in the first and second editions, fragments of sentences and paragraphs missing; an uncorrected 'To' which should be Two; a 'firm star' who should be a film star. There are almost certainly others.

An interview with journalist Nick Cole of the *Scunthorpe Telegraph* on the eve of publication gave scant insight into Lewis's thinking. His answers to Cole's questions seem polite enough, but tired, little more than stock responses he'd given before. The interview, which took place in Lewis's study at Ferriby Road, focused more on *Carter* than *GBH*. Lewis told Cole he thought *GBH* was the best book he'd written. He chain-smoked throughout, mentioning that his agent was considering a proposal to film *Plender*. Asked about the location shift of *Jack's Return Home* to Newcastle, he said he was disappointed. 'Scunthorpe as a town is very interesting with its steelworks, one main street in the centre and the rows of Victorian terrace houses I thought would have made a dramatic backdrop for the film. People are accustomed to seeing violence played out in spectacular locations.' He reeled out often repeated lines about Carter the antihero and his redeeming sardonic humour, his cynicism. He supposed the time had been right for Carter, but that his time had passed. 'Since then, there have been so many spinoffs like *The Sweeney* that everybody knows all about the underworld.' He was keen to point out that *The Rabbit* had sold as many copies worldwide as the Carter novels.

At the conclusion of the interview, Lewis spoke about a book he was working on. Provisionally titled *Other People's Houses*, it told the story of four South Humberside families from 1864 to the present day. The novel, Lewis said, would focus in particular on four children born at the outset of the Second World War. It was intended to be a major piece of work. He had a publisher, and a prospective publication date of 1983. He posed for a photograph at his desk, smartly dressed in white shirt, tie and V-neck sweater, cigarette in hand. His collar length hair is neatly brushed. A collection of spiral bound exercise books is spread across the desk. Between a stack of script files and a desk tidy, hardback editions of *Jack Carter and the Law* and *Jack Carter and the Mafia Pigeon* line up alongside Len Deighton's *Close Up* and Douglas Fairbairn's *Shoot*. In a cubbyhole in the writing desk, a clock reads 3.20pm. The scene is a staged local newspaper staple of the writer at work. When I showed the photograph to Jill Baxter, she recognised the look in Lewis's eyes. 'He'd look at you like that and say something really cutting. He could get you to do anything, just by looking like that.' There is something sad about the photograph. Imagine that January Monday afternoon, the light fading, the struggle to write given over for the day; the book he considers his best work is about to be published and he has been quizzed about a novel published a decade earlier.

For a writer as habitually self-critical as Lewis, it must have hit hard. Cole doesn't recall Lewis as having been drinking that afternoon, but you suspect the deeply felt need to do so must have been on his mind.

Writing in the *Guardian* in 2013, Kate Worsley described *GBH* as Lewis's 'kinkiest, nastiest, most moving novel by miles'. It was, she wrote, 'your genuine east coast noir'. It is a terrifying book, zeroing in on a single location, a man burned by guilt and obsession, and the beginnings and end of madness. From the little Lewis said at the time, it seems *GBH* was intended as a farewell to crime fiction, at least for the time being. What he hoped to kill with the novel's jarring dénouement were characters like Jack Carter and George Fowler. In taking his work to an extreme of violence and deviance, killing Fowler's wife, Jean, by horrific torture and decapitation, mining his own struggles with drink, depression, and the darkness into which it led him, he had exhausted himself. As a genre defining novel, *GBH* would have been difficult to surpass. Novelist and Lewis long-time admirer David Peace has acknowledged the influence of George Fowler's psychological decay in the internal monologues of Brian Clough (*The Damned United*) and Jack Whitehead (*The Red Riding Quartet*). Novelist Stuart Neville has written that Lewis's 'shadow falls on all noir fiction'. In a 1998 edition of the magazine, *Crime Time*, the introduction to a 1991 German language edition of *GBH* by 'the master of the black novel' and Lewis's former fellow Hutchinson new author, Derek Raymond, was reprinted in full. Raymond writes that *GBH* 'is a novel as direct as it is stunning… which never relaxes its grip for a paragraph'. He concluded that Lewis was 'an example of how dangerous writing can really be when it is done properly'.

As far as we know, Lewis drank when he wrote. He certainly did at Theddlethorpe, the last time we have any reliable witness to his working practice. The clarity of purpose and technical adeptness of *GBH* raises the question: did he temporarily find an abstinent space to write each day? If not, the achievement is all the more remarkable.

As I worked on *GBH*, researching its biographical context, bound up in the search for understanding of Lewis's motivations and how he had summoned the energy, discipline and precision to complete the book, I began to question how he had placed himself in the novel: Fowler is an alcoholic with a serious case of the blues in every sense of the word, perhaps clinically depressed, paranoid and alone. That much is evidently a reflection of Lewis's condition. Lewis names Fowler's wife Jean, the name of the girl who had first taken him to bed at the age of 14. Also true. He must have known he was seriously ill by this point, so we assume these are thoughts, feelings and versions of events Lewis very much needs to express. The question to which, once I'd thought of it, I kept returning was whether *GBH* was retelling blow for blow the story of Lewis's experience in the preceding decade. An allegory for the chewing up and spitting out of his life and writing career as he'd experienced and reflected on it. The oppositions littering the text are faithful reflections of his own compartmentalised life in those years: London and the Smoke had lured him in and opened his eyes, but it had corrupted and damaged him too; it had offered the creative opportunities he craved and he had taken them, but they left him with unfulfilled expectations, unremitting guilt and morbid self-doubt. In the end, there is the Sea and the tank on the beach. For Fowler, like Lewis, it represents his own mind and the ghosts that haunt it. For his enemies waiting outside, he is no longer of any use.

GBH is the last great crime novel of the 1970s and the first of the 1980s. Its layers of meaning, intensity, and sheer *knowingness* make it a landmark in British fiction. It is a fiercely independent piece of writing, as fundamental a commentary on the human experience as Camus' *The Stranger*, whose protagonist, the author wrote, was 'condemned because he doesn't play the game'. Lewis changed the game, redefining the possibilities of the psychological noir, using Fowler to represent that part of him that was tormented by his past. Like Fowler, personally and professionally, he felt he had been left for dead. For ten years, he had driven himself, or had been driven, to the brink. *GBH* shows him staring into the abyss.

As the months passed, Lewis's declining health became increasingly obvious to those who knew him well. Sitting in the Volunteer Arms in Barton in 2010, John Dickinson recalled the extent to which Lewis was showing signs of becoming physically ill 'because of the drink'. As far back as Theddlethorpe, he had shown little interest in food, joking with Jill after a visit to Barton that Bertha had cooked for him 'because she thinks I ought to eat dinner'. Jill asked, what had he done? 'He said he'd buried it under the holly tree, the plate, the lot!' But by now he was barely eating at all. Smoking suppressed his appetite. Alcohol was effectively his main source of calories and, in all probability, he was malnourished as a result. His appearance was haggard; he was pale, often unshaven and his complexion took on a yellowish hue. He had little income. Jo believes that Bertha continued to support his drinking in spite of herself. 'She so, so loved Ted and she did protect him. I think latterly she was an *enabler*. You need one if you're an alcoholic and you're going to continue drinking. I'm not saying he would have thought, *I can't get any lower I've got to stop*, but if he's given money he's going to drink.'

Bertha's indulgence is remembered by Nick Turner. 'She loved him and felt sorry for him and forgave him and forgave him and encouraged all of us to come over. Perhaps he was returning to that nest where he knew he'd be safe and looked after.' It's a view borne out by John Dickinson. 'Bertha always made the best of it, but it must have been incredibly hard. He was the worse for wear and she'd have to deal with it. She was a tiny woman, barely five feet tall and quite stooped with age.'

Around this time, Lewis was diagnosed as diabetic. As Nancy puts it, 'his pancreas was shot'. Often lunchtime drinking sessions ended with a ring on Bertha's doorbell at around 3pm. She would open the door to find Lewis, deposited dead drunk on the doorstep. She had neither the strength nor the size to bring him indoors. A mutual friend of Jill Baxter's recalled the period Lewis lived at Ferriby Road. 'We knew Mrs Lewis really well and she used to call my husband out to deal with Ted when he came home drunk and she couldn't move him. He'd collapse on the garden path and my husband used to have to help Mrs Lewis drag him back into the house.' Several times an ambulance was called and Lewis had spells in hospital. Jo recalls, 'They wouldn't know if he was in a diabetic coma or drunk.' When Keith Riseam rang Lewis up to invite him to his fortieth birthday party, he said he would come, but he'd had a drink and couldn't make it. He became a regular at Westfield Lakes, later Reeds Hotel. Set on the periphery of Barton, a mile or so from the nearest houses, it was, in those days, according to Nick Turner, 'a dump, a fisherman's pub, a real dive'. In GBH, Fowler walks into a near empty pub shortly after opening time. There are four other drinkers, none of whom 'is a day under sixty'. Fowler is depressed by the fact that he knows them all. Drinking at Westfield Lakes was, for Lewis, another degree of isolation. Making his way home along an unlit road at night with deep ditches at each side was fraught. He drank heavily, staggering along rough tracks, through dykes and muddy fields back into town, then up to Ferriby Road. As one observer recalled, when he arrived he would be in a 'right state'.

In June 1981, a reunion of former Barton Grammar School staff and pupils was to bring some 60 former classmates and teachers back to Barton for the twenty-fifth anniversary of their leaving school. Lewis was particularly looking forward to meeting Barbara Hewson for the first time since, as 17-year-olds, they'd said goodbye at a friend's party. The day of the reunion, he was determined to be sober in readiness for the evening. He didn't dare go out, fearing he would be unable to walk past the pub. Bertha arranged for one of the girls from Lewis's year, Christine Ellis, to pick him up and drive him to the reunion. At the reunion, when Lewis approached Barbara, she didn't recognise him. 'He said, "You don't know who I am do you?"' Barbara remembers his face was bloated with drink, but his body was thin. 'He said, "Thank God you came – the sun has come out for the first time in months for me."'

It was a difficult evening. Everybody would have known Lewis's story, the books, the film, the success, and all that had gone by the wayside. In contrast to Barbara, who had travelled widely, recently returning from Russia where her husband had been working, Lewis's journey had brought him back to Barton. He and Barbara stayed together that evening, talking mostly about their families. Lewis spoke of his regrets, the breakup of his marriage and not seeing as much of his children as he'd have liked. He told Barbara he wished he could 'turn the clock back and start again'. When their former headmaster, Norman Goddard, approached, Barbara found herself trembling. Lewis put his arm around her and said, 'He can't hurt us now.' Goddard spoke briefly to Barbara. Besides a cursory nod, he ignored Lewis.

Barbara left Lewis's side once that evening to speak to another former pupil, John Bennett. Like Lewis, he had been a brilliant artist. 'He was blond, a handsome boy with very striking blue eyes' who had also been 'quite a ladies' man'. Some years before, Bennett had been driving his open top sports car to London when a fuel lorry in front braked suddenly. Bennett couldn't stop and his car went under the lorry, ripping the fuel tank (other versions of the incident maintain the lorry was carrying some kind of corrosive liquid). He had suffered terrible injuries and been very badly burned, losing his sight. Barbara asked Lewis if he'd mind if she went and talked to Bennett. 'He said he didn't, but he did.' She left her handbag by him as reassurance that she'd be back. 'John couldn't see me, but remembered who I was. He said, "Oh, how lovely, little Barbara!" I did go and have another short chat to him before the evening was over, but Ted didn't like it at all.'

Lewis had written often of car crashes, and seemed to have had a morbid fascination with fire, specifically death by fire. 'You have to be ruthless,' he'd once said about drawing on people he'd known in his writing, acknowledging that it was tantamount to exploitation, but that 'it has to be done'. Perhaps John Bennett provided a little too much reality. At the end of the evening, Barbara and Lewis went their separate ways. Bertha later told Barbara that when Lewis had arrived home drunk that night, and she asked, 'What about the girl?' he said, 'She showed up and didn't recognise me.'

Lewis had been admitted to Scunthorpe General Hospital on at least two previous occasions, but in the first months of 1982, his health deteriorated. On 22 March, he was diagnosed as suffering from severe pneumonia. According to John Dickinson, who visited regularly, 'His general condition wasn't good. His immune system couldn't cope and he was very depressed.' As much as Bertha remained stoical, Dickinson thinks she had seen the end coming. In his last few days, Lewis took to giving away copies of his books. Audrey Hill was an auxiliary at Scunthorpe General, working on Coronary Care Ward 10. Audrey would take patients their tea and she struck up a conversation with Lewis. In return, he gave her a copy of *The Rabbit* with the dedication, 'To Audrey, thanks for your help and kindness, Ted Lewis, 1982.'

Lewis died in hospital on Saturday 27 March 1982. In his final days, an accumulation of fluid had occurred as a result of infection to the lining of his heart; he was also suffering from chronic pancreatitis and cirrhosis of the liver. It seemed he had got out of bed to go to the toilet, suffered a heart attack, and died instantly. Bertha's friend Jean Collingwood registered the death on 29 March. The *Scunthorpe Telegraph* announced the death of 'Ted (Get Carter) Lewis'. The obituary rehashed some of the 1980 interview, but added little else.

Initially, there was confusion over the date of the funeral, which Bertha had inadvertently arranged for the same day as Sally's birthday. It was an association Jo was eager to avoid and she asked Bertha to change the date, which she did. Some of Lewis's friends, including Gil and Doreen Potter, weren't told. Jo also knew that Lewis had wanted to be buried, not cremated – it was something they'd discussed – but, at the time of his death, she felt herself in no position to advise Bertha.

The funeral took place in Scunthorpe at the Woodlands Crematorium on Brumby Wood Lane on 5 April 1982. Jill Baxter remembers it was a 'small affair'. 'I just saw it in the paper. It said the funeral would be at Woodlands and I said to my husband, I've got to go.' Bertha thanked Jill for coming. 'Jo was there. We weren't sitting too near each other. I think we might have said hello, but we didn't really speak and I left straight after the service. There weren't as many there as you'd have thought, just a few local people. People in London wouldn't have known. It was very quick.' She recalls how Lewis had once confessed that he had loved to drink and had known what it was doing to him, and where it would lead. She believes, in all likelihood, he couldn't have stopped even if he'd wanted to.

Inevitably, Bertha felt the loss greatly. She would later tell Barbara Hewson that, in the months before his death, Lewis had visited a priest. 'She felt that Edward had religious beliefs which he'd repressed all his life until then.' Lewis and the priest had talked for many hours and he'd carried out some work in the church grounds – the story circulated that he'd swept leaves in the churchyard. Bertha said that no one had known he'd seen a priest or been to church, and that the priest had visited and told her after his death. She also told Barbara that, when the hospital returned Lewis's personal effects, all his wallet contained, apart from a picture of Nancy and Sally and Toby Eady's business card, was a photograph of Michael Caine.

Lewis had written several chapters of *Other People's Houses*, which Bertha offered to Barbara, along with a synopsis of the rest of the book, either as a keepsake or to finish it. 'I felt honoured that she suggested it, but I knew I had neither the talent nor time to write a saga, especially as I no longer lived in Lincolnshire.' Barbara proposed that Bertha contact Toby Eady for advice. She refused. 'She said that she'd leave it to Jo and the girls after she'd gone and they could decide what to do with it.' Among Lewis's other effects was a proposal for six novels, the 'Jarrett' series, about a man whose thirst for revenge turns him into a ferocious, merciless killer. Presumably, this and the synopsis and manuscript chapters of *Other People's Houses* remain in the family's possession.

In Barton, there were mixed reactions to Lewis's death. In truth, his achievements were not universally recognised; credit for his success was overshadowed by his lifestyle. 'You know how DH Lawrence was received in Nottingham,' says Nick Turner, 'as that mucky bugger who writes mucky books; there were a lot of people in the town who didn't like Ted who thought of him like that, that drunk Ted Lewis, drinking and womanising. But those people didn't really know him.' Six months after Lewis died, shortly before she moved out of Ferriby Road, Bertha told Barbara Hewson that she'd seen him at the bottom of the stairs, looking up as she readied to come down. 'She said, "I knew he was at peace."'

10

Le Serpent
1982–

WHEN RON BURNETT CAME ACROSS A book about British crime authors which included a reference to Ted Lewis, he took it to show Bertha. In return she gave him a Japanese language edition of *Get Carter* she'd been sent. On visits to Lincolnshire, Barbara Hewson spent time with Bertha in the flat in the sheltered accommodation where she moved shortly after her son's death. When Barbara wrote an article about Henry Treece, published in *Lincolnshire Life* magazine, Bertha asked her to write something similar about Lewis, but she was sensitive about his drinking and did not want it referred to in any written account. Barbara found it impossible to write about Lewis without mentioning his alcoholism. 'I would never have written anything Bertha wouldn't have approved of, so it was never written.'

In 1984, Lewis's one time stablemate at Hutchinson, Robin Cook, now writing as Derek Raymond, stepped into the crime averse world of 1980s publishing. There may have been diminishing returns for crime fiction, particularly for what Raymond referred to as the 'black novel', nevertheless his

Factory novels – *He Died with His Eyes Open* (1984); *The Devil's Home on Leave* (1985); *How the Dead Live* (1986); and *I Was Dora Suarez* (1990) – are landmarks in British noir. More elaborate in style than *Carter* or *GBH*, Raymond's visceral, disturbingly violent novels are a grim response to Thatcherite Britain. These are uncompromising underclass chronicles which suggest something of Lewis's spirit was present. In his autobiography, *The Hidden Files*, Raymond gives an insight into how writing *Dora Suarez* had broken him and perhaps, by association, tells us something about Lewis's state of mind. 'I don't mean that it broke me physically or mentally, although it came near to doing both. But it changed me; it separated out for ever what was living and what was dead… if you go down into the darkness, you must expect it to leave traces on you coming up… I know I wondered half way through *Suarez* if I would get through.'

In 1985, Robinson Publishing issued *Jack's Return Home* under its original title for the first time since 1970. For the most part, the 1980s showed little appetite for revisiting the machinations of working class gangsters, even less the retro antistylings and unreconstructed attitudes of the 1970s. There was a staleness about the old world of guv'nors with tightly knotted ties, John Collier suits, and casual racism. Not until Neil Jordan's *Mona Lisa* brought Michael Caine and Bob Hoskins together with Cathy Tyson, in 1986, did a British crime movie gain significant critical attention.

At heart, *Mona Lisa* is a neo-noir love story. Sordid and violent, it pitches George, played by Hoskins, as an ex-con whose naïve sense of right and wrong is set against the twisted moralities of the 1980s sex industry. George's boss, Denny Mortwell, played with misogynistic sleaze by Caine, feeds off the vulnerabilities of junkies, young girls, and fuck-hungry predators. Here Caine is the antithesis of the impeccably tailored 1970s Carter, perhaps a version of the kind of man Carter would have become had he summoned the wherewithal to see off the Fletchers and submitted wholesale to the corruptive influences of their world.

Mona Lisa reacts against the world of sex, crime and money that Lewis's writing inhabited, but in doing so it updates and reaffirms the union of noir and social realist traditions he pioneered. It turns its attention to the harsh realities of those the underworld uses and junks without a second thought. Sympathies are with George, struggling to maintain his humanity as the bloke doing his job and falling for the girl, and with Simone and Cathy, women forced to fight for their lives against victimhood.

Bertha Lewis died in March 1990. She had spent the final few years of her life in sheltered accommodation becoming increasingly detached from all but a handful of close friends. If there had been personal documents and papers relating to her son, most were lost, given away or destroyed. She'd given Lewis's jazz records to John Dickinson and, while there may be a cache of letters and journals to be discovered, you suspect those kinds of literary hoards are the preserve of more self-regarding writers. More written records were lost when local authority boundaries were redrawn and the county of Humberside broken into separate authorities some years later. Barton Grammar School records were destroyed by the new North Lincolnshire Council, depriving us of school reports. History has done its best to wipe the traces. In time, even the sharpest memories grow cloudy.

In 1992, when Allison and Busby reprinted Lewis's most celebrated novel, the title had reverted to *Get Carter*, the book jacket dominated by the black and yellow image of a shotgun toting Michael Caine. To mark the republication, a decade after

Lewis's death, *Arena* magazine published *Brit Grit*, an article by John Williams which told an abridged version of Lewis's story. (Williams, an established novelist and journalist, would be appointed literary executor for Derek Raymond on the author's death in 1994.) In some respects, the article gave the impression of Lewis as some kind of literary hellraiser. Giles Gordon, his first editor, remembered he'd been 'arrogant' and 'boorish'. John McVicar said Lewis had 'lifted stuff' from his prison manuscript. Williams compared *Jack's Return Home* with Dashiell Hammett's masterpiece, *The Glass Key*, naming it the 'finest British crime novel ever written', concluding that Lewis was recognised in Europe as 'one of the lost greats of the hard-boiled style'. The following edition of the magazine published separate letters from the Lewis family and Toby Eady. They had taken exception to the article which Jo described as a 'character assassination' that failed to acknowledge Lewis's personal charm and the crippling guilt and self-doubt which had inhibited him. It would be five years before another Ted Lewis article appeared in print.

As the British cultural resurgence of the 1990s re-engaged with much that the previous decade had written off, films wearing their working class influence found mainstream audiences. The era was documented in *Loaded*, a new magazine first published in May 1994. It signalled the cultural shift, reshaping and repackaging elements of popular culture with a Jam generation emphasis. The first issue featured interviews with Gary Oldman, Paul Weller and Eric Cantona. *Loaded* founding editor, James Brown, a fan of Ted Lewis and *Get Carter*, commissioned respected *Tiger and Jag* and *Roy of the Rovers* comic artists and writers to create a *Get Carter* comic strip. 'We tried everywhere to find who owned rights and couldn't, so we just cracked on in the end.' The strip was hugely popular with readers who'd grown up on a diet of weekly comics and who were eager to revisit *Get Carter*, but there was trouble ahead. 'About four issues in, we had a cease and desist legal letter from Ted Lewis's estate. We showed we had written to film and book companies seeking permission and I got comic experts, including Jonathan Ross, to write about the quality of the art, but they refused to allow us to proceed.'

Nancy Lewis is clear: 'Over the years, other people had been able to find out who owned the rights to dad's books and we were always excited when they showed an interest. Toby sent a letter on our behalf.' The response from *Loaded*, she recalls, was surprisingly dismissive. 'We felt we had no choice but to take legal action.' What Brown couldn't have known was the extent to which comics had been among Lewis's earliest, and most important, inspirations. The boy whose imagination had first been fired by EC crime comics, and whose skills as a graphic artist and illustrator brought him to London, had come full circle. Lewis's greatest character was, briefly, a comic strip antihero.

The critical reappraisal of Lewis began with Issue 9 of *Crime Time* magazine in 1997. In a series of 'grim up north' exclusives under the heading 'GOT CARTER!', Mike Hodges wrote about the impact of reading *Jack's Return Home* for the first time and the development of the script. He gave new insight to the production process, including choice of location and the macabre finds in Dryerdale Hall – the location for Cyril Kinnear's house – previously owned by Vincent Landa, elder brother of Michael Luvaglio, one of the men convicted of Angus Sibbet's murder. There was a sense that the film's moment had come again with Hodges concluding that Carter may have been 'shot dead before our eyes' but he still goes on. 'He is, of course, eternal; he's on film.' In September that year, Hodges introduced a screening of *Get Carter* at the National Film Theatre in London, an event which Steve Chibnall, author of the essential *Get Carter:*

British Film Guide, cites as the beginning of the film's 'formal rehabilitation'.

Accompanying the Hodges *Crime Time* piece was a lengthy article by Paul Duncan, the first of substance to have been written about Ted Lewis. Jo had agreed to an interview. Here, accompanied by new images of the author on the set, Lewis's life and work was placed in context. Jo acknowledged that she had been 'quite blind' to the extent of his drinking, explaining how, in her opinion, he had struggled to face up to their worsening financial situation when book sales didn't materialise. Duncan concluded that Lewis had far more to say than he was able to write, but that he 'wrote crime novels to make money, to support his family', and that there was something admirable in that.

The following year, *Crime Time* issue 12 reprinted Derek Raymond's 1991 introduction to the German edition of *GBH*. Raymond was unequivocal in his praise, writing that 'By preferring to look the street straight in the face instead of peeping at it from behind an upstairs curtain, he [Lewis] cleared a road straight through the black jungle.' It was the kind of recognition, particularly from one of his peers, which had been lacking in his lifetime.

Renewed critical and public interest in *Get Carter* prompted the British Film Institute to release a new print for cinema in June 1999. Hodges admits his relationship with the film was complex. 'Caine's Carter points and doesn't say "please". If he had, I might have been spared 25 years of macho men, on learning I made the film, snapping their fingers at me with the same sinister authority.' Nevertheless, he worked on the new print and the reissue premiered at the National Film Theatre before going on general release. For all the acclaim of rediscovery and critical reappraisal, the DVD release in October

2000 gave Lewis no more credit than the film's original 'based on the novel by' as Carter's tunnel bound train races north. The audio commentary featuring Mike Hodges, Michael Caine and cinematographer Wolfgang Suschitzky barely mentions the novel; and when it does, only in terms of the changes made in the script. Referred to a couple of times as 'the author', Lewis is never mentioned by name.

When writer and theatre director Jonathan Holloway returned to *Jack's Return Home* as the basis for his 2005 stage adaptation of *Get Carter*, with British actor Jack Lord in the lead role, he reconnected strongly with Lewis's original narrative. The production portrayed Carter as an everyman rather than the super-gangster he had become in the movie. 'Jack is a man out of his time and out of his depth,' says Holloway, 'a classic outsider coming home to where he is no longer accepted.' The play features Frank Carter as a character, a ghostly nagging influence from Jack's past. The restoration of Jack's interior monologue and conversations between him, Frank and the Fletchers back in London covers much that Hodges' script had cut. Jack's betrayal of his brother, sleeping with his wife and the guilt which follows his death, emerge as powerful motivation for his vengeance.

For Holloway, who had grown up in Streatham, south London in the 1970s, *Get Carter* recalled an early 70s world of skinheads, suedeheads, hard cases and street violence. Revisiting the novel enabled him to look back at that era and, with sufficient distance, to reappraise social and cultural changes. He was mindful of the impact of the language, the use of drink as a convenience and Carter's deplorable treatment of women, remembering the impact the film and the book had first time around. 'Working class blokes didn't read. If they did it would be *Commando* magazines or cheap pulp sex novels – *Confessions* type novels. *Get Carter* was a book you could read without someone calling you a poof.'

When the production toured in 2005 and 2006, it attracted the kind of audience who wouldn't normally go to the theatre. Holloway remembers it was not particularly well received by the arts establishment, its racist and misogynistic references dismissed as 'hate language'. The Arts Council representative found the play 'old-fashioned' and 'hard to believe in'. But broadsheet critics were more sympathetic. Lyn Gardner in the *Guardian* wrote that it reeked of 'sweat and piss, and disappointed dreams' and that it 'leaves a very nasty taste in the mouth as it captures the not-so-swinging early 70s. But never in an exploitative way.'

The story of *Get Carter* on stage wasn't over. In April 2015, Northern Stage Theatre Company, based in Newcastle, announced a new commission for a play based on *Get Carter*. The writer, Torben Betts, said he would be returning to the original text of Lewis's novel for inspiration, although the play's title would be *Get Carter* and it would be set in the north east. Northern Stage's Artistic Director, Lorne Campbell, was keen to explore the idea of 'a sick man in a sick landscape', restoring the balance between the tortured internalised Jack Carter and the forceful externalised action character portrayed by Michael Caine. He, too, reintroduced Frank Carter to the piece, here a pallid wordless presence, expressing himself now and then at a drum kit, beating out rhythms with brushes, referencing his ambitions to have been a jazz drummer. Alfred Hickling's *Guardian* review noted that Betts' script leaned heavily on Lewis's 'seminal work of northern pulp fiction, *Jack's Return Home*'.

In August 2007, actor Clive Owen, who had become patron of the Electric Palace, a beautifully restored period cinema at Harwich on the Essex Coast, invited Mike Hodges to introduce a double bill of the film *Croupier*, in which Hodges had directed Owen, followed by a question and answer session and a screening of *Get Carter*. 'Ted's wife and daughters attended,' recalled Hodges. 'They were charming but, sadly, I got the distinct feeling they thought I'd taken too much of the credit for the script. In a way they're right.' Hodges confirms he'd never been made aware of Lewis's desire to write the script for *Get Carter*. He said:

Somebody (I can't remember who) told me some years ago that Ted had wanted (maybe expected?) to write the script himself. It saddened me when I heard that. It had simply never occurred to me or Klinger (as far as I know) that he wanted to be involved beyond the deal for the rights. Perhaps I imagined his frustration had been aired at home – and his family feeling aggrieved. Who knows? On the other hand, he seemed delighted with the outcome.

He has clear views on the place denied Lewis in the literary canon:

If Ted had been born in France or America his legacy would have been considerable. He would occupy a place similar to Jim Thompson, Raymond Chandler and the rest of the hard-boiled school of writers. I suspect this will never be the case in Britain. The nation is still incapable of facing the deep malaise that blights it from top to bottom. And let's face it, British literary culture, for what it's worth, is largely middle class, the work of eternal undergraduates. I doubt it will ever encompass the hard-boiled. Especially from one of its own.

Given the French love of noir fiction, it is no surprise that Lewis's writing has remained popular in France. By and large, his books remained in print when, in other territories, they were not. (In the case of the United States, some were not published at all.) Traditions of crime and noir writing and filmmaking had remained strong, part of the French national psyche and ingrained in French culture as a mainline to political and social-realist subjects.

In part it was this subtext, via the existence of a shady right-wing network, which interested French film director Eric Barbier. He had been drawn to Lewis's books after seeing *Get Carter*. 'I started reading *Get Carter* to see where the movie came from. I read the novel and thought Ted Lewis was a great English writer. That's how I read all of Lewis's books, until I read *Plender* – that inspired *Le Serpent*.'

Released in 2006 in France (2007 in the UK) Barbier's French language thriller, starring Yves Attal and Clovis Cornillac, is a mainly faithful retelling of Lewis's original story. Barbier had worked on the script with writer Trân-Minh Nam over a number of years, accentuating the relationship between Vincent (based on Peter Knott), a fashion photographer, and old school friend and nemesis (Joseph) Plender. 'The stories from their childhood gave a real strength... in the sense that there was a love story between the two men who had known each other when they were 12 or 13, and who had created a great rivalry when they were adults. The core of the book is a story of vengeance between the two characters.'

Le Serpent places Lewis's writing in a film tradition stretching back to 1950s noir. Barbier recognised that at the heart of the novel was a thriller which resembled classic movies such as J. Lee Thompson's 1962 *Cape Fear* or Hitchcock's *Strangers on a Train*. Appearing hot on the heels of Guillaume Canet's *Ne Le Dis À Personne* (*Tell No One*), another contemporary French thriller which gained attention in the UK, meant that the two were often compared. They are both stylish and well crafted thrillers. Writing in the *Daily Telegraph*, David Cheal remarked that *Le Serpent* was a film in which 'cunning and cleverness are met with cunning and cleverness, in which violence is the weapon of last, rather than first, resort'.

This was especially so in the film's final 20 minutes, essentially the third act, which owes the least debt to the novel and brings the story to a more visually explosive conclusion than Lewis had envisaged. For all that Barbier adapted the story for contemporary audiences, Clovis Cornillac's Plender remains undeniably a Lewis character, flawed and brilliantly sinister, a man consumed by an adolescent grudge and his quest for retribution.

As Jack Carter entered his fifth decade, the BBC Radio adaptation of *Jack Carter's Law*, narrated by Phil Daniels, abridged Lewis's novel in five 30-minute episodes. First aired in February 2010, repeated on BBC4 Extra in 2011 and 2013, Daniels' reading makes for a distinctly London-voiced version of the novel. Late night broadcasts allowed Lewis's language, whilst abridged, to remain broadly intact, and the adaptation worked well. In the same year, *Get Carter* was placed seventh in the *Guardian*'s list of the greatest crime films of all time. One place below Billy Wilder's *Double Indemnity*, the movie Mike Hodges had initially turned to for inspiration.

In 2012, Lewis was given a brief retrospective in *Lewis's Return Home*, produced for BBC Radio 4 by Beaty Rubens. Presented by poet, critic, novelist and playwright, Sean O'Brien, the 30 minute documentary gave an appraisal of Lewis's life and work, his relationship with the landscape of northern Lincolnshire and the city of Hull. It featured a range of contributors: Jo, Nancy and Sally were interviewed, as were Toby Eady and Ron Burnett. In the panelled room that had once been Henry Treece's classroom, I spoke about Lewis's schooldays. Near a noisy 'top road', where the weather wasn't good and the view across Scunthorpe and the steelworks was its best industrial grey, we explored the inspiration for *Jack's Return Home*. In a tight half hour, memories of Lewis were crystallised into a few phrases by those who knew him. Toby Eady gave an honest appraisal of the Ted Lewis he remembered. 'You wouldn't have noticed him. He was small, he chain-smoked, he drank at least three quarters of a bottle of gin a day, starting in the morning.' Eady felt that London had opened Lewis's mind:

'He achieved what he had achieved, and thought it would continue. Everything he put his hands to, he could do. And no effort. That was the real thing; if he could write a book in a month at the end of the year, that's what he did. But he was too talented for the conventions of this country, because he came from a completely different background. Had he been born an American, he might have had a much bigger readership.'

There was, he concluded, a lingering disappointment in how little *Get Carter* had been attributed to Lewis.

The documentary featured clips from a new radio version of *Jack's Return Home*, adapted by Nick Perry. Hugo Speer played Jack Carter and the production took the story back to its original setting. For the first time in film or fiction, Scunthorpe was named as the location. The production captured the working class north in dialogue, soundscape and music choice. Badfinger's dreary singalong *Come and Get It* evoked pints of brown ale, bri-nylon shirts and factory girls dancing in Scunthorpe Baths Hall. Carter's first person narrative came into its own on radio, although Speer's accent was more West Riding of Yorkshire than northern Lincolnshire. Frank Carter's place was restored and, as with Holloway's and Betts' stage versions, the emotional complexity added to the depth of Jack's character.

In 2004, the *Doctor Who Magazine* Special Edition #9 had chronicled 'the complete fourth doctor'; its second volume included a condensed version of the story of Lewis and *The Shield of Zarak*. Anthony Read is quoted, once again relating the story of the script and making it clear that, in his view, nothing had happened to prevent Lewis working for the BBC. 'There was never any blacklist, or even a preferred list – I was able to commission Douglas Adams, whom nobody had ever heard of, for instance, without seeking anybody's approval.'

The same year saw the release of Shane Meadows' film, *Dead Man's Shoes* (2004), co-written by Meadows, Paddy Considine and Paul Fraser. The film took on the gritty, social realist revenge thriller, reinvigorating Lewis's blueprint. Writing in the *Guardian*, Rob Mackie declared it a 'remorseless revenge tale which starts like *Mean Streets* but turns into more of a *Straw Dogs/Get Carter* hybrid'. Interviewed for Film Four, Meadows explained that Considine's character, the ex-Para Richard, represented 'the darkest side of all of us' and was a projection of his own anger 'unleashed without restraint'. In story, spirit and texture, there are distinct echoes of Lewis's writing. Meadows is unrelenting, as at home in the postindustrial, semi-rural Derbyshire town of Matlock as Lewis was in Scunthorpe.

When Serpent's Tail republished Derek Raymond's *He Died with His Eyes Open*, the first in the series of the author's 'Factory' novels, in 2006, the brief biography recognised he'd been 'widely admired as the godfather of the British noir novel'. In 2009, I'd asked Toby Eady the question I'd been asked numerous times, would Ted Lewis's novels receive a similar reissue? The response suggested not, that the inconsistent quality of Lewis's work made that difficult. Added to which, *All the Way Home and All the Night Through* and *The Rabbit* weren't easily packaged alongside the crime novels.

Late in 2013, Syndicate Books – an imprint of Soho Press in New York – announced they had secured the rights to publish Lewis's novels, until then out of print in the US. Championed by New York publisher, Paul Oliver, the project aimed to bring Lewis's work out of stateside obscurity. *Get Carter* launched the Syndicate editions as the first of the Carter trilogy in June 2014. The novel included a new foreword by Mike Hodges and there were tributes from contemporary crime fiction luminaries, including Dennis Lehane, who wrote, 'Aristotle, when he defined tragedy, mandated that a tragic hero must fall from a great height, but Aristotle never imagined the kind of roadside motels James M. Cain could conjure up or saw the smokestacks rise in the northern English industrial hell of Ted Lewis's *Get Carter*.' The republished novels were reviewed widely and positively. David L. Ulin in the *Los Angeles Times* wrote *Get Carter* 'Sums up the hard-boiled ethos as well as anything I've ever read... as far as classic hard-boiled fiction, *Get Carter* is *sui generis*, the place where British noir begins.'

In May 2015, Soho Press republished *GBH*. In a radio piece for NPR, also published as an article, 'Gangsters, Goons and "Grievous Bodily Harm" in Ted Lewis' London', critic John

Powers described it as 'a pulp-fiction triumph worthy of Jim Thompson or James Ellroy.' 'At his best, [Lewis] achieves something only a handful of crime writers ever do – the chilling sense of cosmic fatality that links noir antiheroes to the likes of Oedipus and Macbeth.' *Washington Post* critic Michael Dirda wrote *GBH* was 'one of the most coldly brilliant crime novels you will ever read'. The novel was 'a mesmerizing story of power, love, hubris and betrayal – but, above all, the portrait of what one might call a tragic villain'. These and others were reviews that Lewis could only have dreamed of in his lifetime, proof of the timeless quality of his best writing, and confirmation of its status as classic noir.

In the UK, Lewis's writing continues to find its way into the mainstream. Russell Lewis, executive producer and writer of the TV series *Endeavour,* the 1960s set stories of the young detective who would become Inspector Morse, acknowledges references to *Jack's Return Home*. Intentionally so with a nod to the 'Fletcher Brothers' in the first series episode *Home*. '*Jack's Return Home* and some of Ted's other novels came across my desk about 20 years ago, with a vague "what about these?" from some TV company or other. I began to dip into them, but the moment passed, and I never got around to reading all of them from cover to cover.' He acknowledges *Get Carter* as 'most likely the finest "British Gangster" movie of the modern era'.

Novelist Ben Myers grew up in Belmont, the Durham suburb where Cliff Brumby's house stood until its demolition in 2008. As youngsters, Myers and his mates would climb the walls to get a look at the house that was in 'that film with Michael Caine'. Later he read Lewis's novel and realised the book had been set in an entirely different place. 'I thought, why have they moved it? The whole point of Scunthorpe, as with all his books, is that the location is vital. That's why I like him so much as a writer, all these dark corners of the north, which are underrepresented in fiction. That sense of place is key to his work.' Myers has written of Lewis's ability to 'transport readers back to a recent northern England of Wimpy bars and stiff whiskies, modernist furnishings and stoic, silent men'. There are resonances of Lewis's rural noir in Myers' own writing: a dark, brutal nature haunts his 'folk crime' novel *Turning Blue*, prompting noir author Cathi Unsworth to recall Lewis, the 'East Riding's lost boy of crime fiction'.

Myers is far from being the only contemporary writer to cite Lewis as an influence. David Peace's landmark noir novels, *The Red Riding Quartet* and *GB84*, revisit the themes, atmospheres and period of Lewis's northern England. In an interview he gave to the BBC in 2003, Peace spoke about the influence of the books on his father's bookshelf – Chandler and Hammett beside John Braine, David Storey and Alan Sillitoe. He maintains *Get Carter* is the finest crime novel he's ever read:

'I was always looking for a book that would combine the plots and style of American Noir with the Northern working class fiction of the post-war and its landscape. I remember watching, and of course loving, the film *Get Carter*, but finding an old Pan paperback edition of the original novel was the revelation. This was the book I'd always been looking for, imagining and hoping for, and it remains my favourite British Crime Novel. When I was writing *Nineteen Seventy Four* and *The Red Riding Quartet*, I was very conscious that I was trying to write something as good as Ellroy's 'LA Quartet', Derek Raymond's 'Factory Series' and the novels of Ted Lewis, particularly *Jack's Return Home* and *GBH*. I know I didn't even come close, but these were the key texts and inspirations for me. And I probably drew the most from Ted

Lewis; not being afraid to set the work in the time and place I had grown up, for a start, and then the dialogue, and the language and texture of that time. I don't think I could have written those books without being inspired by Ted Lewis.'

Peace acknowledges Lewis gave him the confidence to write about the people and places he knew in Yorkshire. 'He was writing a very different kind of crime novel, in a very different but very real world.' Few British writers were writing crime novels set outside London, or outside stately homes and the world of the upper and middle classes. Peace believes Lewis has been hugely underappreciated:

'I think it was sadly inevitable and predictable, and yet another damning indictment of British literary culture then and now. I mean, he was writing at a time when "the crime novel" was not taken seriously, for a start. Secondly, that whole generation of Northern working class writers (as much in subject matter and setting as in the personal backgrounds of the writers) – writers such as Braine, Storey, Barstow and Sillitoe, along with Henry Green and Barry Hines, for example – are also barely in print or read nowadays. If it wasn't for the films of their work, they would be completely forgotten. Because all these writers are casualties in what has been a sustained war on the working class and its culture. But if you go to France, you'll find all Ted Lewis's books in print and revered as classics. C'est la vie!'

Living mostly in and around Hull, there is a crowd of old college friends and jazz fans who got to know each other in the late 1950s and who still keep in touch. They come together for gigs, particularly if Ron Burnett's playing with his band,

The Ron Burnett Mardi Gras Band. Keith Riseam is one of the crowd. He has fond memories of Lewis, but remembers there always seemed to be two sides to his personality, a part of him seeking to escape, or to be someone else. He has more insight than most into Lewis's struggles with drink:

> 'By the time I stopped, I had three months to live. I went to Alcoholics Anonymous, which Ted didn't. I wish he could have made that break like I did. To my knowledge he never tried and that often happens, there's this self-delusion, you start hiding bottles, and it's a death wish. It's a mind changing illness and I'm sure Ted went through the same thing.'

Riseam wonders, what would Lewis have been like? 'We've had our lives, our problems; now we have the time, the security and the memories and we come together again. I know he'd have been part of that.'

In a phone call, Jo Whittle recalled a conversation with Lewis's old friend Alan Smith who reminded her of a time he and Ted were on a train together. 'Ted wanted a drink, but the bar was closed. The chef had obviously had a hard day. Ted gave him some abuse and the chef chased him down the train, knife in hand. Ted pulled the communication cord and stopped the train. The poor chef was arrested and escorted off the train by the police. I'm on the chef's side, but that story still makes me laugh.' It is typical Lewis. Charming and chaotic, he staged his own kind of rebellion, harmless to begin with, as a way to break free of the straitjacket of his upbringing, but then to escape whatever it was that made him drink and keep on drinking, even when he knew it would kill him. He needed people, more importantly, he needed their loyalty, yet did just about everything to exhaust even the most devoted. In the end, he isolated himself until it was him, his mother, writing and drink. There is a consensus that, when he returned to Barton, he felt he had failed. It seemed he was constantly disappointed, always looking for 'the big one'. Had his work been more widely appreciated, would it have made a difference to the way his life ended? Somehow, I doubt it.

But in spite of this sense of it being him against the world, of something always being missing, when pretty much all else had let him down, Ted Lewis was still writing. He loved and was loved in return. He adored his children. Some have said he was a writer who had given up, the perennial lost cause, someone whose gift had been lost or squandered, but I don't agree. He was ill for a long time, longer than those close to him realised, and still wrote. We don't measure writing careers in numbers of books written or copies sold. Fifty years after Lewis wrote Jack Carter into being, he lives on.

Ted Lewis reached further and said more in a handful of novels than most writers ever accomplish. *Jack's Return Home* and *GBH* are among the most authentic British crime novels committed to print. *Plender, Jack Carter's Law* and *The Rabbit* are not far behind. When it comes to the dark extremes of noir fiction, he remains one of its truest and greatest exponents.

*

Acknowledgements

My thanks to Laurie Harvey, whose friendship, shared interest in Lewis, enthusiasm and keen instinct for a lead did so much to help the early research for this book. Thanks also to Jo Whittle, Nancy and Sally Lewis for agreeing to be interviewed; and to Ron and Judy Burnett for welcoming me into their home on numerous occasions, for some great attic finds and, along with Juliet Hiden, for bringing such life to Lewis's time at art school. My appreciation to Toby Eady for his invaluable contributions. And to the Riverbank Boys, particularly Nick Turner, whose memories of Lewis's schooldays gave such clarity and context.

Thanks to Ion Mills, Clare Quinlivan, and Claire Watts at No Exit; and particularly to Steven Mair who has been a meticulous, insightful and understanding editor. I'm indebted to those who read the manuscript and who offered generous insights, suggestions and encouragement along the way: Martin Goodman, Mike Hodges, Brian Lavery, Sean O'Brien, Andrew Spicer, Nick Quantrill, and Cathi Unsworth.

I'm grateful to those who lent photographs, cuttings, and memorabilia, all of which helped to add colour and definition to Lewis's life: Jill Baxter, Ron Burnett, Gwyneth Conroy, Alan Dickinson, Christine Ellis, Barbara Hewson, Nancy Lewis, Martin Turner, Nick Turner.

Thanks to staff at the BFI and Media Archive for Central England at the University of Lincoln for their help in screening Lewis's

Z Cars episodes; BBC Document Archive for help with Lewis's BBC correspondence and joining me in the (so far) fruitless search for the missing *Doctor Who* scripts; also to Hull History Centre, Barton-upon-Humber Library; and Scunthorpe Central Library – particularly Tim Davies for drawing my attention to the *Lincolnshire Times* archive.

Finally, my gratitude to those who listened, encouraged, and, on occasion, kept me from the dark places when I walked a little too far in Lewis's footsteps, especially Beverlea Ayris, Pamela Farrow, Gillian Hobson, Tina Jackson, and Paul Oliver – thank you.

Interviews

I am grateful to the following, many of whom agreed to be interviewed on more than one occasion, all of whom have been instrumental in piecing together Ted Lewis's story:

Alun Armstrong, Richard Armstrong, Jake Arnott, Dr John Ball, Revel Barker, Tom Barling, Jill Baxter, James Brown, Linda Brown, Judy Burnett, Ron Burnett, Brian Case, Janette Chesterman, Nick Cole, Jack Compton, Gwyneth Conroy, Alan Dickinson, John Dickinson, Malcolm Draper, Harry Duffin, Toby Eady, Christine Ellis, David Elvin, Derrick Goodwin, Hilary Green (née Bremner), Nick Hague, Barbara Hewson, Juliet Hiden (née Raahauge), Audrey Hill, Mike Hodges, Jonathan Holloway, Barri Hooper, Brian Jickles, Norman Kauffman, Anthony Klinger, Nancy Lewis, Russell Lewis, Sally Lewis, Karen Maitland, Jane Marling, Chris Miles, Geraldine Moffat, Heather Morton, Brian Moss, Ben Myers, Felicity Myers, Stephanie Nettell, Sean O'Brien, Ralph Parkin, David Peace, Dave Penrose, Doreen Potter, Gil Potter, Victoria Potter, Anthony Read, David Remfry, Derek Ridgers, Keith Riseam, Jackie Scoble, Mike Shucksmith, Neville Smith, Andrew Spicer, Martin Turner, Nick Turner, Lance Wardell, Marlene Wardell, Josephine Whittle, John Williams.

Bibliography

Books

Barling, Tom, *The Smoke* (Corgi 1986)

Brice, Enid, *A Country Grammar School Remembered: A History of Barton-on-Humber Grammar School* 1931–1975 (Hutton Press 2002)

Caine, Michael, *The Autobiography: The Elephant to Hollywood* (Hodder and Stoughton 2011)

Chadder, Viv, 'The higher heel: women and the post-war British crime film' *British Crime Cinema*, Ed. Chibnall, Murphy (Routledge 1999)

Chesterton, GK, *The Club of Queer Trades* (Electronic Classics Series Publication)

Chibnall, Steve, *Get Carter: The British Film Guide 6* (I.B. Tauris & Co. 2003)

Chibnall, Steve; Murphy Robert, 'Parole Overdue: releasing the British crime film into the critical community' *British Crime Cinema*, Ed. Chibnall, Murphy (Routledge 1999)

Cole, Hugh M., *The United States Army in World War II: The Ardennes: Battle of the Bulge* (Office of the Chief of Military History, Department of the Army, Washington D.C. 1965)

Collins, Max Allan 'The Law, Crime and Ted Lewis' (featured in *Jack Carter's Law*, Syndicate Books 2014)

Cooke, Dorian; Hendry, J.F. *Henry Treece, The New Apocalypse: an anthology of criticism, poems and stories* (Fortune Press 1940)

Crandall, Reed; Craig, Johnny; Davis, Jack; Frazetta, Frank; Ingels, Graham; Kurtzman, Harvey; Orlando, Joe;

Williamson, Al; Wood, Wally, *Crime Suspense Stories #1* 1950; *Shock Suspense Stories #6* 1952; *The Haunt of Fear #2* 1950 EC Comics, Russ Cochran, William M. Gaines

Davies, Steven Paul, *Get Carter and Beyond: The Cinema of Mike Hodges* (Batsford Film Books 2002)

Décharné, Max, *Hardboiled Hollywood: The Origins of the Great Crime Films* (No Exit Press 2005)

Delgado, Alan; illustrated by Edward Lewis, *The Hot Water Bottle Mystery* (Brockhampton Press 1962)

Delgado, Alan, illustrated by Edward Lewis, *Return Ticket* (Brockhampton Press 1965)

Dex, Laurie, *Hull and Hull Jazzmen* (Beck Books 1991)

Duncan, Paul, *Noir Fiction: Dark Highways* (Pocket Essentials Literature 2003)

Dyson, Brian, 'Treece, Henry William (1911–1966)', *Oxford Dictionary of National Biography*, Oxford University Press, 2004 (online edn, May 2007)

Foreman, Freddie; Lambrianou, Tony, *Getting it Straight: Villains Talking* (Pan Books 2002)

Greene, Graham, *The Tenth Man* (Penguin Books 1986)

Greene, Graham, *Brighton Rock* (Penguin Books 1987)

Hieronimus, Dr Robert R., *Inside The Yellow Submarine: The Making of the Beatles' Animated Classic* (Krause Publications 2002)

Hodges, Mike, 'Mike Hodges discusses *Get Carter* with the NFT audience, 23 September 1997' *British Crime Cinema*, Ed. Chibnall, Murphy (Routledge 1999)

Hodges, Mike, *Get Carter – a Screenplay by Mike Hodges* (ScreenPress Books 2000)

Hoggart, Richard, *The Uses of Literacy* (Penguin Modern Classics 2009)

Laing, Olivia, *The Trip to Echo Spring: Why Writers Drink*

(Canongate Books Ltd 2013)

Larkin, Philip, 'Here' *The Whitsun Weddings* (Faber and Faber 1964)

Lawrence, DH, *Sons and Lovers* (Wordsworth Classics 1993)

Lay, Samantha, *British Social Realism: From Documentary to Brit Grit* (Wallflower Press 2002)

Lewis, Ted, *All the Way Home and All the Night Through* (Hutchinson New Authors 1965)

Lewis, Ted, 'The Rabbit' *Argosy* (Fleetway Productions 1966)

Lewis, Ted, *Carter* (Pan Books 1971)

Lewis, Ted 'Kings, Queens and Pawns' *Men Only – Volume 38, Number 11* (Paul Raymond Publications 1974)

Lewis, Ted 'With This Song, Baby, It Don't Matter' *Men Only – Volume 40, Number 3* (Paul Raymond Publications 1975)

Lewis, Ted, *The Rabbit* (Michael Joseph 1975)

Lewis, Ted, *Billy Rags* (Sphere Books 1975)

Lewis, Ted, *The Rabbit* (Sphere Books 1976)

Lewis, Ted, *Jack Carter's Law* (Sphere Books 1978)

Lewis, Ted, *Boldt* (Sphere Books 1978)

Lewis, Ted, *Jack's Return Home* (Constable and Robinson 1985)

Lewis, Ted, *GBH* (Allison and Busby 1993)

Lewis, Ted, *Jack Carter and the Mafia Pigeon* (Allison and Busby 1994)

Lewis, Ted, *Plender* (Allison and Busby 1997)

Lewis, Ted, *Get Carter* (Allison and Busby 1998)

Lewis, Ted, *Get Carter* (Allison and Busby 2013)

Lewis, Ted, *Get Carter* (Syndicate Books 2014)

Lewis, Ted, *Jack Carter's Law* (Syndicate Books 2014)

Lewis, Ted, *Jack Carter and the Mafia Pigeon* (Syndicate Books 2014)

Lewis, Ted, *GBH* (Soho Press 2015)

MacInnes, Colin, *Absolute Beginners* (Allison and Busby 1980)

MacInnes, Colin, *England, Half English* (Hogarth Press 1986)

Mackendrick, Alexander; Ed. Paul Cronin, *On Film Making: An Introduction to the Craft of the Director* (Faber and Faber 2004)

Marnham, Patrick, *Wild Mary: A Life of Mary Wesley* (Vintage 2007)

McVicar, John, *McVicar: By Himself* (A Jot Publishing 2007)

Miles, Barry, *London Calling: A Countercultural History of London since 1945* (Atlantic Books 2010)

Moore, Alan; O'Neill, Kevin, *The League of Extraordinary Gentlemen Century: 1969* (Top Shelf, Knockabout 2011)

Morton, James, *Gangland Volume 2: The Underworld in Britain and Ireland* (Warner Books 1996)

Murphy, Robert, 'A revenger's tragedy – *Get Carter*' *British Crime Cinema*, Ed. Chibnall, Murphy (Routledge 1999)

Nuttall, Jeff, *Bomb Culture* (Paladin 1972)

O'Brien, Sean, 'The Ferry' from *The Drowned Book* (Picador 2007)

Peace, David, *1977* (Serpent's Tail 2000)

Pearson, John, *The Profession of Violence: The Rise and Fall of the Kray Twins* (Harper Collins 1995)

Reason, Joyce, *Bran the Bronze Smith* (Dent 1939)

Richardson, Charlie; with Bob Long, *My Manor: The Autobiography of Charlie Richardson* (Sidgwick and Jackson 1991)

Richardson, Neil, *Home to Stay: An Account of Stretford in the Second World War* (From the diaries of J.G. Atherton, 1991)

Richardson, Neil, *Luftwaffe Over Manchester: The Blitz Years 1940–44* (2003)

Shires, Linda M., *British Poetry of the Second World War (Studies in Twentieth-Century Literature)* (Palgrave 1985)

Sillince, WA, *We're All In It* (Collins 1941)

Sillince, WA, *We're Still All In It* (Collins 1942)

Sillince, WA, *Minor Relaxations* (Collins 1945)

Sillince, WA, *Comic Drawing* (Pitman 1950)

Sole, Deanne, 'Author Appreciation: Henry Treece' *Pop Matters* (13 August 2007)

Spicer, Andrew, *Typical Men: The Representation of Masculinity in Popular British Cinema* (IB Tauris & Co. 2003)

Spicer, Andrew; AT McKenna, *The Man Who Got Carter: Michael Klinger, Independent Production and the British Film Industry, 1960–1980* (IB Tauris & Co. 2013)

Spillane, Mickey, *The Mike Hammer Omnibus Volume 1: I, the Jury* (Allison and Busby 2006)

Thomas, Dylan, *The Collected Letters*, Ed. Paul Ferris (Paladin 1987)

Treece, Henry, *The Golden Strangers* (Savoy Books Ltd. 1980)

Wilson, Andrew, *Beautiful Shadow: A Life of Patricia Highsmith* (Bloomsbury 2003)

Worthen, John, *DH Lawrence: The Life of an Outsider* (Counterpoint Press 2005)

Articles

Berlins, Marcel, 'What is it about Albert Camus' The Outsider that makes it such an enduring favourite with men?' The *Guardian* (12 April 2006)

Campbell, Duncan, 'Charlie Richardson Obituary' The *Guardian* (20 September 2012)

Corliss, Richard, 'The Glory and Horror of EC Comics' *Time Magazine* (29 April 2004)

Danziger, Danny, 'The Worst of Times: A trust destroyed: Toby Eady talks to Danny Danziger' The *Independent* (16 May 1994)

DeNeefe, Janet, 'Toby Eady: a life less ordinary' *Jakarta Post* (14

February 2008)

Duncan, Paul, 'All the Way Home: Ted Lewis' *Crime Time Issue 9* (Oldcastle Books 1997)

Du Noyer, Paul, 'The time has come, the jester said ...' *Q* magazine interview with Spike Milligan, Van Morrison (August 1989)

French, Philip 'Blacklisted but unbowed' the *Observer* – celebrating the centenary of Joseph Losey (24 May 2009)

Gardner, Lyn, 'Get Carter – Old Town Hall, Hemel Hempstead' the *Guardian* (11 March 2006)

Gee, Catherine 'My Favourite Charles Dickens character: Bill Sikes from Oliver Twist (1838)' the *Telegraph* (15 February 2012)

Hall, Stuart, 'Notes on Deconstructing "the Popular"' (1981); *Cultural Theory: An Anthology* ed. Szeman, Imre; Kaposy, Timothy (Wiley-Blackwell 2010)

Harris, John, 'All that jazz' the *Guardian* (21 May 2011)

Herron, Alec, 'Manchester's Trafford Park, the world's first industrial estate – a history of cities in 50 buildings, day 26' the *Guardian* (29 April 2015)

Hodges, Mike, 'Getting Carter' *Crime Time Issue 9* (Oldcastle Books 1997)

Myers, Ben, 'Mapping the fictional north' the *Guardian* (25 April 2012)

Myers, Ben, 'Shelf space' *Big Issue North* (3 December 2012)

Nette, Andrew, '"Get Carter", Again: The Story of a Noir Icon' *Los Angeles Review of Books* (1 December 2014)

O'Hagan, Andrew 'Short Cuts' *London Review of Books* (12 September 2013)

Powers, John, 'Gangsters, Goons and "Grievous Bodily Harm" in Ted Lewis' London' *NPR Book Review* (7 May 2015)

Raymond, Derek, 'On Ted Lewis' *Crime Time Issue 12* (Oldcastle

Books 1998)

Rosenthal, Tom, 'Obituary: Edmund Fisher' the *Independent* (4 March 1995)

Sweet, David, 'Obituary: James Neal' the *Guardian* (16 November 2011)

Taylor, Charles, 'Ted Lewis and his Kitchen Sink Killers' *Barnes & Noble* (22 April 2015)

Ulin, David L. '"Get Carter" and the birth of British noir' *Los Angeles Times* (2 September 2014)

Uncredited, 'Obituary: Charles Richardson' the *Telegraph* (20 September 2012)

Uncredited, 'Obituary: Frankie Fraser' the *Telegraph* (26 November 2014)

Waugh, Auberon, 'Criminal Connection' *The Spectator* (3 March 1973)

Williams, John, 'Brit Grit: John Williams on British crime writer Ted Lewis' *Arena Magazine Winter 92/93 Dec/Jan* (ABC Consumer Press 1992)

York, Peter, 'Bigger! Better! Richer! The golden age of advertising' the *Independent* (1 March 2008)

Websites

www.21stcenturyradio.com/yellowsub/ – website of Dr Robert R. Hieronimus

www.bartoncivicsociety.co.uk

www.fantasticfiction.co.uk/b/tom-barling

www.film4.com – Shane Meadows on *Dead Man's Shoes*

www.grahamlord.com – website of the late author and journalist.

www.hulltrawler.net – Details of Hull fishing trawlers

www.hullwebs.co.uk – Hull history 1902 – 2000

www.jfkfacts.org/assassination/experts/josiah-thompsons – Josiah Thompson discusses his book *Six Seconds in Dallas*.

www.magforum.com – *Teen Magazines*

www.michaelklingerpapers.uwe.ac.uk/ Catalogued archive of Michael Klinger material at University of the West of England

www.noiroftheweek.com – *Shack Out on 101* (1955) Steve Eifert

www.offthetelly.co.uk – *Noise! Adventure! Glitter!* – *TJ Worthington remembers Zokko!* TJ Worthington, May 2007

www.original-political-cartoon.com – *William Augustus Sillince 1906–1974*

www.pacific.edu/Library – *Jazz-Diplomacy Tour 1958*

www.parishes.lincolnshire.gov.uk/Theddlethorpe – *Theddlethorpe Parish Council*

www.paul-gibson.com/social-history – Social history guide to the clubs and pubs of Hull

www.reelstreets.com – *Get Carter* locations

www.sabotagetimes.com – *Three Day Millionaires: Stories from the Golden Age of Deep Sea Fishing* (2015) Russ Litten

www.screenonline.org.uk – BFI online resource: *The Criminal* (1960) Melanie Williams; *Z Cars* (1962–78) Mark Duguid

www.shannonsullivan.com/drwho/serials/5d.html – *A Brief History of Time – Travel: Androids of Tara* Shannon Patrick Sullivan, 31 December 2012

www.shortlist.com – *Get Carter: 40th Anniversary* Rob Crossan

www.staudrysproject.wordpress.com – St Audry's Project *Telling it like it is: the story of a psychiatric hospital in Suffolk*

www.theddlethorpe.org.uk

www.thedoctorwhosite.co.uk

www.thefictionstroker.wordpress.com – *The Fiction Stroker Speaks To... Ian Kennedy Martin* (20 November 2012)

Film

The Big Heat (1953) – Director, Fritz Lang

Shack Out on 101 (1955) – Director, Edward Dein

Bad Day at Black Rock (1955) – Director, John Sturges

Seven Men From Now (1956) – Director, Budd Boetticher (mentioned in *The Rabbit*)

Hell Drivers (1956) Director, Cy Endfield

The Criminal (1960) – Director, Joseph Losey

The Man Who Shot Liberty Valance – Director, John Ford

The Killers (1964) – Director, Don Siegel; starring Lee Marvin

Dying for a Smoke (1967) – short film: Director – John Halas, Script – Joy Batchelor, backgrounds Ted Lewis (BFI Archive)

Get Carter (1971) – (DVD commentary, Michael Caine, Mike Hodges, Wolfgang Suchitzky)

Dead Man's Shoes (2004) – Director, Shane Meadows

Le Serpent (2007) – Director, Eric Barbier (with DVD commentary by the director)

Yellow Submarine (1968) – Director, George Dunning; Animation Clean-up Supervisor, Ted Lewis

Radio

Jack Carter's Law – BBC Radio 7/4 Extra TX: 13, 20, 27 February, 6, 13 March 2011; repeated 11 June – 9 July 2011; 5 January – 2 February 2013

Lewis's Return Home – BBC Radio 4 TX: 27 August 2012

Jack's Return Home – BBC Radio 4 TX: 28 August, 5, 12, 17 September 2012

Other Sources

Lewis, Ted – *The Zodiac Factor: Plender*, draft of screenplay commissioned by the BBC (1976)

Lewis, Ted – *Thirteen Women – Mary: 1972*, draft of screenplay [Estimated date 1976/77]

Lewis, Ted – BBC Television Script Unit – Drama Writer's File

at the BBC Document archive – Various correspondence;
contracts; script extracts
Lincolnshire and South Humber Times – (28 October 1961)
Philip Larkin, speaking on BBC's Monitor, 15 December 1964
Treece, Henry, *Notes on Perception and Vision* (Notes from a
lecture given at Regional College of Art, Hull, 1 June 1966.
Reproduced by kind permission Savoy Web Publishing)

Index

315

INDEX